ILTS Science: Biology
105 Teacher Certification Exam

By: Sharon Wynne, M.S.

XAMonline, INC.
Boston

Copyright © 2013 XAMonline, Inc.

All rights reserved. No part of the material protected by this copyright notice may be reproduced or utilized in any form or by any means, electronic or mechanical, including photocopying, recording or by any information storage and retrievable system, without written permission from the copyright holder.

To obtain permission(s) to use the material from this work for any purpose including workshops or seminars, please submit a written request to:

XAMonline, Inc.
25 First Street, Suite 106
Cambridge, MA 02141
Toll Free 1-800-301-4647
Email: info@xamonline.com
Web www.xamonline.com

Library of Congress Cataloging-in-Publication Data

Wynne, Sharon A.
    Science: Biology 105: Teacher Certification / Sharon A. Wynne. -2nd ed.
    ISBN: 978-1-58197-978-7
    1. Science: Biology 105.   2. Study Guides.   3. ILTS
    4. Teachers' Certification & Licensure.   5. Careers

Disclaimer:

The opinions expressed in this publication are the sole works of XAMonline and were created independently from the Pearson Corporation, National Education Association, Educational Testing Service, any State Department of Education, National Evaluation Systems or other testing affiliates.

Between the time of publication and printing, state specific standards as well as testing formats and website information may change that is not included in part or in whole within this product. Sample test questions are developed by XAMonline and reflect similar content as on real tests; however, they are not former tests. XAMonline assembles content that aligns with state standards but makes no claims nor guarantees teacher candidates a passing score. Numerical scores are determined by testing companies such as NES or ETS and then are compared with individual state standards. A passing score varies from state to state.

Printed in the United States of America   œ-1
ILTS Science: Biology 105
ISBN: 978-1-58197-978-7

TEACHER CERTIFICATION STUDY GUIDE

| COMPETENCY # | TABLE OF CONTENTS | PG # |

SUBAREA I.   **SCIENCE AND TECHNOLOGY**

0001 Understand and apply knowledge of science as inquiry...............................1

0002 Understand and apply knowledge of the concepts, principles, and processes of technological design 6

0003 Understand and apply knowledge of accepted practices of science............8

0004 Understand and apply knowledge of the interactions among science, technology, and society..14

0005 Understand and apply knowledge of the major unifying concepts of all sciences and how these concepts relate to other disciplines.......................18

SUBAREA II.   **LIFE SCIENCE**

0006 Understand and apply knowledge of cell structure and function 23

0007 Understand and apply knowledge of the principles of heredity and biological evolution..34

0008 Understand and apply knowledge of the characteristics and life functions of organisms...41

0009 Understand and apply knowledge of how organisms interact with each other and with their environment...45

SUBAREA III.   **PHYSICAL SCIENCE**

0010 Understand and apply knowledge of the nature and properties of energy in its various forms 50

0011 Understand and apply knowledge of the structure and properties of matter 53

0012 Understand and apply knowledge of forces and motion..............................60

0013 Understand and apply knowledge of electricity, magnetism, and waves......70

SCIENCE: BIOLOGY

TEACHER CERTIFICATION STUDY GUIDE

SUBAREA IV.   **EARTH SYSTEMS AND THE UNIVERSE**

0014 Understand and apply knowledge of Earth's land, water, atmospheric systems and the history of Earth 77

0015 Understand and apply knowledge of the dynamic nature of Earth 83

0016 Understand and apply knowledge of objects in the universe and their dynamic interactions 90

0017 Understand and apply knowledge of the origins of and changes in the universe... 93

SUBAREA V.   **CELL BIOLOGY, HEREDITY, AND EVOLUTION**

0018 Understand and apply knowledge of the concepts of cell biology 96

0019 Understand and apply knowledge of the molecular basis of heredity and the associated mathematical probabilities... 107

0020 Understand and apply knowledge of the historical progression of cellular biology and genetics and the basic research methods and technologies used in these areas... 115

0021 Understand and apply knowledge of biological evolution and diversity........ 117

SUBAREA VI.   **ORGANISMAL BIOLOGY AND ECOLOGY**

0022 Understand and apply knowledge of organismal biology, using examples from each kingdom... 123

0023 Understand and apply knowledge of biological diversity in terms of the structure, function, and nomenclature of the major groups of organisms..... 128

0024 Understand and apply knowledge of ecological concepts........................... 134

0025 Understand and apply knowledge of matter, energy, and organization in living systems... 140

Sample Test.. 145

Answer Key 171

Rationales with Sample Questions 172

SCIENCE: BIOLOGY   ii

TEACHER CERTIFICATION STUDY GUIDE

Great Study and Testing Tips!

What to study in order to prepare for the subject assessments is the focus of this study guide but equally important is *how* you study.

You can increase your chances of truly mastering the information by taking some simple, but effective steps.

Study Tips:

1. Some foods aid the learning process. Foods such as milk, nuts, seeds, rice, and oats help your study efforts by releasing natural memory enhancers called CCKs (*cholecystokinin*) composed of *tryptopha*n, *choline*, and *phenylalanine*. All of these chemicals enhance the neurotransmitters associated with memory. Before studying, try a light, protein-rich meal of eggs, turkey, and fish. All of these foods release the memory enhancing chemicals. The better the connections, the more you comprehend.

Likewise, before you take a test, stick to a light snack of energy boosting and relaxing foods. A glass of milk, a piece of fruit, or some peanuts all release various memory-boosting chemicals and help you to relax and focus on the subject at hand.

2. Learn to take great notes. A by-product of our modern culture is that we have grown accustomed to getting our information in short doses (i.e. TV news sound bites or USA Today style newspaper articles).

Consequently, we've subconsciously trained ourselves to assimilate information better in neat little packages. If your notes are scrawled all over the paper, it fragments the flow of the information. Strive for clarity. Newspapers use a standard format to achieve clarity. Your notes can be much clearer through the use of proper formatting. A very effective format is called *"Cornell Method."*

> Take a sheet of loose-leaf lined notebook paper and draw a line all the way down the paper about 1-2" from the left-hand edge.
>
> Draw another line across the width of the paper about 1-2" up from the bottom. Repeat this process on the reverse side of the page.

Look at the highly effective result. You have ample room for notes, a left hand margin for special emphasis items or inserting supplementary data from the textbook, a large area at the bottom for a brief summary, and a little rectangular space for just about anything you want.

3. **Get the concept then the details.** Too often we focus on the details and don't gather an understanding of the concept. However, if you simply memorize only dates, places, or names, you may well miss the whole point of the subject.

A key way to understand things is to put them in your own words. If you are working from a textbook, automatically summarize each paragraph in your mind. If you are outlining text, don't simply copy the author's words.

Rephrase them in your own words. You remember your own thoughts and words much better than someone else's and subconsciously tend to associate the important details to the core concepts.

4. **Ask Why?** Pull apart written material paragraph by paragraph and don't forget the captions under the illustrations.

Example: If the heading is "Stream Erosion", flip it around to read "Why do streams erode?" Then answer the questions.

If you train your mind to think in a series of questions and answers, not only will you learn more, but it also helps to lessen the test anxiety because you are used to answering questions.

5. **Read for reinforcement and future needs.** Even if you only have 10 minutes, put your notes or a book in your hand. Your mind is similar to a computer; you have to input data in order to have it processed. *By reading, you are creating the neural connections for future retrieval.* The more times you read something, the more you reinforce the learning of ideas.

Even if you don't fully understand something on the first pass, *your mind stores much of the material for later recall.*

6. **Relax to learn so go into exile.** Our bodies respond to an inner clock called biorhythms. Burning the midnight oil works well for some people, but not everyone.

If possible, set aside a particular place to study that is free of distractions. Shut off the television, cell phone, and pager and exile your friends and family during your study period.

If you really are bothered by silence, try background music. Light classical music at a low volume has been shown to aid in concentration over other types. Music that evokes pleasant emotions without lyrics are highly suggested. Try just about anything by Mozart. It relaxes you.

TEACHER CERTIFICATION STUDY GUIDE

7. Use arrows not highlighters. At best, it's difficult to read a page full of yellow, pink, blue, and green streaks. Try staring at a neon sign for a while and you'll soon see that the horde of colors obscure the message.

A quick note, a brief dash of color, an underline, and an arrow pointing to a particular passage is much clearer than a horde of highlighted words.

8. Budget your study time. Although you shouldn't ignore any of the material, *allocate your available study time in the same ratio that topics may appear on the test.*

TEACHER CERTIFICATION STUDY GUIDE

Testing Tips:

1. <u>**Get smart, play dumb.**</u> **Don't read anything into the question.** Don't make an assumption that the test writer is looking for something other than what is asked. Stick to the question as written and don't read extra things into it.

2. <u>**Read the question and all the choices *twice* before answering the question.**</u> You may miss something by not carefully reading and then re-reading both the question and the answers.

If you really don't have a clue as to the right answer, leave it blank on the first time through. Go on to the other questions, as they may provide a clue as to how to answer the skipped questions.

If later on, you still can't answer the skipped ones . . . **Guess.** The only penalty for guessing is that you *might* get it wrong. Only one thing is certain; if you don't put anything down, you will get it wrong!

3. <u>**Turn the question into a statement.**</u> Look at the way the questions are worded. The syntax of the question usually provides a clue. Does it seem more familiar as a statement rather than as a question? Does it sound strange?

By turning a question into a statement, you may be able to spot if an answer sounds right, and it may also trigger memories of material you have read.

4. <u>**Look for hidden clues.**</u> It's actually very difficult to compose multiple-foil (choice) questions without giving away part of the answer in the options presented.

In most multiple-choice questions you can often readily eliminate one or two of the potential answers. This leaves you with only two real possibilities and automatically your odds go to Fifty-Fifty for very little work.

5. <u>**Trust your instincts.**</u> For every fact that you have read, you subconsciously retain something of that knowledge. On questions that you aren't really certain about, go with your basic instincts. **Your first impression on how to answer a question is usually correct.**

6. <u>**Mark your answers directly on the test booklet.**</u> Don't bother trying to fill in the optical scan sheet on the first pass through the test.

Just be very careful not to miss-mark your answers when you eventually transcribe them to the scan sheet.

7. <u>**Watch the clock!**</u> You have a set amount of time to answer the questions. Don't get bogged down trying to answer a single question at the expense of 10 questions you can more readily answer.

SCIENCE: BIOLOGY

TEACHER CERTIFICATION STUDY GUIDE

SUBAREA I   SCIENCE AND TECHNOLOGY

COMPETENCY 0001   UNDERSTAND AND APPLY KNOWLEDGE OF
                   SCIENCE AS INQUIRY

Skill 1.1   Recognize assumptions, processes, purposes, requirements, and tools of scientific inquiry.

Scientific inquiry is an understanding of science through questioning, experimentation and drawing conclusions.

The basic skills involved in this important process are:

1. Observing
2. Identifying problem
3. Gathering information/research
4. Hypothesizing
5. Experimental design, which includes identifying control, constants, independent and dependent variables
6. Conducting an experiment and repeating the experiment for validity
7. Interpreting, analyzing, and evaluating data
8. Drawing conclusions
9. Communicating conclusions

What are the uses of scientific inquiry?

1. Finding solutions for world problems
2. Encouraging problem solving approach to thinking, learning and understanding
3. To apply math and language skills
4. To confirm by experimentation that which is already known to the scientific community
5. Offer explanations, conclusions, and critical evaluations
6. Encourage the use of modern technology for research, experiments, analysis, and to communicate data
7. To be up to date with recent advances in science

The simplest form of science inquiry involves the following steps:

1. A question

2. Hypothesis
(A plausible explanation/an educated guess)

3. Experimental design
(Identifying control, constants, independent and dependent variables)

4. Experimenting and repeating the experiment for reliability

5. Data
(Analysis and evaluation)

6. Conclusions
Hypothesis correct/incorrect

7. Communicating the conclusions
(Visual, models, written and oral)

Scientific inquiry is a very powerful and highly interesting tool to teach and learn.

Skill 1.2   Use evidence and logic in developing proposed explanations that address scientific questions and hypotheses.

Armed with knowledge of the subject matter, students can effectively conduct investigations. They need to learn to think critically and logically to connect evidence with explanations. This includes deciding what evidence should be used and accounting for unusual data. Based upon data collected during experimentation, basic statistical analysis and measures of probability can be used to make predictions and develop interpretations.

Students should be able to review the data, summarize, and form a logical argument about the cause-and-effect relationships. It is important to differentiate between causes and effects and determine when causality is uncertain.

When developing proposed explanations, the students should be able to express their level of confidence in the proposed explanations and point out possible sources of uncertainty and error. When formulating explanations, it is important to distinguish between error and unanticipated results. Possible sources of error would include assumptions of models and measuring techniques or devices.

With confidence in the proposed explanations, the students need to identify what would be required to reject the proposed explanations. Based upon their experience, they should develop new questions to promote further inquiry.

Skill 1.3   **Identify various approaches to conducting scientific investigations and their applications**

Different types of questions and hypotheses require different approaches to conducting scientific investigations. Some investigations involve making models; some involve discovery of new phenomena and objects; some involve observing and describing objects, organisms, or events; some involve experiments; some involve collecting specimens; and some involve seeking more information.

Different scientific domains use different methods, core theories, and standards.

Scientific investigations sometimes result in new ideas and phenomena to be studied, generate new procedures or methods for an investigation, or develop new technologies to improve data collection. All of these results can lead to new investigations.

Skill 1.4   **Use tools and mathematical and statistical methods for collecting, managing, analyzing (e.g., average, curve fit, error determination), and communicating results of investigations.**

The procedure used to obtain data is important to the outcome. Experiments consist of **controls** and **variables**. A control is the experiment run under normal conditions. The variable includes a factor that is changed. In biology, the variable may be light, temperature, pH, time, etc. The differences in tested variables may be used to make a prediction or form a hypothesis. Only one variable should be tested at a time. One would not alter both the temperature and pH of the experimental subject.

An **independent variable** is one that is changed or manipulated by the researcher. This could be the amount of light given to a plant or the temperature at which bacteria is grown. The **dependent variable** is that which is influenced by the independent variable.

Average, or arithmetic mean is, the sum of all measurements in the data set divided by the number of observations in the data set.

When one graphs data points, one should follow through by connecting the dots with as smooth a line as possible. The connected points will create either a line or a curve, or appear totally random (you would not be able to connect truly random points). It is possible that not all points will be exactly on the line. Points that do not fall on the line are outliers. If the line is rounded, it is called a **curve fit**. If it is straight, the variables are said to have a linear relationship.

There are many ways in which **errors** could creep into measurements. Errors in measurements could occur because –
1. Improper use of instruments used for measuring – weighing etc.
2. Parallax error – not positioning the eyes during reading of measurements
3. Not using same instruments and methods of measurement during an experiment
4. Not using the same source of materials, resulting in the content of a certain compound used for experimentation being different

Besides these mentioned above, there could be other possible sources of error as well.

When erroneous results are used for interpreting data, the conclusions are not reliable. An experiment is valid only when all the constants (like time, place, method of measurement etc.) are strictly controlled. Experimental uncertainty is due to either random errors or systematic errors.

Random errors are defined as statistical fluctuations in the measured data due to the precision limitations of the measurement device. Random errors usually result from the experimenter's inability to take the same measurement in exactly the same way to get exactly the same number.

Systematic errors, by contrast, are defined as reproducible inaccuracies that are consistently in the same direction. Systematic errors are often due to a problem, which persists throughout the entire experiment.

Science uses the **metric system** as it is accepted worldwide and allows easier comparison among experiments done by scientists around the world.

The meter is the basic metric unit of length. One meter is 1.1 yards. The liter is the basic metric unit of volume. 1 gallon is 3.846 liters. The gram is the basic metric unit of mass. 1000 grams is 2.2 pounds.

The following prefixes are used to describe the multiples of the basic metric units.

deca- 10X the base unit
hecto- 100X the base unit
kilo- 1,000X the base unit
mega- 1,000,000X the base unit
giga- 1,000,000,000X the base unit
tera- 1,000,000,000,000X the base unit

deci - 1/10 the base unit
centi - 1/100 the base unit
milli - 1/1,000 the base unit
micro- 1/1,000,000 the base unit
nano- 1/1,000,000,000 the base unit
pico- 1/1,000,000,000,000 the base unit

The common instrument used for measuring volume is the graduated cylinder. The unit of measurement is usually in milliliters (mL). It is important for accurate measurement to read the liquid in the cylinder at the bottom of the meniscus, the curved surface of the liquid.

SCIENCE: BIOLOGY

The common instrument used in measuring mass is the triple beam balance. The triple beam balance is measured in as low as tenths of a gram and can be estimated to the hundredths of a gram.

The ruler or meter sticks are the most commonly used instruments for measuring length. Measurements in science should always be measured in metric units. Be sure when measuring length that the metric units are used.

Skill 1.5   Demonstrate knowledge of ways to report, display, and defend the results of an investigation.

The type of graphic representation used to display observations depends on the data that is collected. **Line graphs** are used to compare different sets of related data or to predict data that has yet to be measured. An example of a line graph would be comparing the rate of activity of different enzymes at varying temperatures. A **bar graph** or **histogram** is used to compare different items and make comparisons based on this data. An example of a bar graph would be comparing the ages of children in a classroom. A **pie chart** is useful when organizing data as part of a whole. A good use for a pie chart would be displaying the percent of time students spend on various after-school activities.

As noted before, the independent variable is controlled by the experimenter. This variable is placed on the x-axis (horizontal axis). The dependent variable is influenced by the independent variable and is placed on the y-axis (vertical axis). It is important to choose the appropriate units for labeling the axes. It is best to take the largest value to be plotted and divide it by the number of blocks, and rounding to the nearest whole number.

Careful research and statistically significant figures will be your best allies should you need to defend your work. For this reason, make sure to use controls, work in a systematic fashion, keep clear records, and have reproducible results.

COMPETENCY 0002 UNDERSTAND AND APPLY KNOWLEDGE OF THE CONCEPTS, PRINCIPLES, AND PROCESSES OF TECHNOLOGICAL DESIGN.

Skill 2.1 Recognize the capabilities, limitations, and implications of technology and technological design and redesign.

Science and technology are interdependent as advances in technology often lead to new scientific discoveries and new scientific discoveries often lead to new technologies. Scientists use technology to enhance the study of nature and solve problems that nature presents. Technological design is the identification of a problem and the application of scientific knowledge to solve the problem.

While technology and technological design can provide solutions to problems faced by humans, technology must exist within nature and cannot contradict physical or biological principles. In addition, technological solutions are temporary and new technologies typically provide better solutions in the future. Monetary costs, available materials, time, and available tools also limit the scope of technological design and solutions. Finally, technological solutions have intended benefits and unexpected consequences. Scientists must attempt to predict the unintended consequences and minimize any negative impact on nature or society.

Skill 2.2 Identify real-world problems or needs to be solved through technological design.

The problems and needs, ranging from very simple to highly complex, that technological design can solve are nearly limitless. Disposal of toxic waste, routing of rainwater, crop irrigation, and energy creation are but a few examples of real-world problems that scientists address or attempt to address with technology.

Skill 2.3 Apply a technological design process to a given problem situation.

The technological design process has five basic steps:

1. Identify a problem
2. Propose designs and choose between alternative solutions
3. Implement the proposed solution
4. Evaluate the solution and its consequences
5. Report results

After the identification of a problem, the scientist must propose several designs and choose between the alternatives. Scientists often utilize simulations and models in evaluating possible solutions.

Implementation of the chosen solution involves the use of various tools depending on the problem, solution, and technology. Scientists may use physical tools, objects and computer software.

After implementation of the solution, scientists evaluate the success or failure of the solution against pre-determined criteria. In evaluating the solution, scientists must consider the negative consequences as well as the planned benefits.

Finally, scientists must communicate results in different ways – orally, written, models, diagrams, and demonstrations.

Example:

Problem – toxic waste disposal
Chosen solution – genetically engineered microorganisms to digest waste
Implementation – use genetic engineering technology to create organism capable of converting waste to environmentally safe product
Evaluate – introduce organisms to waste site and measure formation of products and decrease in waste; also evaluate any unintended effects
Report – prepare a written report of results complete with diagrams and figures

Skill 2.4 Identify a design problem and propose possible solutions, considering such constraints as tools, materials, time, costs, and laws of nature.

In addition to finding viable solutions to design problems, scientists must consider such constraints as tools, materials, time, costs, and laws of nature. Effective implementation of a solution requires adequate tools and materials. Scientists cannot apply scientific knowledge without sufficient technology and appropriate materials (e.g. construction materials, software). Technological design solutions always have costs. Scientists must consider monetary costs, time costs, and the unintended effects of possible solutions. Types of unintended consequences of technological design solutions include adverse environmental impact and safety risks. Finally, technology cannot contradict the laws of nature. Technological design solutions must work within the framework of the natural world.

Skill 2.5 Evaluate various solutions to a design problem.

In evaluating and choosing between potential solutions to a design problem, scientists utilize modeling, simulation, and experimentation techniques. Small-scale modeling and simulation help test the effectiveness and unexpected consequences of proposed solutions while limiting the initial costs. Modeling and simulation may also reveal potential problems that scientists can address prior to full-scale implementation of the solution. Experimentation allows for evaluation of proposed solutions in a controlled environment where scientists can manipulate and test specific variables.

COMPETENCY 0003 UNDERSTAND AND APPLY KNOWLEDGE OF ACCEPTED PRACTICES OF SCIENCE.

Skill 3.1 Demonstrate an understanding of the nature of science (e.g., tentative, replicable, historical, empirical) and recognize how scientific knowledge and explanations change over time.

The combination of science, mathematics and technology forms the scientific endeavor and makes science a success. It is impossible to study science on its own without the support of other disciplines like mathematics, technology, geology, physics, and other disciplines as well.

Science is tentative. By definition it is searching for information by making educated guesses. It must be replicable. Another scientist must be able to achieve the same results under the same conditions at a later time. The term empirical means it must be assessed through tests and observations. Science changes over time. New technologies gather previously unavailable data and enable us to build upon current theories with new information.

Ancient history followed the geocentric theory, which was displaced by the heliocentric theory developed by Copernicus, Ptolemy and Kepler. Newton's laws of motion by Isaac Newton were based on mass, force and acceleration. They state that the force of gravity between any two objects in the universe depends upon their mass and distance; they are still widely used to date. In the 20th century, Albert Einstein was the most outstanding scientist for his work on relativity, which led to his theory that $E=mc2$. Early in the 20th century, Alfred Wegener proposed his theory of continental drift, stating that continents moved away from the super continent, Pangaea. This theory was accepted in 1960s when more evidence was collected on this. John Dalton and Lavosier made significant contributions in the field of atoms and matter. The Curies and Ernest Rutherford contributed greatly to radioactivity and the splitting of atom, which have lot of practical applications. Charles Darwin proposed his theory of evolution and Gregor Mendel's experiments on peas helped us to understand heredity. The most significant was the industrial revolution in Britain, in which science was applied practically to increase the productivity and also introduced a number of social problems like child labor.

The nature of science mainly consists of three important things:

1. The scientific world view
This includes some very important issues like – it is possible to understand this highly organized world and its complexities with the help of latest technology. Scientific ideas are subject to change. After repeated experiments, a theory is established, but this theory could be changed or supported in future. Only laws that occur naturally do not change.

Scientific knowledge may not be discarded but is modified – e.g., Albert Einstein didn't discard the Newtonian principles but modified them in his theory of relativity.

Also science can't answer all our questions. We can't find answers to questions related to our beliefs, moral values and our norms.

2. Scientific inquiry

Scientific inquiry starts with a simple question. This simple question leads to information gathering, an educated guess otherwise known as hypothesis. To prove the hypothesis, an experiment has to be conducted, which yields data and the conclusion. All experiments must be repeated at least twice to get reliable results. Thus scientific inquiry leads to new knowledge or to verifying established theories. Science requires proof or evidence. Science is dependent on accuracy, not bias or prejudice. In science, there is no place for preconceived ideas or premeditated results. By using their senses and modern technology, scientists will be able to get reliable information. Science is a combination of logic and imagination. A scientist needs to think and imagine and be able to reason. Science explains, reasons and predicts. These three are interwoven and are inseparable. While reasoning is absolutely important for science, there should be no bias or prejudice. Science is not authoritarian because it has been shown that scientific authority can be wrong. No one can determine or make decisions for others on any issue.

3. Scientific enterprise

Science is a complex activity involving various people and places. A scientist may work alone or in a laboratory, classroom or for that matter, anywhere. Mostly it is a group activity requiring a lot of social skills of cooperation, communication of results or findings, consultations, discussions etc.

Science demands a high degree of communication to the governments, funding authorities and to public.

Skill 3.2 **Compare scientific hypotheses, predictions, laws, theories, and principles and recognize how they are developed and tested.**

Science may be defined as a body of knowledge that is systematically derived from study, observations, and experimentation. Its goal is to identify and establish principles and theories that may be applied to solve problems. Pseudoscience, on the other hand, is a belief that is not warranted. There is no scientific methodology or application. Some of the more classic examples of pseudoscience include witchcraft, alien encounters or any topic that is explained by hearsay.

Scientific theory and experimentation must be repeatable. It is also possible to be disproved and is capable of change. Science depends on communication, agreement, and disagreement among scientists. It is composed of theories, laws, and hypotheses.

theory - the formation of principles or relationships which have been verified and accepted.

law - an explanation of events that occur with uniformity under the same conditions (laws of nature, law of gravitation).

hypothesis - an unproved theory or educated guess followed by research to best explain a phenomena. A theory is a proven hypothesis.

Science is limited by the available technology. An example of this would be the relationship of the discovery of the cell and the invention of the microscope. As our technology improves, more hypotheses will become theories and possibly laws. Science is also limited by the data that is able to be collected. Data may be interpreted differently on different occasions. Science limitations cause explanations to be changeable as new technologies emerge.

The first step in scientific inquiry is posing a question to be answered. Next, a hypothesis is formed to provide a plausible explanation. An experiment is then proposed and performed to test this hypothesis. A comparison between the predicted and observed results is the next step. Conclusions are then formed and it is determined whether the hypothesis is correct or incorrect. If incorrect, the next step is to form a new hypothesis and the process is repeated.

Skill 3.3 Recognize examples of valid and biased thinking in reporting of scientific research.

Scientific research can be biased in the choice of what data to consider, in the reporting or recording of the data, and/or in how the data are interpreted. The scientist's emphasis may be influenced by his/her nationality, sex, ethnic origin, age, or political convictions. For example, when studying a group of animals, male scientists may focus on the social behavior of the males and typically male characteristics.

Although bias related to the investigator, the sample, the method, or the instrument may not be completely avoidable in every case, it is important to know the possible sources of bias and how bias could affect the evidence. Moreover, scientists need to be attentive to possible bias in their own work as well as that of other scientists.

Objectivity may not always be attained. However, one precaution that may be taken to guard against undetected bias is to have many different investigators or groups of investigators working on a project. By different, it is meant that the groups are made up of various nationalities, ethnic origins, ages, and political convictions and composed of both males and females. It is also important to note one's aspirations, and to make sure to be truthful to the data, even when grants, promotions, and notoriety are at risk.

Skill 3.4 Recognize the basis for and application of safety practices and regulations in the study of science.

All science labs should contain the following items of **safety equipment**. Those marked with an asterisk are requirements by state laws.

* fire blanket which is visible and accessible
*Ground Fault Circuit Interrupters (GCFI) within two feet of water supplies
*signs designating room exits
*emergency shower capable of providing a continuous flow of water
*emergency eye wash station which can be activated by the foot or forearm
*eye protection for every student and a means of sanitizing equipment
*emergency exhaust fans providing ventilation to the outside of the building
*master cut-off switches for gas, electric and compressed air. Switches must have permanently attached handles. Cut-off switches must be clearly labeled.
*an ABC fire extinguisher
*storage cabinets for flammable materials
-chemical spill control kit
-fume hood with a motor which is spark proof
-protective laboratory aprons made of flame retardant material
-signs which will alert potential hazardous conditions
-containers for broken glassware, flammables, corrosives, and waste. Containers should be labeled.

Students should wear safety goggles when performing dissections, heating, or while using acids and bases. Hair should always be tied back and objects should never be placed in the mouth. Food should not be consumed while in the laboratory. Hands should always be washed before and after laboratory experiments. In case of an accident, eye washes and showers should be used for eye contamination or a chemical spill that covers the student's body. Small chemical spills should only be contained and cleaned by the teacher. Kitty litter or a chemical spill kit should be used to clean spill. For large spills, the school administration and the local fire department should be notified. Biological spills should also be handled only by the teacher. Contamination with biological waste can be cleaned by using bleach when appropriate.

Accidents and injuries should always be reported to the school administration and local health facilities. The severity of the accident or injury will determine the course of action to pursue.

It is the responsibility of the teacher to provide a safe environment for their students. Proper supervision greatly reduces the risk of injury and a teacher should never leave a class for any reason without providing alternate supervision. After an accident, two factors are considered; **foreseeability** and **negligence**. Foreseeability is the anticipation that an event may occur under certain circumstances. Negligence is the failure to exercise ordinary or reasonable care. Safety procedures should be a part of the science curriculum and a well managed classroom is important to avoid potential lawsuits.

All laboratory solutions should be prepared as directed in the lab manual. Care should be taken to avoid contamination. All glassware should be rinsed thoroughly with distilled water before using and cleaned well after use. All solutions should be made with distilled water as tap water contains dissolved particles that may affect the results of an experiment. Unused solutions should be disposed of according to local disposal procedures.

The "Right to Know Law" covers science teachers who work with potentially hazardous chemicals. Briefly, the law states that employees must be informed of potentially toxic chemicals. An inventory must be made available if requested. The inventory must contain information about the hazards and properties of the chemicals. This inventory is to be checked against the "Substance List". Training must be provided on the safe handling and interpretation of the Material Safety Data Sheet.

The following chemicals are potential carcinogens and are not allowed in school facilities: Acrylonitriel, Arsenic compounds, Asbestos, Bensidine, Benzene, Cadmium compounds, Chloroform, Chromium compounds, Ethylene oxide, Ortho-toluidine, Nickel powder, and Mercury.

Chemicals should not be stored on bench tops or heat sources. They should be stored in groups based on their reactivity with one another and in protective storage cabinets. All containers within the lab must be labeled. Suspect and known carcinogens must be labeled as such and segregated within trays to contain leaks and spills.

Chemical waste should be disposed of in properly labeled containers. Waste should be separated based on their reactivity with other chemicals.

Biological material should never be stored near food or water used for human consumption. All biological material should be appropriately labeled. All blood and body fluids should be put in a well-contained container with a secure lid to prevent leaking. All biological waste should be disposed of in biological hazardous waste bags.

Material safety data sheets are available for every chemical and biological substance. These are available directly from the company of acquisition or the internet. The manuals for equipment used in the lab should be read and understood before using them.

COMPETENCY 0004 UNDERSTAND AND APPLY KNOWLEDGE OF THE INTERACTIONS AMONG SCIENCE, TECHNOLOGY, AND SOCIETY.

Skill 4.1 Recognize the historical and contemporary development of major scientific ideas and technological innovations.

Anton van Leeuwenhoek is known as the father of microscopy. In the 1650s, Leeuwenhoek began making tiny lenses which gave magnifications up to 300x. He was the first to see and describe bacteria, yeast, plants, and the microscopic life found in water. Over the years, light microscopes have advanced to produce greater clarity and magnification. The scanning electron microscope (SEM) was developed in the 1950s. Instead of light, a beam of electrons passes through the specimen. Scanning electron microscopes have a resolution about one thousand times greater than light microscopes. The disadvantage of the SEM is that the chemical and physical methods used to prepare the sample result in the death of the specimen.

In the late 1800s, Pasteur discovered the role of microorganisms in the cause of disease, pasteurization, and the rabies vaccine. Koch took this observation one step further by formulating the idea that specific diseases were caused by specific pathogens. **Koch's postulates** are still used as guidelines in the field of microbiology: the same pathogen must be found in every diseased person, the pathogen must be isolated and grown in culture, the disease is induced in experimental animals from the culture, and the same pathogen must be isolated from the experimental animal.

DNA structure was another key event in biological study. In the 1950s, James Watson and Francis Crick discovered the structure of a DNA molecule as that of a double helix. This structure made it possible to explain DNA's ability to replicate and to control the synthesis of proteins.

The use of animals in biological research has expedited many scientific discoveries. Animal research has allowed scientists to learn more about animal biological systems, including the circulatory and reproductive systems. One significant use of animals is for the testing of drugs, vaccines, and other products (such as perfumes and shampoos) before use or consumption by humans. Along with the pros of animal research, the cons are also very significant. The debate about the ethical treatment of animals has been ongoing since the introduction of animals in research. Many people believe the use of animals in research is cruel and unnecessary. Animal use is federally and locally regulated. The purpose of the Institutional Animal Care and Use Committee (IACUC) is to oversee and evaluate all aspects of an institution's animal care and use program.

Skill 4.2 Demonstrate and understanding of the ways that science and technology affect people's everyday lives, societal values and systems, the environment, and new knowledge.

Society as a whole impacts biological research. The pressure from the majority of society has led to bans and restrictions on human cloning research. Human cloning has been restricted in the United States and many other countries. The U.S. legislature has banned the use of federal funds for the development of human cloning techniques. Some individual states have banned human cloning regardless of where the funds originate.

The demand for genetically modified crops by society and industry has steadily increased over the years. Genetic engineering in the agricultural field has led to improved crops for human use and consumption. Crops are genetically modified for increased growth and insect resistance because of the demand for larger and greater quantities of produce.

With advances in biotechnology come those in society who oppose it. Ethical questions come into play when discussing animal and human research. Does it need to be done? What are the effects on humans and animals? There are no right or wrong answers to these questions. There are governmental agencies in place to regulate the use of humans and animals for research.

Science and technology are often referred to as a "double-edged sword". Although advances in medicine have greatly improved the quality and length of life, certain moral and ethical controversies have arisen. Unforeseen environmental problems may result from technological advances. Advances in science have led to an improved economy through biotechnology as applied to agriculture, yet it has put our health care system at risk and has caused the cost of medical care to skyrocket. Society depends on science, yet is necessary that the public be scientifically literate and informed in order to allow potentially unethical procedures to occur. Especially vulnerable are the areas of genetic research and fertility. It is important for science teachers to stay abreast of current research and to involve students in critical thinking and ethics whenever possible.

Skill 4.3 Analyze the processes of scientific and technological breakthroughs and their effects on other fields of study, careers, and job markets.

Scientific and technological breakthroughs greatly influence other fields of study and the job market. All academic disciplines utilize computer and information technology to simplify research and information sharing. In addition, advances in science and technology influence the types of available jobs and the desired work skills. For example, machines and computers continue to replace unskilled laborers and computer and technological literacy is now a requirement for many jobs and careers. Finally, science and technology continue to change the very nature of careers. Because of science and technology's great influence on all areas of the economy, and continuing scientific and technological breakthroughs, careers are far less stable than in past eras. Workers can thus expect to change jobs and companies much more often than in the past.

Skill 4.4 Analyze issues related to science and technology at the local, state, national, and global levels (e.g., environmental policies, genetic research).

Local, state, national, and global governments and organizations must increasingly consider policy issues related to science and technology. For example, local and state governments must analyze the impact of proposed development and growth on the environment. Governments and communities must balance the demands of an expanding human population with the local ecology to ensure sustainable growth.

In addition, advances in science and technology create challenges and ethical dilemmas that national governments and global organizations must attempt to solve. Genetic research and manipulation, antibiotic resistance, stem cell research, and cloning are but a few of the issues facing national governments and global organizations.

In all cases, policy makers must analyze all sides of an issue and attempt to find a solution that protects society while limiting scientific inquiry as little as possible. For example, policy makers must weigh the potential benefits of stem cell research, genetic engineering, and cloning (e.g. medical treatments) against the ethical and scientific concerns surrounding these practices. Also, governments must tackle problems like antibiotic resistance, which can result from the indiscriminate use of medical technology (i.e. antibiotics) in order to prevent medical treatments from becoming obsolete.

Skill 4.5 Evaluate the credibility of scientific claims made in various forms (e.g., the media, public debates, advertising).

Because people often attempt to use scientific evidence in support of political or personal agendas, the ability to evaluate the credibility of scientific claims is a necessary skill in today's society. In evaluating scientific claims made in the media, public debates, and advertising, one should follow several guidelines.

First, scientific, peer-reviewed journals are the most accepted source for information on scientific experiments and studies. One should carefully scrutinize any claim that does not reference peer-reviewed literature.

Second, the media and those with an agenda to advance (advertisers, debaters, etc.) often overemphasize the certainty and importance of experimental results. One should question any scientific claim that sounds fantastical or overly certain.

Finally, knowledge of experimental design and the scientific method is important in evaluating the credibility of studies. For example, one should look for the inclusion of control groups and the presence of data to support the given conclusions.

TEACHER CERTIFICATION STUDY GUIDE

COMPETENCY 0005   **UNDERSTAND AND APPLY KNOWLEDGE OF THE MAJOR UNIFYING CONCEPTS OF ALL SCIENCES AND HOW THESE CONCEPTS RELATE TO OTHER DISCIPLINES.**

Skill 5.1   **Identify the major unifying concepts of the sciences (e.g., systems, order, and organization; constancy, change, measurement) and their applications in real-life situations.**

The following are the concepts and processes generally recognized as common to all scientific disciplines:

- Systems, order, and organization
- Evidence, models, and explanation
- Constancy, change, and measurement
- Evolution and equilibrium
- Form and function

Because the natural world is so complex, the study of science involves the **organization** of items into smaller groups based on interaction or interdependence. These groups are called **systems**. Examples of organization are the periodic table of elements and the five-kingdom classification scheme for living organisms. Examples of systems are the solar system, cardiovascular system, Newton's laws of force and motion, and the laws of conservation.

Order refers to the behavior and measurability of organisms and events in nature. The arrangement of planets in the solar system and the life cycle of bacterial cells are examples of order.

Scientists use **evidence** and **models** to form **explanations** of natural events. Models are miniaturized representations of a larger event or system. Evidence is anything that furnishes proof.

Constancy and **change** describe the observable properties of natural organisms and events. Scientists use different systems of **measurement** to observe change and constancy. For example, the freezing and melting points of given substances and the speed of sound are constant under constant conditions. Growth, decay, and erosion are all examples of natural change.

Evolution is the process of change over a long period of time. While biological evolution is the most common example, one can also classify technological advancement, changes in the universe, and changes in the environment as evolution.

Equilibrium is the state of balance between opposing forces of change. Homeostasis and ecological balance are examples of equilibrium.

SCIENCE: BIOLOGY

Form and **function** are properties of organisms and systems that are closely related. The function of an object usually dictates its form and the form of an object usually facilitates its function. For example, the form of the heart (e.g. muscle, valves) allows it to perform its function of circulating blood through the body.

Skill 5.2   Recognize connections within and among traditional scientific disciplines.

Because biology is the study of living things, we can easily apply the knowledge of biology to daily life and personal decision-making. For example, biology greatly influences the health decisions humans make everyday. What foods to eat, when and how to exercise, and how often to bathe are just three of the many decisions we make everyday that are based on our knowledge of biology. Other areas of daily life where biology affects decision-making are parenting, interpersonal relationships, family planning, and consumer spending.

Skill 5.3   Apply fundamental mathematical language, knowledge, and skills at the level of algebra and statistics in scientific contexts.

The knowledge and use of basic mathematical concepts and skills is a necessary aspect of scientific study. Science depends on data and the manipulation of data requires knowledge of mathematics. Understanding of basic statistics, graphs and charts, and algebra are of particular importance. Scientists must be able to understand and apply the statistical concepts of mean, median, mode, and range to sets of scientific data. In addition, scientists must be able to represent data graphically and interpret graphs and tables. Finally, scientists often use basic algebra to solve scientific problems and design experiments. For example, the substitution of variables is a common strategy in experiment design. Also, the ability to determine the equation of a curve is valuable in data manipulation, experimentation, and prediction.

Modern science uses a number of disciplines to understand it better. Statistics is one of those subjects, which is absolutely essential for science.

Mean: Mean is the mathematical average of all the items. To calculate the mean, all the items must be added up and divided by the number of items. This is also called the arithmetic mean or more commonly as the "average".

Median: The median depends on whether the number of items is odd or even. If the number is odd, then the median is the value of the item in the middle. This is the value that denotes that the number of items having higher or equal value to that is same as the number of items having equal or lesser value than that. If the number of the items is even, the median is the average of the two items in the middle, such that the number of items having values higher or equal to it is same as the number of items having values equal or less than that.

Mode: Mode is the value of the item that occurs the most often, if there are not many items. Bimodal is a situation where there are two items with equal frequency.

Range: Range is the difference between the maximum and minimum values. The range is the difference between two extreme points on the distribution curve.

Scientists use mathematical tools and equations to model and solve scientific problems. Solving scientific problems often involves the use of quadratic, trigonometric, exponential, and logarithmic functions.

Quadratic equations take the standard form $ax^2 + bx + c = 0$. The most appropriate method of solving quadratic equations in scientific problems is the use of the quadratic formula. The quadratic formula produces the solutions of a standard form quadratic equation.

$$x = \frac{-b \pm \sqrt{b^2 - 4ac}}{2a} \quad \{\text{Quadratic Formula}\}$$

One common application of quadratic equations is the description of biochemical reaction equilibriums. Consider the following problem.

Example 1

80.0 g of ethanoic acid (MW = 60g) reacts with 85.0 g of ethanol (MW = 46g) until equilibrium. The equilibrium constant is 4.00. Determine the amounts of ethyl acetate and water produced at equilibrium.

$$CH_3COOH + CH_3CH_2OH = CH_3CO_2C_2H_5 + H_2O$$

The equilibrium constant, K, describes equilibrium of the reaction, relating the concentrations of products to reactants.

$$K = \frac{[CH_3CO_2C_2H_5][H_2O]}{[CH_3CO_2H][CH_3CH_2OH]} = 4.00$$

The equilibrium values of reactants and products are listed in the following table.

	CH_3COOH	CH_3CH_2OH	$CH_3CO_2C_2H_5$	H_2O
Initial	80/60 = 1.33 mol	85/46 = 1.85 mol	0	0
Equilibrium	1.33 − x	1.85 − x	x	x

Thus, $K = \dfrac{[x][x]}{[1.33-x][1.85-x]} = \dfrac{x^2}{2.46 - 3.18x + x^2} = 4.00$.

Rearrange the equation to produce a standard form quadratic equation.

$$\frac{x^2}{2.46 - 3.18x + x^2} = 4.00$$

$$x^2 = 4.00(2.46 - 3.18x + x^2) = 9.84 - 12.72x + 4x^2$$

$$0 = 3x^2 - 12.72x + 9.84$$

Use the quadratic formula to solve for x.

$$x = \frac{-(-12.72) \pm \sqrt{(-12.72)^2 - 4(3)(9.84)}}{2(3)} = 3.22 \text{ or } 1.02$$

3.22 is not an appropriate answer, because we started with only 3.18 moles of reactants. Thus, the amount of each product produced at equilibrium is 1.02 moles.

Scientists use trigonometric functions to define angles and lengths. For example, field biologists can use trigonometric functions to estimate distances and directions. The basic trigonometric functions are sine, cosine, and tangent. Consider the following triangle describing these relationships.

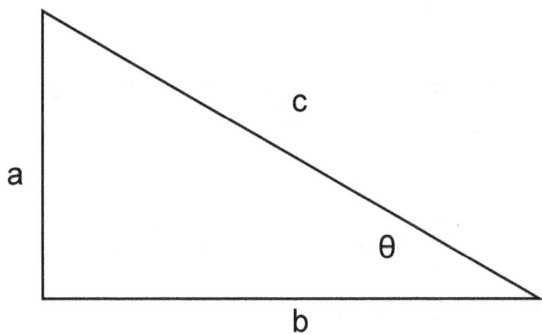

$$\sin \theta = \frac{a}{c}, \cos \theta = \frac{b}{c}, \tan \theta = \frac{a}{b}$$

Exponential functions are useful in modeling many scientific phenomena. For example, scientists use exponential functions to describe bacterial growth and radioactive decay. The general form of exponential equations is $f(x) = Ca^x$ (C is a constant). Consider the following problem involving bacterial growth.

Example 2

Determine the number of bacteria present in a culture inoculated with a single bacterium after 24 hours if the bacterial population doubles every 2 hours. Use $N(t) = N_0 e^{kt}$ as a model of bacterial growth where N(t) is the size of the population at time t, N_0 is the initial population size, and k is the growth constant.

We must first determine the growth constant, k. At t = 2, the size of the population doubles from 1 to 2. Thus, we substitute and solve for k.

$$2 = 1(e^{2k})$$

$\ln 2 = \ln e^{2k}$ Take the natural log of each side.

$\ln 2 = 2k(\ln e) = 2k$ $\ln e = 1$

$k = \dfrac{\ln 2}{2}$ Solve for k.

The population size at t = 24 is

$$N(24) = e^{(\frac{\ln 2}{2})24} = e^{12 \ln 2} = 4096.$$

Finally, logarithmic functions have many applications to science and biology. One simple example of a logarithmic application is the pH scale. Scientists define pH as follows.

     pH = - $\log_{10}$ [H+], where [H+] is the concentration of hydrogen ions

Thus, we can determine the pH of a solution with a [H+] value of 0.0005 mol/L by using the logarithmic formula.

     pH = - $\log_{10}$ [0.0005] = 3.3

Skill 5.4   Recognize the fundamental relationships among the natural sciences and the social sciences.

The fundamental relationship between the natural and social sciences is the use of the scientific method and the rigorous standards of proof that both disciplines require. This emphasis on organization and evidence separates the sciences from the arts and humanities. Natural science, particularly biology, is closely related to social science, the study of human behavior. Biological and environmental factors often dictate human behavior and accurate assessment of behavior requires a sound understanding of biological factors.

SUBAREA II.   LIFE SCIENCE

COMPETENCY 0006   UNDERSTAND AND APPLY KNOWLEDGE OF CELL STRUCTURE AND FUNCTION.

Skill 6.1   Compare and contrast the structures of viruses and prokaryotic and eukaryotic cells.

The cell is the basic unit of all living things. There are three types of cells. They are prokaryotes, eukaryotes, and archaea. Archaea have some similarities with prokaryotes, but are as distantly related to prokaryotes as prokaryotes are to eukaryotes.

PROKARYOTES

Prokaryotes consist only of bacteria and cyanobacteria (formerly known as blue-green algae). The classification of prokaryotes is in the diagram below.

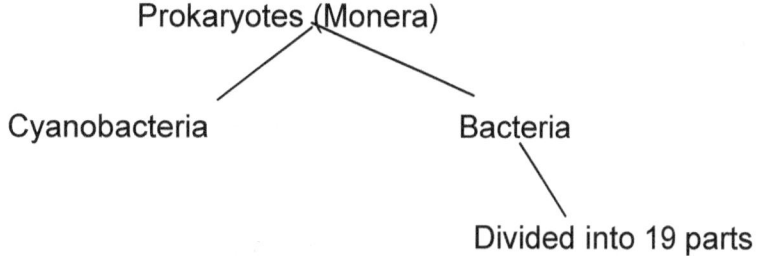

These cells have no defined nucleus or nuclear membrane. The DNA, RNA, and ribosomes float freely within the cell. The cytoplasm has a single chromosome condensed to form a **nucleoid**. Prokaryotes have a thick cell wall made up of amino sugars (glycoproteins). This is for protection, to give the cell shape, and to keep the cell from bursting. It is the **cell wall** of bacteria that is targeted by the antibiotic penicillin. Penicillin works by disrupting the cell wall, thus killing the cell.

The cell wall surrounds the **cell membrane** (plasma membrane). The cell membrane consists of a lipid bilayer that controls the passage of molecules in and out of the cell. Some prokaryotes have a capsule made of polysaccharides that surrounds the cell wall for extra protection from higher organisms.

Many bacterial cells have appendages used for movement called **flagella**. Some cells also have **pili**, which are protein strands used for attachment of the bacteria. Pili may also be used for sexual conjugation (where the DNA from one bacterial cell is transferred to another bacterial cell).

Prokaryotes are the most numerous and widespread organisms on earth. Bacteria were most likely the first cells and date back in the fossil record to 3.5 billion years ago. Their ability to adapt to the environment allows them to thrive in a wide variety of habitats.

EUKARYOTES

Eukaryotic cells are found in protists, fungi, plants, and animals. Most eukaryotic cells are larger than prokaryotic cells. They contain many organelles, which are membrane bound areas for specific functions. Their cytoplasm contains a cytoskeleton which provides a protein framework for the cell. The cytoplasm also supports the organelles and contains the ions and molecules necessary for cell function. The cytoplasm is contained by the plasma membrane. The plasma membrane allows molecules to pass in and out of the cell. The membrane can bud inward to engulf outside material in a process called endocytosis. Exocytosis is a secretory mechanism, the reverse of endocytosis. The most significant differentiation between prokaryotes and eukaryotes is that eukaryotes have a **nucleus**.

VIRUSES

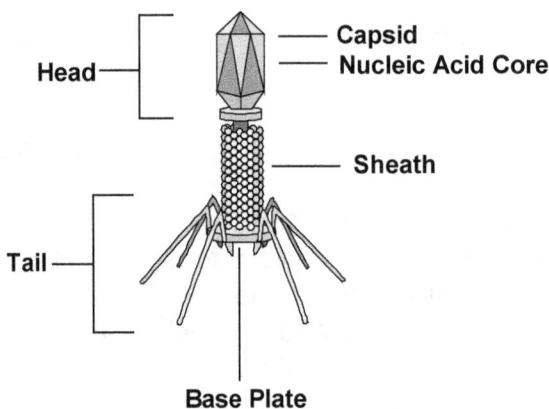

Bacteriophage

All viruses have a head or protein capsid that contains genetic material. This material is encoded in the nucleic acid and can be DNA, RNA, or even a limited number of enzymes. Some viruses also have a protein tail region. The tail aids in binding to the surface of the host cell and penetrating the surface of the host in order to introduce the virus's genetic material.

Other examples of viruses and their structures:

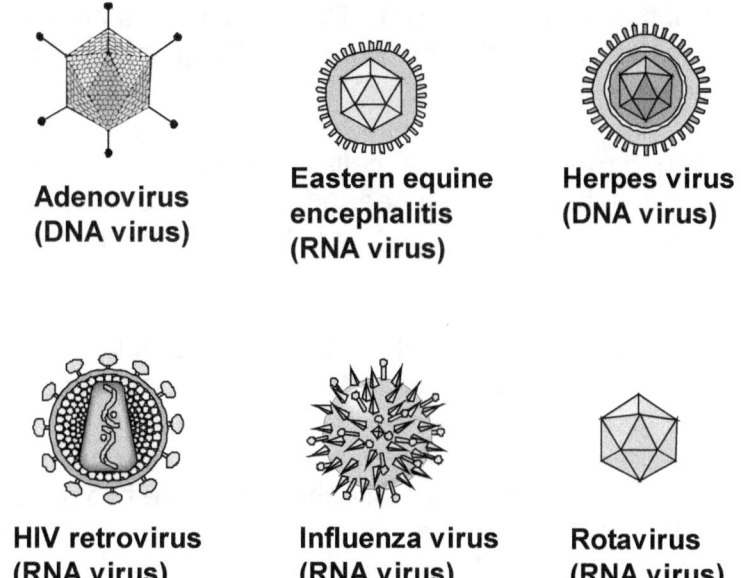

Skill 6.2   Identify the structures and functions of cellular organelles.

The **nucleus** is the brain of the cell that contains all of the cell's genetic information. The chromosomes consist of chromatin, which is a complex of DNA and proteins. The chromosomes are tightly coiled to conserve space while providing a large surface area. The nucleus is the site of transcription of the DNA into RNA. The **nucleolus** is where ribosomes are made. There is at least one of these dark-staining bodies inside the nucleus of most eukaryotes. The nuclear envelope is two membranes separated by a narrow space. The envelope contains many pores that let RNA out of the nucleus.

Ribosomes are the site for protein synthesis. Ribosomes may be free-floating in the cytoplasm or attached to the endoplasmic reticulum. There may be up to a half a million ribosomes in a cell, depending on how much protein is made by the cell.

The **endoplasmic reticulum** (ER) is folded and provides a large surface area. It is the "roadway" of the cell and allows for transport of materials through and out of the cell. There are two types of ER. Smooth endoplasmic reticulum contains no ribosomes on its surface. This is the site of lipid synthesis. Rough endoplasmic reticulum has ribosomes on its surface. They aid in the synthesis of proteins that are membrane bound or destined for secretion.

Many of the products made in the ER proceed on to the Golgi apparatus. The **Golgi apparatus** functions to sort, modify, and package molecules that are made in the other parts of the cell (like the ER). These molecules are either sent out of the cell or to other organelles within the cell. The Golgi apparatus is a stacked structure to increase the surface area.

Lysosomes are found mainly in animal cells. These contain digestive enzymes that break down food, substances not needed, viruses, damaged cell components and eventually the cell itself. It is believed that lysosomes are responsible for the aging process.

Mitochondria are large organelles that are the site of cellular respiration, where ATP is made to supply energy to the cell. Muscle cells have many mitochondria because they use a great deal of energy. Mitochondria have their own DNA, RNA, and ribosomes and are capable of reproducing by binary fission if there is a greater demand for additional energy. Mitochondria have two membranes: a smooth outer membrane and a folded inner membrane. The folds inside the mitochondria are called cristae. They provide a large surface area for cellular respiration to occur.

Plastids are found only in photosynthetic organisms. They are similar to the mitochondria due to the double membrane structure. They also have their own DNA, RNA, and ribosomes and can reproduce if the need for the increased capture of sunlight becomes necessary. There are several types of plastids. **Chloroplasts** are the site of photosynthesis. The stroma is the chloroplast's inner membrane space. The stroma encloses sacs called thylakoids that contain the photosynthetic pigment chlorophyll. The chlorophyll traps sunlight inside the thylakoid to generate ATP that is used in the stroma to produce carbohydrates and other products. The **chromoplasts** make and store yellow and orange pigments. They provide color to leaves, flowers, and fruits. The **amyloplasts** store starch and are used as a food reserve. They are abundant in roots like potatoes.

The Endosymbiotic Theory states that mitochondria and chloroplasts were once free living and possibly evolved from prokaryotic cells. At some point in our evolutionary history, they entered the eukaryotic cell and maintained a symbiotic relationship with the cell, with both the cell and organelle benefiting from the relationship. The fact that they both have their own DNA, RNA, ribosomes, and are capable of reproduction helps to confirm this theory.

Found in plant cells only, the **cell wall** is composed of cellulose and fibers. It is thick enough for support and protection, yet porous enough to allow water and dissolved substances to enter. **Vacuoles** are found mostly in plant cells. They hold stored food and pigments. Their large size allows them to fill with water in order to provide turgor pressure. Lack of turgor pressure causes a plant to wilt.

The **cytoskeleton**, found in both animal and plant cells, is composed of protein filaments attached to the plasma membrane and organelles. They provide a framework for the cell and aid in cell movement. They constantly change shape and move about. Three types of fibers make up the cytoskeleton:

1. **Microtubules** – the largest of the three, they make up cilia and flagella for locomotion. Some examples are sperm cells, cilia that line the fallopian tubes and tracheal cilia. Centrioles are also composed of microtubules. They aid in cell division to form the spindle fibers that pull the cell apart into two new cells. Centrioles are not found in the cells of higher plants.

2. **Intermediate filaments** – intermediate in size, they are smaller than microtubules but larger than microfilaments. They help the cell to keep its shape.

3. **Microfilaments** – smallest of the three, they are made of actin and small amounts of myosin (like in muscle tissue). They function in cell movement like cytoplasmic streaming, endocytosis, and ameboid movement. These structures pinch the two cells apart after cell division, forming two new cells.

The following is a diagram of a generalized animal cell.

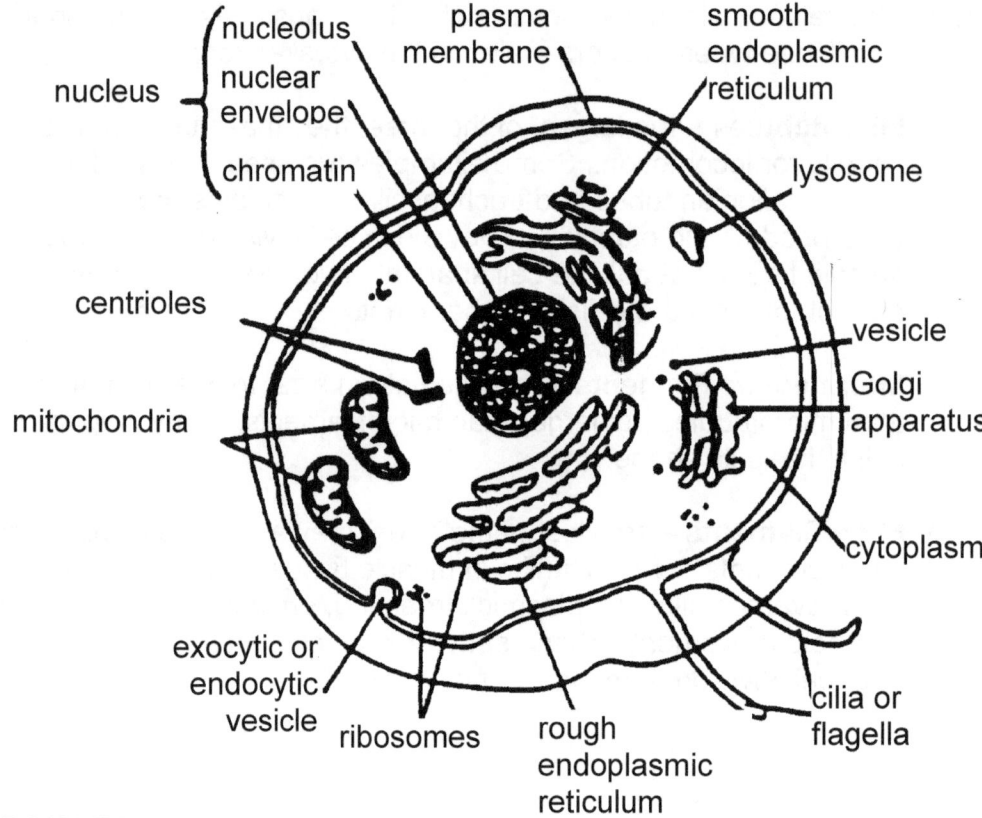

ARCHAEA

There are three kinds of organisms with archaea cells: **methanogens** are obligate anaerobes that produce methane, **halobacteria** can live only in concentrated brine solutions, and **thermoacidophiles** can only live in acidic hot springs.

Skill 6.3   Describe the processes of the cell cycle.

The purpose of cell division is to provide growth and repair in body (somatic) cells and to replenish or create sex cells for reproduction. There are two forms of cell division. **Mitosis** is the division of somatic cells and **meiosis** is the division of sex cells (eggs and sperm).

Mitosis is divided into two parts: the **mitotic (M) phase** and **interphase**. In the mitotic phase, mitosis and cytokinesis divide the nucleus and cytoplasm, respectively. This phase is the shortest phase of the cell cycle. Interphase is the stage where the cell grows and copies the chromosomes in preparation for the mitotic phase. Interphase occurs in three stages of growth: **G1** (growth) period is when the cell is growing and metabolizing, the **S** period (synthesis) is where new DNA is being made and the **G2** phase (growth) is where new proteins and organelles are being made to prepare for cell division.

The mitotic phase is a continuum of change, although it is described as occurring in five stages: prophase, prometaphase, metaphase, anaphase, and telophase. During **prophase**, the cell proceeds through the following steps continuously, with no stopping. The chromatin condenses to become visible chromosomes. The nucleolus disappears and the nuclear membrane breaks apart. Mitotic spindles form that will eventually pull the chromosomes apart. They are composed of microtubules. The cytoskeleton breaks down and the spindles are pushed to the poles or opposite ends of the cell by the action of centrioles. During **prometaphase**, the nuclear membrane fragments and allows the spindle microtubules to interact with the chromosomes. Kinetochore fibers attach to the chromosomes at the centromere region. (Sometimes prometaphase is grouped with metaphase). When the centrosomes are at opposite ends of the cell, the division is in **metaphase**. The centromeres of all the chromosomes are aligned with one another. During **anaphase**, the centromeres split in half and homologous chromosomes separate. The chromosomes are pulled to the poles of the cell, with identical sets at either end. The last stage of mitosis is **telophase**. Here, two nuclei form with a full set of DNA that is identical to the parent cell. The nucleoli become visible and the nuclear membrane reassembles. A cell plate is seen in plant cells, whereas a cleavage furrow is formed in animal cells. The cell is pinched into two cells. Cytokinesis, or division of the cytoplasm and organelles, occurs.

Below is a diagram of mitosis.

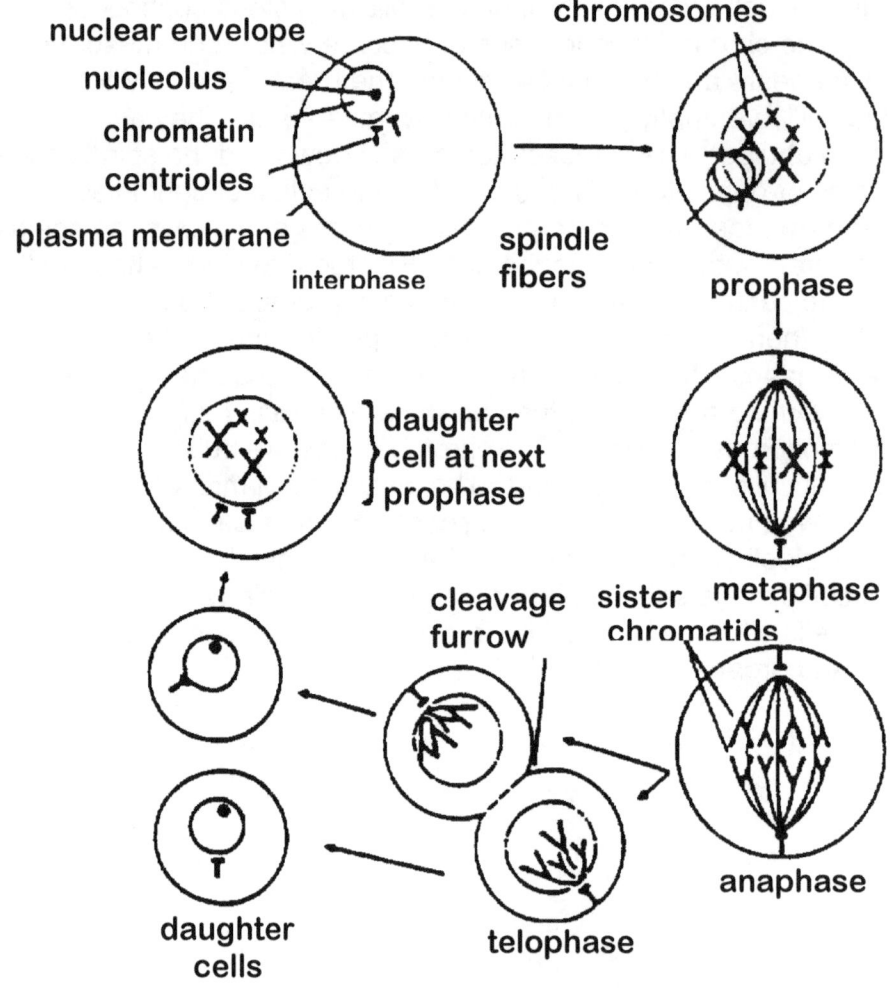

Mitosis in an Animal Cell

Meiosis is similar to mitosis, but there are two consecutive cell divisions, meiosis I and meiosis II in order to reduce the chromosome number by one half. This way, when the sperm and egg join during fertilization, the haploid number is reached.

Similar to mitosis, meiosis is preceded by an interphase during which the chromosome replicates. The steps of meiosis are as follows:

1. **Prophase I** – the replicated chromosomes condense and pair with homologues in a process called synapsis. This forms a tetrad. Crossing over, the exchange of genetic material between homologues to further increase diversity, occurs during prophase I.
2. **Metaphase I** – the homologous pairs attach to spindle fibers after lining up in the middle of the cell.
3. **Anaphase I** – the sister chromatids remain joined and move to the poles of the cell.
4. **Telophase I** – the homologous chromosome pairs continue to separate. Each pole now has a haploid chromosome set. Telophase I occurs simultaneously with cytokinesis. In animal cells, cleavage furrows form and cell plate appear in plant cells.
5. **Prophase II** – a spindle apparatus forms and the chromosomes condense.
6. **Metaphase II** – sister chromatids line up in center of cell. The centromeres divide and the sister chromatids begin to separate.
7. **Anaphase II** – the separated chromosomes move to opposite ends of the cell.
8. **Telophase II** – cytokinesis occurs, resulting in four haploid daughter cells.

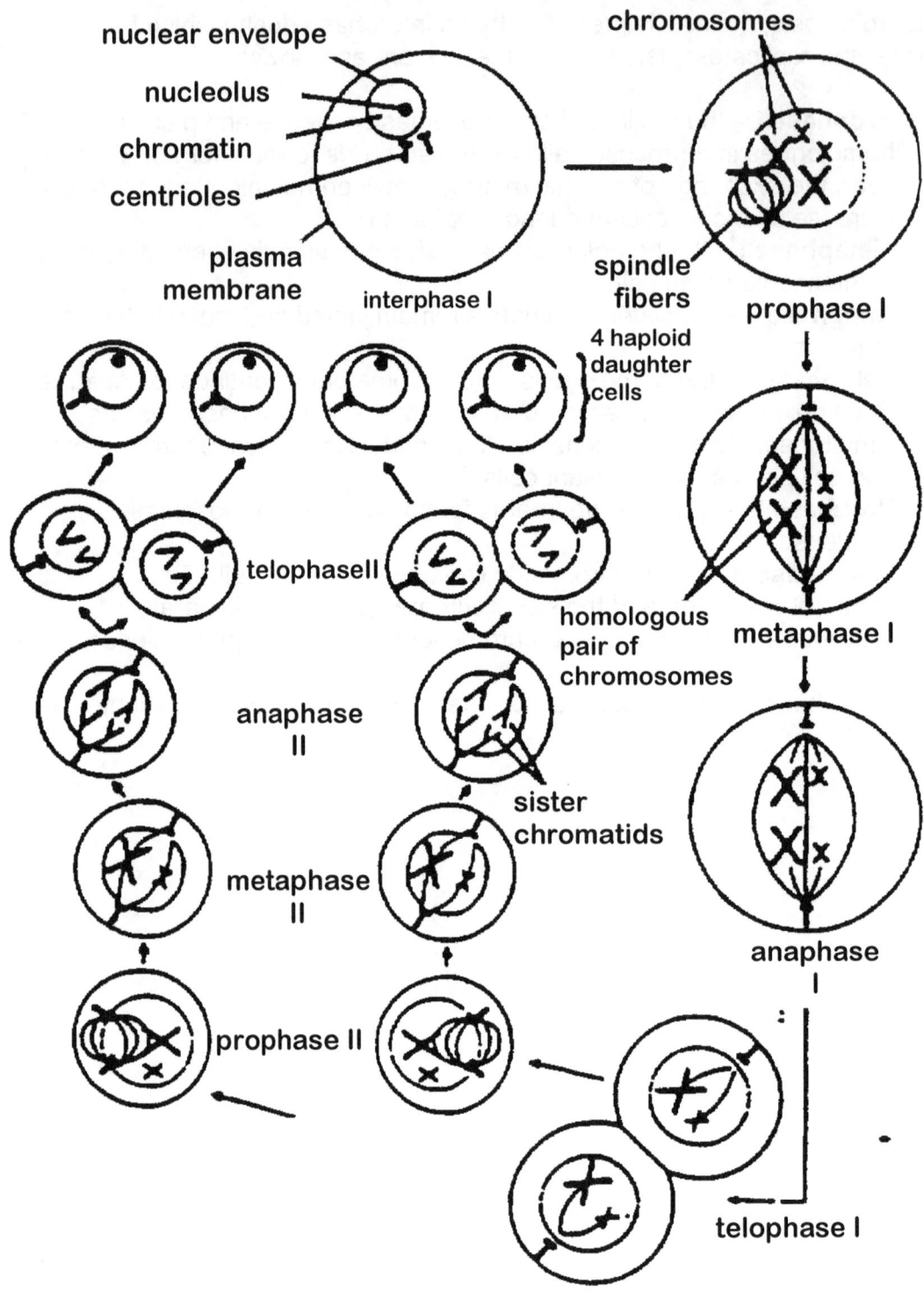

Skill 6.4 **Explain the functions and applications of the instruments and technologies used to study the life sciences at the molecular and cellular level.**

Gel electrophoresis is a method for analyzing DNA. Electrophoresis separates DNA or protein by size or electrical charge. The DNA runs towards the positive charge as it separates the DNA fragments by size. The gel is treated with a DNA-binding dye that fluoresces under ultraviolet light. A picture of the gel can be taken and used for analysis.

One of the most widely used genetic engineering techniques is **polymerase chain reaction (PCR)**. PCR is a technique in which a piece of DNA can be amplified into billions of copies within a few hours. This process requires primer to specify the segment to be copied, and an enzyme (usually taq polymerase) to amplify the DNA. PCR has allowed scientists to perform several procedures on the smallest amount of DNA.

COMPETENCY 0007 UNDERSTAND AND APPLY KNOWLEDGE OF THE PRINCIPLES OF HEREDITY AND BIOLOGICAL EVOLUTION.

Skill 7.1 Recognize the nature and function of the gene, with emphasis on the molecular basis of inheritance and gene expression.

Gregor Mendel is recognized as the father of genetics. His work in the late 1800s is the basis of our knowledge of genetics. Although unaware of the presence of DNA or genes, Mendel realized there were factors (now known as **genes**) that were transferred from parents to their offspring. Mendel worked with pea plants and fertilized the plants himself, keeping track of subsequent generations which led to the Mendelian laws of genetics. Mendel found that two "factors" governed each trait, one from each parent. Traits or characteristics came in several forms, known as **alleles**. For example, the trait of flower color had white alleles (*pp*) and purple alleles (*PP*). Mendel formed two laws: the law of segregation and the law of independent assortment.

In bacterial cells, the *lac* operon is a good example of the control of gene expression. The *lac* operon contains the genes that encode for the enzymes used to convert lactose into fuel (glucose and galactose). The *lac* operon contains three genes, *lac Z*, *lac Y*, and *lac A*. *Lac Z* encodes an enzyme for the conversion of lactose into glucose and galactose. *Lac Y* encodes for an enzyme that causes lactose to enter the cell. *Lac A* encodes for an enzyme that acetylates lactose.

The *lac* operon also contains a promoter and an operator that is the "off and on" switch for the operon. A protein called the repressor switches the operon off when it binds to the operator. When lactose is absent, the repressor is active and the operon is turned off. The operon is turned on again when allolactose (formed from lactose) inactivates the repressor by binding to it.

Skill 7.2 Analyze the transmission of genetic information (e.g., Punnett squares, sex-linked traits, pedigree analysis).

The **law of segregation** states that only one of the two possible alleles from each parent is passed on to the offspring. If the two alleles differ, then one is fully expressed in the organism's appearance (the dominant allele) and the other has no noticeable effect on appearance (the recessive allele). The two alleles for each trait segregate into different gametes. A Punnet square can be used to show the law of segregation. In a Punnet square, one parent's genes are put at the top of the box and the other parent's genes on the side. Genes combine in the squares just like numbers are added in addition tables. This Punnet square shows the result of the cross of two F_1 hybrids.

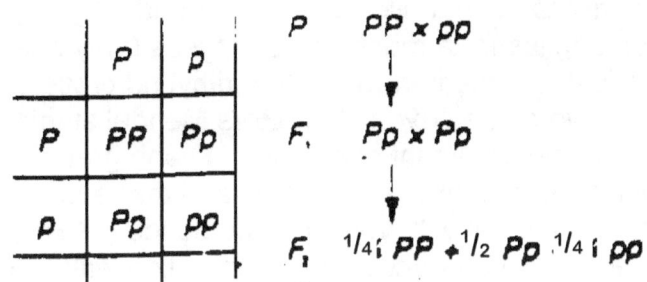

This cross results in a 1:2:1 ratio of F_2 offspring. Here, the *P* is the dominant allele and the *p* is the recessive allele. The F_1 cross produces three offspring with the dominant allele expressed (two *PP* and *Pp*) and one offspring with the recessive allele expressed (*pp*). Some other important terms to know:

> **Homozygous** – having a pair of identical alleles. For example, *PP* and *pp* are homozygous pairs.
> **Heterozygous** – having two different alleles. For example, *Pp* is a heterozygous pair.
> **Phenotype** – the organism's physical appearance.
> **Genotype** – the organism's genetic makeup. For example, *PP* and *Pp* have the same phenotype (purple in color), but different genotypes.

The **law of independent assortment** states that alleles sort independently of each other. The law of segregation applies for a monohybrid crosses (only one character, in this case flower color, is experimented with). In a dihybrid cross, two characters are being explored. Two of the seven characters Mendel studied were seed shape and color. Yellow is the dominant seed color (*Y*) and green is the recessive color (*y*). The dominant seed shape is round (*R*) and the recessive shape is wrinkled (*r*). A cross between a plant with yellow round seeds (*YYRR*) and a plant with green wrinkled seeds (*yyrr*) produces an F_1 generation with the genotype *YyRr*. The production of F_2 offspring results in a 9:3:3:1 phenotypic ratio.

F_2

	YR	Yr	yR	yr
YR	YYRR	YYRr	YyRR	YyRr
Yr	YYRr	YYrr	YyRr	Yyrr
yR	YyRR	YyRr	yyRR	yyRr
yr	YyRr	Yyrr	yyRr	yyrr

P   YYRR × yyrr

↓

F_1 YyRr

↓

F_2 YYRR - 1
     YYRr - 2 } 9 yellow round
     YyRR - 2
     YyRr - 4

     yyRR - 1 } 3 green round
     yyRr - 2

     YYrr - 1 } 3 yellow wrinkled
     Yyrr - 2

     yyrr - 1 } 1 green wrinkled

Based on Mendelian genetics, the more complex hereditary pattern of **dominance** was discovered. In Mendel's law of segregation, the F_1 generation has either purple or white flowers. This is an example of **complete dominance**. **Incomplete dominance** is when the F_1 generation results in an appearance somewhere between the two parents. For example, red flowers are crossed with white flowers, resulting in an F_1 generation with pink flowers. The red and white traits are still carried by the F_1 generation, resulting in an F_2 generation with a phenotypic ration of 1:2:1. In **codominance,** the genes may form new phenotypes. The ABO blood grouping is an example of codominance. A and B are of equal strength and O is recessive. Therefore, type A blood may have the genotypes of AA or AO, type B blood may have the genotypes of BB or BO, type AB blood has the genotype A and B, and type O blood has two recessive O genes.

A **family pedigree** is a collection of a family's history for a particular trait. As you work your way through the pedigree of interest, the Mendelian inheritance theories are applied. In tracing a trait, the generations are mapped in a pedigree chart, similar to a family tree but with the alleles present. In a case where both parent have a particular trait and one of two children also express this trait, then the trait is due to a dominant allele. In contrast, if both parents do not express a trait and one of their children do, that trait is due to a recessive allele.

Sex linked traits - the Y chromosome found only in males (XY) carries very little genetic information, whereas the X chromosome found in females (XX) carries very important information. Since men have no second X chromosome to cover up a recessive gene, the recessive trait is expressed more often in men. Women need the recessive gene on both X chromosomes to show the trait. Examples of sex linked traits include hemophilia and color-blindness.

Skill 7.3 Analyze the processes of change at the microscopic and macroscopic levels.

In order to fully understand heredity and biological evolution, students need to comprehend the material on both a smaller (microscopic) and a larger (macroscopic) scale. For example, smaller items would include molecules, DNA, and genes and larger items might include organisms and the biosphere.

The teaching of molecular biology is important to the understanding of the chemical basis of life. Students tend to associate molecules with physical science, not realizing that living systems are made of molecules as well as cells. At the macroscopic level, students learn species as a basis for classifying organisms; in order to understand species at the microscopic level, they need to comprehend the genetic basis of the species.

Microscopic Level:

Atoms, molecules, chemical processes and reactions, bacteria, viruses, protists, cells, tissues, chromosomes, genes, meiosis, mitosis, mutations, comparative embryology, molecular evolution.

Macroscopic Level:

Comparative anatomy, natural selection, convergent evolution, divergent evolution, taxonomy, organs, organisms, body systems, animal and plant structure and function, animal behavior, populations, communities, food chains and webs, biomes.

Skill 7.4 Identify scientific evidence from various sources, such as the fossil records, comparative anatomy, and biochemical similarities, to demonstrate knowledge of theories about processes of biological evolution.

The hypothesis that life developed on Earth from nonliving materials is the most widely accepted theory on the origin of life. The transformation from nonliving materials to life had four stages. The first stage was the nonliving (abiotic) synthesis of small monomers such as amino acids and nucleotides. In the second stage, these monomers combine to form polymers, such as proteins and nucleic acids. The third stage is the accumulation of these polymers into droplets called protobionts. The last stage is the origin of heredity, with RNA as the first genetic material.

The first stage of this theory was hypothesized in the 1920s. A. I. Oparin and J. B. S. Haldane were the first to theorize that the primitive atmosphere was a reducing atmosphere with no oxygen present. The gases were rich in hydrogen, methane, water and ammonia. In the 1950s, Stanley Miller proved Oparin's theory in the laboratory by combining the above gases. When given an electrical spark, he was able to synthesize simple amino acids. It is commonly accepted that amino acids appeared before DNA. Other laboratory experiments have supported the theory that other stages in the origin of life theory could have happened.

Other scientists believe simpler hereditary systems originated before nucleic acids. In 1991, Julius Rebek was able to synthesize a simple organic molecule that replicates itself. According to his theory, this simple molecule may be the precursor of RNA.

Prokaryotes are the simplest life form. Their small genome size limits the number of genes that control metabolic activities. Over time, some prokaryotic groups became multicellular organisms for this reason. Prokaryotes then evolved to form complex bacterial communities where species benefit from one another.

The **endosymbiotic theory** of the origin of eukaryotes states that eukaryotes arose from symbiotic groups of prokaryotic cells. According to this theory, smaller prokaryotes lived within larger prokaryotic cells, eventually evolving into chloroplasts and mitochondria. Chloroplasts are the descendant of photosynthetic prokaryotes and mitochondria are likely to be the descendants of bacteria that were aerobic heterotrophs. Serial endosymbiosis is a sequence of endosymbiotic events. Serial endosymbiosis may also play a role in the progression of life forms to become eukaryotes.

Fossils are the key to understanding biological history. They are the preserved remnants left by an organism that lived in the past. Scientists have established the geological time scale to determine the age of a fossil. The geological time scale is broken down into four eras: the Precambrian, Paleozoic, Mesozoic, and Cenozoic. The eras are further broken down into periods that represent a distinct age in the history of Earth and its life. Scientists use rock layers called strata to date fossils. The older layers of rock are at the bottom. This allows scientists to correlate the rock layers with the era they date back to. Radiometric dating is a more precise method of dating fossils. Rocks and fossils contain isotopes of elements accumulated over time. The isotope's half-life is used to date older fossils by determining the amount of isotope remaining and comparing it to the half-life.

Dating fossils is helpful to construct and evolutionary tree. Scientists can arrange the succession of animals based on their fossil record. The fossils of an animal's ancestors can be dated and placed on its evolutionary tree. For example, the branched evolution of horses shows the progression of the modern horse's ancestors to be larger, to have a reduced number of toes, and have teeth modified for grazing.

Comparative anatomical studies reveal that some structural features are basically similar – e.g., flowers generally have sepals, petals, stigma, style and ovary but the size, color, number of petals, sepals etc., may differ from species to species.

The degree of resemblance between two organisms indicates how closely they are related in evolution.

- Groups with little in common are supposed to have diverged from a common ancestor much earlier in geological history than groups which have more in common

- To decide how closely two organisms are, anatomists look for the structures which may serve different purpose in the adult, but are basically similar (homologous)

- In cases where similar structures serve different functions in adults, it is important to trace their origin and embryonic development

When a group of organisms share a homologous structure, which is specialized, to perform a variety of functions in order to adapt to different environmental conditions are called adaptive radiation. The gradual spreading of organisms with adaptive radiation is known as divergent evolution.

Examples of divergent evolution are the pentadactyl limb and insect mouthparts.

Under similar environmental conditions, fundamentally different structures in different groups of organisms may undergo modifications to serve similar functions. This is called convergent evolution. The structures, which have no close phylogenetic links but showing adaptation to perform the same functions, are called analogous.

Examples are – wings of bats, bird and insects, jointed legs of insects and vertebrates, eyes of vertebrates and cephalopods.

Vestigial organs: Organs that are smaller and simpler in structure than corresponding parts in the ancestral species are called vestigial organs. They are usually degenerated or underdeveloped. These were functional in ancestral species but now have become non functional, e.g., vestigial hind limbs of whales, vestigial leaves of some xerophytes, vestigial wings of flightless birds like ostriches, etc.

COMPETENCY 0008 UNDERSTAND AND APPLY KNOWLEDGE OF THE CHARACTERISTICS AND LIFE FUNCTIONS OF ORGANISMS.

Skill 8.1 Identify the levels of organization of various types of organisms and the structures and functions of cells, tissues, organs, and organ systems.

Life has defining properties. Some of the more important processes and properties associated with life are as follows:

*Order – an organism's complex organization.
*Reproduction – life only comes from life (biogenesis).
*Energy utilization – organisms use and make energy to do many kinds of work.
*Growth and development – DNA-directed growth and development.
*Adaptation to the environment – occurs by homeostasis (ability to maintain a certain status), response to stimuli, and evolution.

Life is highly organized. The organization of living systems builds on levels from small to increasingly more large and complex. All aspects, whether it is a cell or an ecosystem, have the same requirements to sustain life. Life is organized from simple to complex in the following way:

Atoms ⮕ molecules ⮕ organelles ⮕ cells ⮕ tissues ⮕ organs ⮕ organ systems ⮕ organism

Skill 8.2 Analyze the strategies and adaptations used by organisms to obtain the basic requirements of life.

Members of the five different kingdoms of the classification system of living organisms often differ in their basic life functions. Here we compare and analyze how members of the five kingdoms obtain nutrients, excrete waste, and reproduce.

Bacteria are prokaryotic, single-celled organisms that lack cell nuclei. The different types of bacteria obtain nutrients in a variety of ways. Most bacteria absorb nutrients from the environment through small channels in their cell walls and membranes (chemotrophs) while some perform photosynthesis (phototrophs). Chemoorganotrophs use organic compounds as energy sources while chemolithotrophs can use inorganic chemicals as energy sources. Depending on the type of metabolism and energy source, bacteria release a variety of waste products (e.g. alcohols, acids, carbon dioxide) into the environment through diffusion.

All bacteria reproduce through binary fission (asexual reproduction) producing two identical cells. Bacteria reproduce very rapidly, dividing or doubling every twenty minutes in optimal conditions. Asexual reproduction does not allow for genetic variation, but bacteria achieve genetic variety by absorbing DNA from ruptured cells and conjugating or swapping chromosomal or plasmid DNA with other cells.

Animals are multicellular, eukaryotic organisms. All animals obtain nutrients by eating food (ingestion). Different types of animals derive nutrients from eating plants, other animals, or both. Animal cells perform respiration that converts food molecules, mainly carbohydrates and fats, into energy. The excretory systems of animals, like animals themselves, vary in complexity. Simple invertebrates eliminate waste through a single tube, while complex vertebrates have a specialized system of organs that process and excrete waste.

Most animals, unlike bacteria, exist in two distinct sexes. Members of the female sex give birth or lay eggs. Some less developed animals can reproduce asexually. For example, flatworms can divide in two and some unfertilized insect eggs can develop into viable organisms. Most animals reproduce sexually through various mechanisms. For example, aquatic animals reproduce by external fertilization of eggs, while mammals reproduce by internal fertilization. More developed animals possess specialized reproductive systems and cycles that facilitate reproduction and promote genetic variation.

Plants, like animals, are multi-cellular, eukaryotic organisms. Plants obtain nutrients from the soil through their root systems and convert sunlight into energy through photosynthesis. Many plants store waste products in vacuoles or organs (e.g. leaves, bark) that are discarded. Some plants also excrete waste through their roots.

More than half of the plant species reproduce by producing seeds from which new plants grow. Depending on the type of plant, flowers or cones produce seeds. Other plants reproduce by spores, tubers, bulbs, buds, and grafts. The flowers of flowering plants contain the reproductive organs. Pollination is the joining of male and female gametes that is often facilitated by movement by wind or animals.

Fungi are eukaryotic, mostly multi-cellular organisms. All fungi are heterotrophs, obtaining nutrients from other organisms. More specifically, most fungi obtain nutrients by digesting and absorbing nutrients from dead organisms. Fungi secrete enzymes outside of their body to digest organic material and then absorb the nutrients through their cell walls.

Most fungi can reproduce asexually and sexually. Different types of fungi reproduce asexually by mitosis, budding, sporification, or fragmentation. Sexual reproduction of fungi is different from sexual reproduction of animals. The two mating types of fungi are plus and minus, not male and female. The fusion of hyphae, the specialized reproductive structure in fungi, between plus and minus types produces and scatters diverse spores.

Protists are eukaryotic, single-celled organisms. Most protists are heterotrophic, obtaining nutrients by ingesting small molecules and cells and by digesting them in vacuoles. All protists reproduce asexually by either binary or multiple fission. Like bacteria, protists achieve genetic variation by exchange of DNA through conjugation.

Skill 8.3 **Analyze factors (e.g., physiological, behavioral) that influence homeostasis within an organism.**

Animal behavior is responsible for courtship leading to mating, communication between species, territoriality, and aggression between animals and dominance within a group. Behaviors may include body posture, mating calls, display of feathers or fur, coloration or bearing of teeth and claws.

Innate behaviors are inborn or instinctual. An environmental stimulus such as the length of day or temperature results in a behavior. Hibernation among some animals is an innate behavior, as is a change in color known as camouflage.

Learned behavior is modified behavior due to past experience.

Skill 8.4 **Demonstrate an understanding of the human as a living organism with life functions comparable to those of other life forms.**

Humans are living organisms that display the basic properties of life. Humans share functional characteristics with all living organisms, from simple bacteria to complex mammals. The basic functions of living organisms include reproduction, growth and development, metabolism, and homeostasis/response to the environment.

Reproduction – All living organisms reproduce their own kind. Life arises only from other life. Humans reproduce through sexual reproduction, requiring the interaction of a male and a female. Human sexual reproduction is nearly identical to reproduction in other mammals. In addition, while simpler organisms have different methods of reproduction, they all reproduce. For example, the major mechanism of bacterial reproduction is asexual binary fission in which the cell divides in half, producing two identical cells.

Growth and Development – Growth and development, as directed by DNA, produces an organism characteristic of its species. In humans and other higher-level mammals, growth and development is a very complex process. In humans, growth and development requires differentiation of cells into many different types to form the various organs, structures, and functional elements. While differentiation is unique to higher level organisms, all living organisms grow. For example, the simplest bacterial cell grows in size until it divides into two organisms. Human body cells undergo a similar process, growing in size until division is necessary.

Metabolism – Metabolism is the sum of all chemical reactions that occur in a living organism. Catabolism is the breaking down of complex molecules to release energy. Anabolism is the utilization of the energy from catabolism to build complex molecules. Cellular respiration, the basic mechanism of catabolism in humans, is common to many living organisms of varying levels of complexity.

Homeostasis/Response to the Environment – All living organisms respond and adapt to their environments. Homeostasis is the result of regulatory mechanisms that help maintain an organism's internal environment within tolerable limits. For example, in humans and mammals, constriction and dilation of blood vessels near the skin help maintain body temperature.

TEACHER CERTIFICATION STUDY GUIDE

COMPETENCY 0009 UNDERSTAND AND APPLY KNOWLEDGE OF HOW ORGANISMS INTERACT WITH EACH OTHER AND WITH THEIR ENVIRONMENT.

Skill 9.1 Identify living and nonliving components of the environment and how they interact with one another.

Succession is an orderly process of replacing a community that has been damaged or has begun where no life previously existed. Primary succession occurs where life never existed before, as in a flooded area or a new volcanic island. Secondary succession takes place in communities that were once flourishing but disturbed by some source, either man or nature, but not totally stripped. A climax community is a community that is established and flourishing.

Abiotic and biotic factors play a role in succession. **Biotic factors** are living things in an ecosystem: plants, animals, bacteria, fungi, etc. **Abiotic factors** are non-living aspects of an ecosystem: soil quality, rainfall, temperature, etc.

Abiotic factors affect succession by way of the species that colonize the area. Certain species will or will not survive depending on the weather, climate, or soil makeup. Biotic factors such as inhibition of one species due to another may occur. This may be due to some form of competition between the species.

Skill 9.2 Recognize the concepts of populations, communities, ecosystems, and ecoregions and the role of biodiversity in living systems.

A **population** is a group of individuals of one species that live in the same general area. Many factors can affect the population size and its growth rate. Population size can depend on the total amount of life a habitat can support. This is the carrying capacity of the environment. Once the habitat runs out of food, water, shelter, or space, the carrying capacity decreases, and then stabilizes.

Skill 9.3 Analyze factors (e.g., ecological, behavioral) that influence interrelationships among organisms.

Ecological and behavioral factors affect the interrelationships among organisms in many ways. Two important ecological factors are environmental conditions and resource availability. Important types of organismal behaviors include competitive, instinctive, territorial, and mating.

Environmental conditions, such as climate, influence organismal interrelationships by changing the dynamic of the ecosystem. Changes in climate such as moisture levels and temperature can alter the environment, changing the characteristics that are advantageous to some species but not others. For example, an increase in temperature will favor those organisms that can tolerate the temperature change. Thus, those organisms gain a competitive advantage. In addition, the availability of necessary resources influences interrelationships. For example, when necessary resources are scarce, interrelationships are more competitive than when resources are abundant.

SCIENCE: BIOLOGY

Types of behavior that influence interrelationships:

Competitive – As previously mentioned, organisms compete for scarce resources. In addition, organisms compete with members of their own species for mates and territory. Many competitive behaviors involve rituals and dominance hierarchies. Rituals are symbolic activities that often settle disputes without undue harm. For example, dogs bare their teeth, erect their ears, and growl to intimidate competitors. A dominance hierarchy, or "pecking order", organizes groups of animals, simplifying interrelationships, conserving energy, and minimizing the potential for harm in a community.

Instinctive – Instinctive, or innate, behavior is common to all members of a given species and is genetically preprogrammed. Environmental differences do not affect instinctive behaviors. For example, baby birds of many types and species beg for food by raising their heads and opening their beaks.

Territorial – Many animals act aggressively to protect their territory from other animals. Animals protect territories for use in feeding, mating, and rearing of young.

Mating – Mating behaviors are very important interspecies interactions. The search for a mate with which to reproduce is an instinctive behavior. Mating interrelationships often involve ritualistic and territorial behaviors that are often competitive.

Skill 9.4 Develop a model or explanation that shows the relationships among organisms in the environment (e.g., food web, food chain, ecological pyramid).

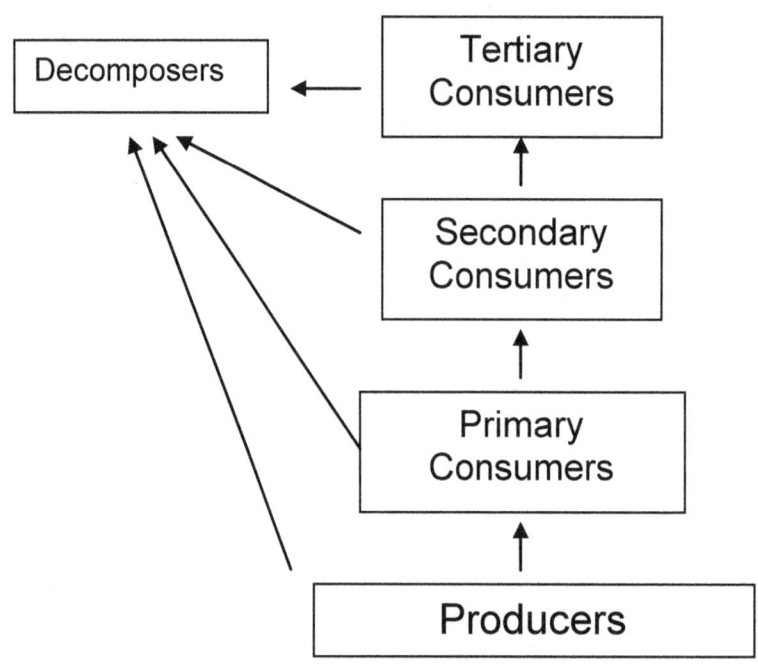

Skill 9.5 **Recognize the dynamic nature of the environment, including how communities, ecosystems, and ecoregions change over time.**

The environment is ever changing because of natural events and the actions of humans, animals, plants, and other organisms. Even the slightest changes in environmental conditions can greatly influence the function and balance of communities, ecosystems, and ecoregions. For example, subtle changes in salinity and temperature of ocean waters over time can greatly influence the range and population of certain species of fish. In addition, a slight increase in average atmospheric temperature can promote tree growth in a forest, but a corresponding increase in the viability of pathogenic bacteria can decrease the overall growth and productivity of the forest.

Another important concept in ecological change is succession. Ecological succession is the transition in the composition of species in an ecosystem, often after an ecological disturbance in the community. Primary succession begins in an environment virtually void of life, such as a volcanic island. Secondary succession occurs when a natural event disrupts an ecosystem, leaving the soil intact. An example of secondary succession is the reestablishment of a forest after destruction by a forest fire.

Factors that drive the process of succession include interspecies competition, environmental conditions, inhibition, and facilitation. In a developing ecosystem, species compete for scarce resources. The species that compete most successfully dominate. Environmental conditions, as previously discussed, influence species viability. Finally, the activities of certain species can inhibit or facilitate the growth and development of other species. Inhibition results from exploitative competition or interference competition. In facilitation, a species or group of species lays the foundation for the establishment of other, more advanced species. For example, the presence of a certain bacterial population can change the pH of the soil, allowing for the growth of different types of plants and trees.

Skill 9.6 **Analyze interactions of humans with their environment.**

The human population has been growing exponentially for centuries. People are living longer and healthier lives than ever before. Better health care and nutrition practices have helped in the survival of the population.

Human activity affects parts of the nutrient cycles by removing nutrients from one part of the biosphere and adding them to another. This results in nutrient depletion in one area and nutrient excess in another. This affects water systems, crops, wildlife, and humans.

Humans are responsible for the depletion of the ozone layer. This depletion is due to chemicals used for refrigeration and aerosols. The consequences of ozone depletion will be severe. Ozone protects the Earth from the majority of UV radiation. An increase of UV will promote skin cancer and unknown effects on wildlife and plants.

Humans have a tremendous impact on the world's natural resources. The world's natural water supplies are affected by human use. Waterways are major sources for recreation and freight transportation. Oil and wastes from boats and cargo ships pollute the aquatic environment. The aquatic plant and animal life is affected by this contamination.

Deforestation for urban development has resulted in the extinction or relocation of several species of plants and animals. Animals are forced to leave their forest homes or perish amongst the destruction. The number of plant and animal species that have become extinct due to deforestation is unknown. Scientists have only identified a fraction of the species on Earth. It is known that if the destruction of natural resources continues, there may be no plants or animals successfully reproducing in the wild.

Humans are continuously searching for new places to form communities. This encroachment on the environment leads to the destruction of wildlife communities. Conservationists focus on endangered species, but the primary focus should be on protecting the entire biome. If a biome becomes extinct, the wildlife dies or invades another biome.

Preservations established by the government aim at protecting small parts of biomes. While beneficial in the conservation of a few areas, the majority of the environment is still unprotected.

Skill 9.7   Explain the functions and applications of the instruments and technologies used to study the life sciences at the organism and ecosystem level.

Biologists use a variety of tools and technologies to perform tests, collect and display data, and analyze relationships at the organismal and ecosystem level. Examples of commonly used tools include computer-linked probes, computerized tracking devices, computer models and databases, and spreadsheets.

Biologists use computer-linked probes to measure various environmental factors including temperature, dissolved oxygen, pH, ionic concentration, and pressure. The advantage of computer-linked probes, as compared to more traditional observational tools, is that the probes automatically gather data and present it in an accessible format. This property of computer-linked probes eliminates the need for constant human observation and manipulation.

Biologists use computerized tracking devices to study the behavior of animals in an ecosystem. Biologists can implant computer chips on animals to track movement and migration, population changes, and general behavioral characteristics.

Computer models allow biologists to use data and information they collect in the field to make predictions and projections about the future of ecosystems and organisms. Because ecosystems are large and change very slowly, direct observation is not a suitable strategy for ecological studies. For example, while a scientist cannot reasonably expect to observe and gather data over an entire ecosystem, she can collect samples and use computer databases and models to make projections about the ecosystem as a whole.

Finally, biologists use spreadsheets to organize, analyze, and display data. For example, conservation ecologists use spreadsheets to model population growth and development, apply sampling techniques, and create statistical distributions to analyze relationships. Spreadsheet use simplifies data collection and manipulation and allows the presentation of data in a logical and understandable format.

SUBAREA III.   **PHYSICAL SCIENCE**

COMPETENCY 0010   **UNDERSTAND AND APPLY KNOWLEDGE OF THE NATURE AND PROPERTIES OF ENERGY IN ITS VARIOUS FORMS.**

Skill 10.1   **Describe the characteristics of and relationships among thermal, acoustical, radiant, electrical, chemical, mechanical, and nuclear energies through conceptual questions.**

Thermal energy is the total internal energy of objects created by the vibration and movement of atoms and molecules. Heat is the transfer of thermal energy.

Acoustical energy, or sound energy, is the movement of energy through an object in waves. Energy that forces an object to vibrate creates sound.

Radiant energy is the energy of electromagnetic waves. Light, visible and otherwise, is an example of radiant energy.

Electrical energy is the movement of electrical charges in an electromagnetic field. Examples of electrical energy are electricity and lightning.

Chemical energy is the energy stored in the chemical bonds of molecules. For example, the energy derived from gasoline is chemical energy.

Mechanical energy is the potential and kinetic energy of a mechanical system. Rolling balls, car engines, and body parts in motion exemplify mechanical energy.

Nuclear energy is the energy present in the nucleus of atoms. Division, combination, or collision of nuclei release nuclear energy.

Skill 10.2   **Analyze the processes by which energy is exchanged or transformed through conceptual questions.**

Interacting objects in the universe constantly exchange and transform energy. Total energy remains the same, but the form of the energy readily changes. Energy often changes from kinetic (motion) to potential (stored) or potential to kinetic. In reality, available energy, energy that is easily utilized, is rarely conserved in energy transformations. Heat energy is an example of relatively "useless" energy often generated during energy transformations. Exothermic reactions release heat and endothermic reactions require heat energy to proceed. For example, the human body is notoriously inefficient in converting chemical energy from food into mechanical energy. The digestion of food is exothermic and produces substantial heat energy.

Skill 10.3   Apply the three laws of thermodynamics to explain energy transformations, including basic algebraic problem solving.

The three laws of thermodynamics are as follows:

1. The total amount of energy in the universe is constant, energy cannot be created or destroyed, but can merely change form.

    Equation:
    $\Delta E = Q + W$
    Change in energy = (Heat energy entering or leaving) + (work done)

2. In energy transformations, entropy (disorder) increases and useful energy is lost (as heat).

    Equation:
    $\Delta S = \Delta Q / T$
    Change in entropy = (Heat transfer) / (Temperature)

3. As the temperature of a system approaches absolute zero, entropy (disorder) approaches a constant.

Sample Problems:
1. A car engine burns gasoline to power the car. An amount of gasoline containing 2000J of stored chemical energy produced 1500J of mechanical energy to power the engine. How much heat energy did the engine release?

Solution:
$\Delta E = Q + W$	the first law of thermodynamics
2000J = Q + 1500J	apply the first law
Q (work) = 500J	solve

2. 18200J of heat leaks out of a hot oven. The temperature of the room is 25°C (298K). What is the increase in entropy resulting from this heat transfer?

Solution:
$\Delta S = \Delta Q / T$	the second law of thermodynamics
ΔS = 18200J / 298K	apply the second law
= 61.1 J/K	solve

Skill 10.4　Apply the principle of conservation as it applies to energy through conceptual questions and solving basic algebraic problems.

The law of conservation of energy states that energy is neither created nor destroyed. Thus, energy changes form when energy transactions occur in nature. Because the total energy in the universe is constant, energy continually transitions between forms. For example, an engine burns gasoline converting the chemical energy of the gasoline into mechanical energy, a plant converts radiant energy of the sun into chemical energy found in glucose, or a battery converts chemical energy into electrical energy.

COMPETENCY 0011 UNDERSTAND AND APPLY KNOWLEDGE OF THE STRUCTURE AND PROPERTIES OF MATTER.

Skill 11.1 Describe the nuclear and atomic structure of matter, including the three parts of the atom.

An **atom** is a nucleus surrounded by a cloud with moving electrons.

The **nucleus** is the center of the atom. The positive particles inside the nucleus are called **protons.** The mass of a proton is about 2,000 times that of the mass of an electron. The number of protons in the nucleus of an atom is called the **atomic number**. All atoms of the same element have the same atomic number.

Neutrons are another type of particle in the nucleus. Neutrons and protons have about the same mass, but neutrons have no charge. Neutrons were discovered because scientists observed that not all atoms in neon gas have the same mass. They had identified isotopes. **Isotopes** of an element have the same number of protons in the nucleus, but have different masses. Neutrons explain the difference in mass. They have mass but no charge.

The mass of matter is measured against a standard mass such as the gram. Scientists measure the mass of an atom by comparing it to that of a standard atom. The result is relative mass. The **relative mass** of an atom is its mass expressed in terms of the mass of the standard atom. The isotope of the element carbon is the standard atom. It has six (6) neutrons and is called carbon-12. It is assigned a mass of 12 atomic mass units (amu). Therefore, the **atomic mass unit (amu)** is the standard unit for measuring the mass of an atom. It is equal to the mass of a carbon atom.

The **mass number** of an atom is the sum of its protons and neutrons. In any element, there is a mixture of isotopes, some having slightly more or slightly fewer protons and neutrons. The **atomic mass** of an element is an average of the mass numbers of its atoms.

The following table summarizes the terms used to describe atomic nuclei:

Term	Example	Meaning	Characteristic
Atomic Number	# protons (p)	same for all atoms of a given element	Carbon (C) atomic number = 6 (6p)
Mass number	# protons + # neutrons (p + n)	changes for different isotopes of an element	C-12 (6p + 6n) C-13 (6p + 7n)
Atomic mass	average mass of the atoms of the element	usually not a whole number	atomic mass of carbon equals 12.011

Each atom has an equal number of electrons (negative) and protons (positive). Therefore, atoms are neutral. Electrons orbiting the nucleus occupy energy levels that are arranged in order and the electrons tend to occupy the lowest energy level available. A **stable electron arrangement** is an atom that has all of its electrons in the lowest possible energy levels.

Each energy level holds a maximum number of electrons. However, an atom with more than one level does not hold more than 8 electrons in its outermost shell.

Level	Name	Max. # of Electrons
First	K shell	2
Second	L shell	8
Third	M shell	18
Fourth	N shell	32

This can help explain why chemical reactions occur. Atoms react with each other when their outer levels are unfilled. When atoms either exchange or share electrons with each other, these energy levels become filled and the atom becomes more stable.

As an electron gains energy, it moves from one energy level to a higher energy level. The electron can not leave one level until it has enough energy to reach the next level. **Excited electrons** are electrons that have absorbed energy and have moved farther from the nucleus.

Electrons can also lose energy. When they do, they fall to a lower level. However, they can only fall to the lowest level that has room for them. This explains why atoms do not collapse.

SCIENCE: BIOLOGY

Skill 11.2 **Analyze the properties of materials in relation to their chemical or physical structures (e.g., periodic table trends, relationships, and properties) and evaluate uses of the materials based on their properties.**

The **periodic table of elements** is an arrangement of the elements in rows and columns so that it is easy to locate elements with similar properties. The elements of the modern periodic table are arranged in numerical order by atomic number.

The **periods** are the rows down the left side of the table. They are called first period, second period, etc. The columns of the periodic table are called **groups**, or **families.** Elements in a family have similar properties.

There are three types of elements that are grouped by color: metals, nonmetals, and metalloids.

Element Key

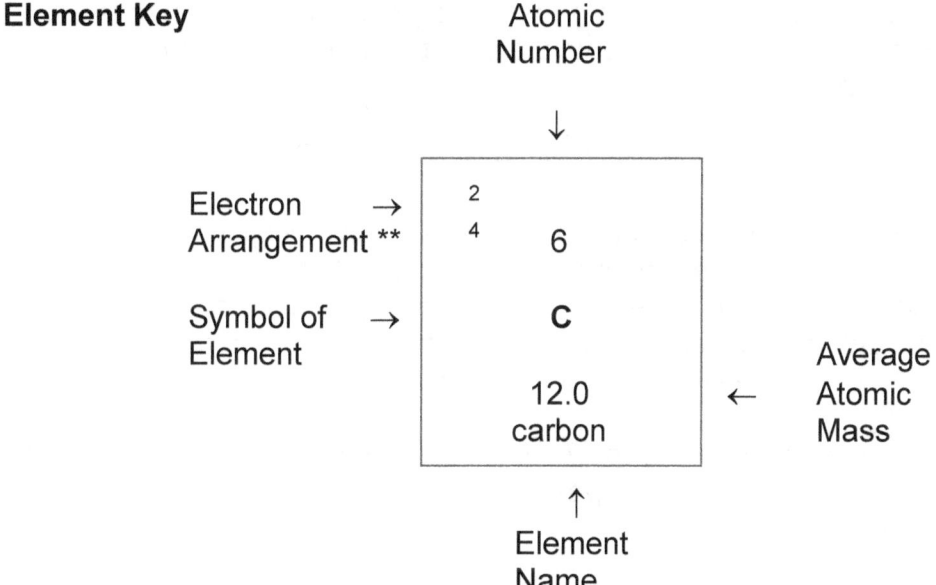

** Number of electrons on each level. Top number represents the innermost level.

The periodic table arranges metals into families with similar properties. The periodic table has its columns marked IA - VIIIA. These are the traditional group numbers. Arabic numbers 1 - 18 are also used, as suggested by the Union of Physicists and Chemists. The Arabic numerals will be used in this text.

Metals:

With the exception of hydrogen, all elements in Group 1 are **alkali metals**. These metals are shiny, softer, less dense, and the most chemically active.

Group 2 metals are the **alkaline earth metals.** They are harder, denser, have higher melting points, and are chemically active.

The **transition elements** can be found by finding the periods (rows) from 4 to 7 under the groups (columns) 3 - 12. They are metals that do not show a range of properties as you move across the chart. They are hard and have high melting points. Compounds of these elements are colorful, such as silver, gold, and mercury.

Elements can be combined to make metallic objects. An **alloy** is a mixture of two or more elements having properties of metals. The elements do not have to be all metals. For instance, steel is made up of the metal iron and the non-metal carbon.

Nonmetals:

Nonmetals are not as easy to recognize as metals because they do not always share physical properties. However, in general the properties of nonmetals are the opposite of metals. They are not shiny, are brittle, and are not good conductors of heat and electricity.

Nonmetals are solids, gases, and one liquid (bromine).

Nonmetals have four to eight electrons in their outermost energy levels and tend to attract electrons to their outer energy levels. As a result, the outer levels usually are filled with eight electrons. This difference in the number of electrons is what caused the differences between metals and nonmetals. The outstanding chemical property of nonmetals is that react with metals.

The **halogens** can be found in Group 17. Halogens combine readily with metals to form salts. Table salt, fluoride toothpaste, and bleach all have an element from the halogen family.

The **Noble Gases** got their name from the fact that they did not react chemically with other elements, much like the nobility did not mix with the masses. These gases (found in Group 18) will only combine with other elements under very specific conditions. They are **inert** (inactive).

In recent years, scientists have found this to be only generally true, since chemists have been able to prepare compounds of krypton and xenon.

Metalloids:

Metalloids have properties in between metals and nonmetals. They can be found in Groups 13 - 16, but do not occupy the entire group. They are arranged in stair steps across the groups.

Physical Properties:
1. All are solids having the appearance of metals.
2. All are white or gray, but not shiny.
3. They will conduct electricity, but not as well as a metal.

Chemical Properties:
1. Have some characteristics of metals and nonmetals.
2. Properties do not follow patterns like metals and nonmetals. Each must be studied individually.

Boron is the first element in Group 13. It is a poor conductor of electricity at low temperatures. However, increase its temperature and it becomes a good conductor. By comparison, metals, which are good conductors, lose their ability as they are heated. It is because of this property that boron is so useful. Boron is a semiconductor. **Semiconductors** are used in electrical devices that have to function at temperatures too high for metals.

Silicon is the second element in Group 14. It is also a semiconductor and is found in great abundance in the earth's crust. Sand is made of a silicon compound, silicon dioxide. Silicon is also used in the manufacture of glass and cement.

Skill 11.3 Apply the principle of conservation as it applies to mass and charge through conceptual questions.

The principle of conservation states that certain measurable properties of an isolated system remain constant despite changes in the system. Two important principles of conservation are the conservation of mass and charge.

The principle of conservation of mass states that the total mass of a system is constant. Examples of conservation in mass in nature include the burning of wood, rusting of iron, and phase changes of matter. When wood burns, the total mass of the products, such as soot, ash, and gases, equals the mass of the wood and the oxygen that reacts with it. When iron reacts with oxygen, rust forms. The total mass of the iron-rust complex does not change. Finally, when matter changes phase, mass remains constant. Thus, when a glacier melts due to atmospheric warming, the mass of liquid water formed is equal to the mass of the glacier.

The principle of conservation of charge states that the total electrical charge of a closed system is constant. Thus, in chemical reactions and interactions of charged objects, the total charge does not change. Chemical reactions and the interaction of charged molecules are essential and common processes in living organisms and systems.

Skill 11.4 Analyze bonding and chemical, atomic, and nuclear reactions (including endothermic and exothermic reactions) in natural and man-made systems and apply basic stoichiometric principles.

Chemical reactions are the interactions of substances resulting in chemical change and change in energy. Chemical reactions involve changes in electron motion and the breaking and forming of chemical bonds. Reactants are the original substances that interact to form distinct products. Endothermic chemical reactions consume energy while exothermic chemical reactions release energy with product formation. Chemical reactions occur continually in nature and are also induced by man for many purposes.

Nuclear reactions, or **atomic reactions**, are reactions that change the composition, energy, or structure of atomic nuclei. Nuclear reactions change the number of protons and neutrons in the nucleus. The two main types of nuclear reactions are fission (splitting of nuclei) and fusion (joining of nuclei). Fusion reactions are exothermic, releasing heat energy. Fission reactions are endothermic, absorbing heat energy. Fission of large nuclei (e.g. uranium) releases energy because the products of fission undergo further fusion reactions. Fission and fusion reactions can occur naturally, but are most recognized as man-made events. Particle acceleration and bombardment with neutrons are two methods of inducing nuclear reactions.

Stoichiometry is the calculation of quantitative relationships between reactants and products in chemical reactions. Scientists use stoichiometry to balance chemical equations, make conversions between units of measurement (e.g. grams to moles), and determine the correct amount of reactants to use in chemical reactions.

Example:

The reaction of iron (Fe) and hydrochloric acid (HCl) produces H_2 and $FeCl_2$. Determine the amount of HCl required to react with 200g of Fe.

$Fe + HCl = H_2 + FeCl_2$

$Fe + 2HCl = H_2 + FeCl_2$ Balance equation (equal number of atoms on each side)

$$\frac{200 g\ Fe}{1} \cdot \frac{1\ mol\ Fe}{55.8 g\ Fe} \cdot \frac{2\ mol\ HCl}{1\ mol\ Fe} \cdot \frac{36.5 g\ HCl}{1\ mol\ HCl}$$ Perform stoichiometric calculations

= 262 g of HCl required to react completely with 200 g Fe   Solve

Skill 11.5 Apply kinetic theory to explain interactions of energy with matter, including conceptual questions on changes in state.

The kinetic theory states that matter consists of molecules, possessing kinetic energies, in continual random motion. The state of matter (solid, liquid, or gas) depends on the speed of the molecules and the amount of kinetic energy the molecules possess. The molecules of solid matter merely vibrate allowing strong intermolecular forces to hold the molecules in place. The molecules of liquid matter move freely and quickly throughout the body and the molecules of gaseous matter move randomly and at high speeds.

Matter changes state when energy is added or taken away. The addition of energy, usually in the form of heat, increases the speed and kinetic energy of the component molecules. Faster moving molecules more readily overcome the intermolecular attractions that maintain the form of solids and liquids. In conclusion, as the speed of molecules increases, matter changes state from solid to liquid to gas (melting and evaporation).

As matter loses heat energy to the environment, the speed of the component molecules decreases. Intermolecular forces have greater impact on slower moving molecules. Thus, as the speed of molecules decrease, matter changes from gas to liquid to solid (condensation and freezing).

Skill 11.6 Explain the functions and applications of the instruments and technologies used to study matter and energy.

Scientists utilize various instruments and technologies to study matter and energy. Commonly used instruments include spectrometers, basic measuring devices, thermometers, and calorimeters.

Spectroscopy is the study of absorption and emission of energy of different frequencies by molecules and atoms. The spectrometer is the instrument used in spectroscopy. Because different molecules and atoms have different spectroscopic properties, spectroscopy helps scientists determine the molecular composition of matter.

Basic devices, like scales and rulers, measure the physical properties of matter. Scientists often measure the size, volume, and mass of different forms of matter.

Thermometers and calorimeters measure the energy exchanged in chemical reactions. Temperature change during chemical reactions is indicative of the flow of energy into or out of a system of reactants and products.

TEACHER CERTIFICATION STUDY GUIDE

COMPETENCY 0012 UNDERSTAND AND APPLY KNOWLEDGE OF FORCES AND MOTION.

Skill 12.1 Demonstrate an understanding of the concepts and interrelationships of position, time, velocity, and acceleration through conceptual questions, algebra-based kinematics, and graphical analysis.

Position is relative. Your position in the center of the room is relative to the size of the room. A car's position on a track is relative to the determination of the track's start and end points. The velocity of an object can be defined as its speed in a particular direction. Both speed and direction are required to velocity. The symbol for velocity is v. It is the measurement of the rate of change of displacement from a fixed point. Acceleration (symbol: a) is defined as the rate of change (with respect to time) of velocity. Acceleration is measured in units of length/time², usually meters/second^2. To accelerate an object is to change its velocity, which is accomplished by altering either its speed or direction with respect to time. Acceleration has to do with changing how fast an object is moving. If an object is not changing its velocity, then the object is not accelerating. If an object is moving northward at a velocity of 10 m/s at 1 sec, and 20 m/s one second later (t= 2 sec), it is accelerating.

Skill 12.2 Demonstrate an understanding of the concepts and interrelationships of force (including gravity and friction), inertia, work, power, energy, and momentum.

Entropy is the measure of how much energy or heat is available for work. Work occurs only when heat is transferred from hot to cooler objects. Once this is done, no more work can be extracted. The energy is still being conserved, but is not available for work as long as the objects are the same temperature. Theory has it that, eventually, all things in the universe will reach the same temperature. If this happens, energy will no longer be usable.

Forces
Dynamics is the study of the relationship between motion and the forces affecting motion. **Force** causes motion.
Mass and weight are not the same quantities. An object's **mass** gives it a reluctance to change its current state of motion. It is also the measure of an object's resistance to acceleration. The force that the earth's gravity exerts on an object with a specific mass is called the object's weight on earth. Weight is a force that is measured in Newtons. Weight (W) = mass times acceleration due to gravity (**W = mg**). To illustrate the difference between mass and weight, picture two rocks of equal mass on a balance scale. If the scale is balanced in one place, it will be balanced everywhere, regardless of the gravitational field. However, the weight of the stones would vary on a spring scale, depending upon the gravitational field.

SCIENCE: BIOLOGY

In other words, the stones would be balanced both on earth and on the moon. However, the weight of the stones would be greater on earth than on the moon.

Newton's laws of motion:

Newton's first law of motion is also called the law of inertia. It states that an object at rest will remain at rest and an object in motion will remain in motion at a constant velocity unless acted upon by an external force.

Newton's second law of motion states that if a net force acts on an object, it will cause the acceleration of the object. The relationship between force and motion is Force equals mass times acceleration. **(F = ma).**

Newton's third law states that for every action there is an equal and opposite reaction. Therefore, if an object exerts a force on another object, that second object exerts an equal and opposite force on the first.

Surfaces that touch each other have a certain resistance to motion. This resistance is **friction.**
1. The materials that make up the surfaces will determine the magnitude of the frictional force.
2. The frictional force is independent of the area of contact between the two surfaces.
3. The direction of the frictional force is opposite to the direction of motion.
4. The frictional force is proportional to the normal force between the two surfaces in contact.

Static friction describes the force of friction of two surfaces that are in contact but do not have any motion relative to each other, such as a block sitting on an inclined plane. **Kinetic friction** describes the force of friction of two surfaces in contact with each other when there is relative motion between the surfaces.

When an object moves in a circular path, a force must be directed toward the center of the circle in order to keep the motion going. This constraining force is called **centripetal force**. Gravity is the centripetal force that keeps a satellite circling the earth.

Push and pull –Pushing a volleyball or pulling a bowstring applies muscular force when the muscles expand and contract. Elastic force is when any object returns to its original shape (for example, when a bow is released).

Rubbing – Friction opposes the motion of one surface past another. Friction is common when slowing down a car or sledding down a hill.

Pull of gravity – is a force of attraction between two objects. Gravity questions can be raised not only on earth but also between planets and even black hole discussions.

Forces on objects at rest – The formula F= m/a is shorthand for force equals mass over acceleration. An object will not move unless the force is strong enough to move the mass. Also, there can be opposing forces holding the object in place. For instance, a boat may want to be forced by the currents to drift away but an equal and opposite force is a rope holding it to a dock.

Forces on a moving object - Overcoming inertia is the tendency of any object to oppose a change in motion. An object at rest tends to stay at rest. An object that is moving tends to keep moving.

Inertia and circular motion – The centripetal force is provided by the high banking of the curved road and by friction between the wheels and the road. This inward force that keeps an object moving in a circle is called centripetal force.

Simple machines include the following:

1. Inclined plane
2. Lever
3. Wheel and axle
4. Pulley

Compound machines are two or more simple machines working together. A wheelbarrow is an example of a complex machine. It uses a lever and a wheel and axle. Machines of all types ease workload by changing the size or direction of an applied force. The amount of effort saved when using simple or complex machines is called mechanical advantage or MA.

Work is done on an object when an applied force moves through a distance.

Power is the work done divided by the amount of time that it took to do it. (Power = Work / time)

Skill 12.3   **Describe and predict the motions of bodies in one and two dimensions in inertial and accelerated frames of reference in a physical system, including projectile motion but excluding circular motion.**

The science of describing the motion of bodies is known as **kinematics**. The motion of bodies is described using words, diagrams, numbers, graphs, and equations.

The following words are used to describe motion: vectors, scalars, distance, displacement, speed, velocity, and acceleration.

The two categories of mathematical quantities that are used to describe the motion of objects are scalars and vectors. **Scalars** are quantities that are fully described by magnitude alone. Examples of scalars are 5m and 20 degrees Celsius. **Vectors** are quantities that are fully described by magnitude and direction. Examples of vectors are 30m/sec, and 5 miles north.

Distance is a scalar quantity that refers to how much ground an object has covered while moving. **Displacement** is a vector quantity that refers to the object's change in position.

   Example:

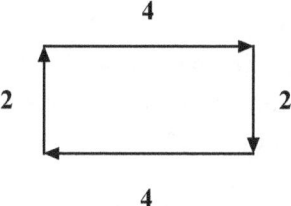

Jamie walked 2 miles north, 4 miles east, 2 miles south, and then 4 miles west. In terms of distance, she walked 12 miles. However, there is no displacement because the directions cancelled each other out, and she returned to her starting position.

Speed is a scalar quantity that refers to how fast an object is moving (ex. the car was traveling 60 mi./hr). **Velocity** is a vector quantity that refers to the rate at which an object changes its position. In other words, velocity is speed with direction (ex. the car was traveling 60 mi./hr east).

$$\text{Average speed} = \frac{\text{Distance traveled}}{\text{Time of travel}}$$

$$v = \frac{d}{t}$$

$$\text{Average velocity} = \frac{\Delta \text{position}}{\text{time}} = \frac{\text{displacement}}{\text{time}}$$

Instantaneous Speed - speed at any given instant in time.

Average Speed - average of all instantaneous speeds, found simply by a distance/time ratio.

Acceleration is a vector quantity defined as the rate at which an object changes its velocity.

$$a = \frac{\Delta velocity}{time} = \frac{v_f - v_i}{t}$$ where f = the final velocity and i = the initial velocity

Since acceleration is a vector quantity, it always has a direction associated with it. The direction of the acceleration vector depends on

- whether the object is speeding up or slowing down
- whether the object is moving in the positive or negative direction.

Newton's Three Laws of Motion:

First Law: An object at rest tends to stay at rest and an object in motion tends to stay in motion with the same speed and in the same direction unless acted upon by an unbalanced force, for example, when riding on a descending elevator that suddenly stops, blood rushes from your head to your feet. **Inertia** is the resistance an object has to a change in its state of motion.

Second Law: The acceleration of an object depends directly upon the net force acting upon the object, and inversely upon the mass of the object. As the net force increases, so will the object's acceleration. However, as the mass of the object increases, its acceleration will decrease.

$$F_{net} = m * a$$

Third Law: For every action, there is an equal and opposite reaction, for example, when a bird is flying, the motion of its wings pushes air downward; the air reacts by pushing the bird upward.

Projectile Motion

By definition, a **projectile** has only one force acting upon it – the force of gravity.

Gravity influences the vertical motion of the projectile, causing vertical acceleration. The horizontal motion of the projectile is the result of the tendency of any object in motion to remain in motion at constant velocity. (Remember, there are no horizontal forces acting upon the projectile. By definition, gravity is the only force acting upon the projectile.)

Projectiles travel with a parabolic trajectory due to the fact that the downward force of gravity accelerates them downward from their otherwise straight-line trajectory. Gravity affects the vertical motion, not the horizontal motion, of the projectile. Gravity causes a downward displacement from the position that the object would be in if there were no gravity.

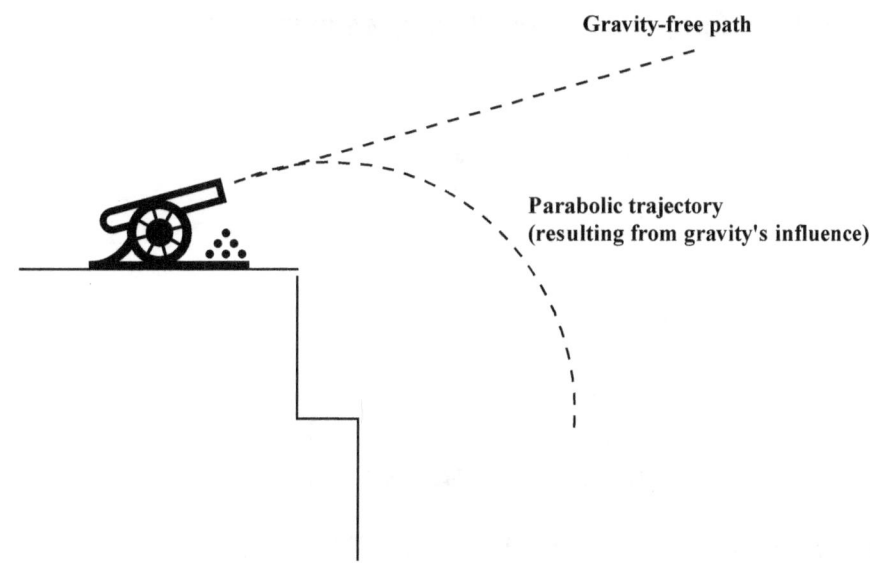

Skill 12.4 Analyze and predict motions and interactions of bodies involving forces within the context of conservation of energy and/or momentum through conceptual questions and algebra-based problem solving.

The Law of **Conservation of Energy** states that energy may neither be created nor destroyed. Therefore, the sum of all energies in the system is a constant.

Example:

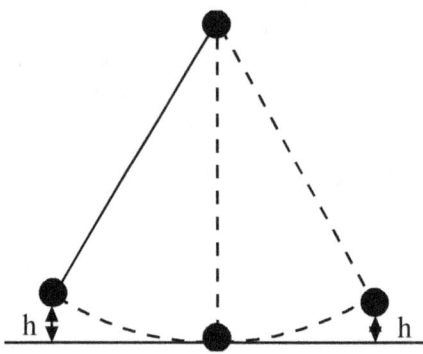

The formula to calculate the potential energy is PE = mgh.

The mass of the ball = 20kg
The height, h = 0.4m
The acceleration due to gravity, g = 9.8 m/s^2

PE = mgh
PE = 20(.4)(9.8)
PE = 78.4J (Joules, units of energy)

The position of the ball on the left is where the Potential Energy (PE) = 78.4J resides while the Kinetic Energy (KE) = 0. As the ball is approaching the center position, the PE is decreasing while the KE is increasing. At exactly halfway between the left and center positions, the PE = KE.

The center position of the ball is where the Kinetic Energy is at its maximum while the Potential Energy (PE) = 0. At this point, theoretically, the entire PE has transformed into KE. Now the KE = 78.4J while the PE = 0.

The right position of the ball is where the Potential Energy (PE) is once again at its maximum and the Kinetic Energy (KE) = 0.

We can now say that:

$$PE + KE = 0$$
$$PE = -KE$$

The sum of PE and KE is the **total mechanical energy**:

Total Mechanical Energy = PE + KE

The law of **momentum conservation** can be stated as follows: For a collision occurring between object 1 and object 2 in an isolated system, the total momentum of the two objects before the collision is equal to the total momentum of the two objects after the collision. That is, the momentum lost by object 1 is equal to the momentum gained by object 2.

Example:

A 90 kg soccer player moving west at 4 m/s collides with an 80 kg soccer player moving east at 5 m/s. After the collision, both players move east at 3 m/s. Draw a vector diagram in which the before and after collision momenta of each player is represented by a momentum vector.

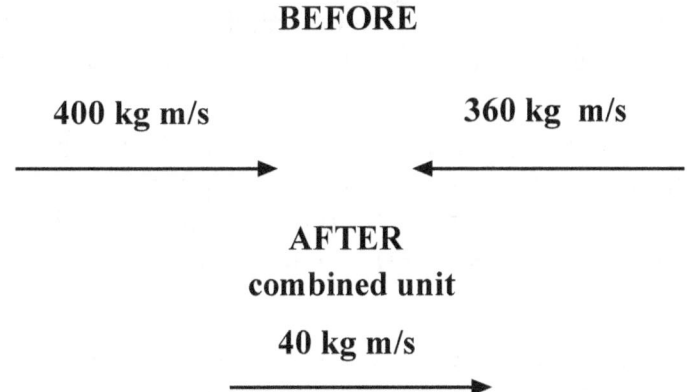

The combined momentum before the collision is +400 kg m/s + (- 360 kg m/s) or 40 kg m/s. According to the law of conservation of momentum, the combined momentum after a collision must be equal to the combined momentum before the collision.

Skill 12.5 Describe the effects of gravitational and nuclear forces in real-life situations through conceptual questions.

Gravitational and the two nuclear forces make up three of the four fundamental forces of nature, with electromagnetic force being the fourth.

Gravitational force is defined as the force of attraction between all masses in the universe. Every object exerts gravitational force on every other object. This force depends on the masses of the objects and the distance between them. The gravitational force between any two masses is given by Newton's law of universal gravitation, which states that the force is inversely proportional to the square of the distance between the masses. Near the surface of the Earth, the acceleration of an object due to gravity is independent of the mass of the object and therefore constant.

It is the gravitational attraction of the Earth that gives weight to objects with mass and causes them to fall to the ground when dropped. Gravity is responsible for the existence of the objects in our solar system. Without it, the celestial bodies would not be held together. It keeps the Earth and all the other planets in orbit around the sun, keeps the moon in orbit around the Earth, and causes the formation of the tides.

Examples of mechanisms that utilize gravity to some degree are intravenous drips and water towers where the height difference provides a pressure differential in the liquid. The gravitational potential energy of water is also used to generate hydroelectricity. Pendulum clocks depend upon gravity to regulate time.

There are two types of nuclear forces: strong and weak. The strong force is an interaction that binds protons and neutrons together in atomic nuclei. The strong force only acts on elementary particles directly, but is observed between hadrons (subatomic particles) as the nuclear force.

The weak force is an interaction between elementary particles involving neutrinos or antineutrinos. Its most familiar effects are beta decay and the associated radioactivity.

Skill 12.6   Explain the functions and applications of the instruments and technologies used to study force and motion in everyday life.

The **speedometer** in a car indicates how fast the car is going at any moment (instantaneous speed).

Tachometers measure the speed of rotation of a shaft or disk. In an automobile, this assists the driver in choosing gear settings with a manual transmission. Tachometers are also used in medicine to measure blood flow.

Gravity gradiometers are used in petroleum exploration to determine areas of higher or lower density in the earth's crust.

An **accelerometer** is a device for measuring acceleration. Accelerometers are used along with gyroscopes in inertial guidance systems for rocket programs. One of the most common uses for accelerometers is in airbag deployment systems in automobiles. The accelerometers are used to detect rapid deceleration of the vehicle to determine when a collision has occurred and the severity of the collision. Research is currently being done on the use of accelerometers to improve Global Positioning Systems (GPS). An accelerometer can infer position in places such as tunnels where the GPS cannot detect it. They are incorporated into Tablet PCs to align the screen based upon the direction in which the PC is being held and in many laptop computers to detect falling and protect the data on the hard drive. Accelerometers are incorporated into sports watches to indicate speed and distance (useful to runners).

A **gravimeter** is a device used to measure the local gravitational field. They are much more sensitive than accelerometers. Measurements of the surface gravity of the earth are part of geophysical analysis, which includes the study of earthquakes.

Weighing scales, such as spring scales, are sometimes used to measure force rather than mass or weight.

TEACHER CERTIFICATION STUDY GUIDE

COMPETENCY 0013 UNDERSTAND AND APPLY KNOWLEDGE OF ELECTRICITY, MAGNETISM, AND WAVES.

Skill 13.1 Recognize the nature and properties of electricity and magnetism, including static charge, moving charge, basic RC circuits, fields, conductors, and insulators.

An **electric circuit** is a path along which electrons flow. A simple circuit can be created with a dry cell, wire, a bell, or a light bulb. When all are connected, the electrons flow from the negative terminal, through the wire to the device and back to the positive terminal of the dry cell. If there are no breaks in the circuit, the device will work. The circuit is closed. Any break in the flow will create an open circuit and cause the device to shut off.

The device (bell, bulb) is an example of a **load**. A load is a device that uses energy. Suppose that you also add a buzzer so that the bell rings when you press the buzzer button. The buzzer is acting as a **switch**. A switch is a device that opens or closes a circuit. Pressing the buzzer makes the connection complete and the bell rings. When the buzzer is not engaged, the circuit is open and the bell is silent.

A **series circuit** is one where the electrons have only one path along which they can move. When one load in a series circuit goes out, the circuit is open. An example of this is a set of Christmas tree lights that is missing a bulb. None of the bulbs will work.

A **parallel circuit** is one where the electrons have more than one path to move along. If a load goes out in a parallel circuit, the other load will still work because the electrons can still find a way to continue moving along the path.

When an electron goes through a load, it does work and therefore loses some of its energy. The measure of how much energy is lost is called the **potential difference**. The potential difference between two points is the work needed to move a charge from one point to another.

Potential difference is measured in a unit called the volt. **Voltage** is potential difference. The higher the voltage, the more energy the electrons have. This energy is measured by a device called a voltmeter. To use a voltmeter, place it in a circuit parallel with the load you are measuring.

Current is the number of electrons per second that flow past a point in a circuit. Current is measured with a device called an ammeter. To use an ammeter, put it in series with the load you are measuring.

SCIENCE: BIOLOGY

As electrons flow through a wire, they lose potential energy. Some is changed into heat energy because of resistance. **Resistance** is the ability of the material to oppose the flow of electrons through it. All substances have some resistance, even if they are a good conductor such as copper. This resistance is measured in units called **ohms**. A thin wire will have more resistance than a thick one because it will have less room for electrons to travel. In a thicker wire, there will be more possible paths for the electrons to flow. Resistance also depends upon the length of the wire. The longer the wire, the more resistance it will have. Potential difference, resistance, and current form a relationship know as **Ohm's Law**. Current **(I)** is measured in amperes and is equal to potential difference **(V)** divided by resistance **(R)**.

$$I = V / R$$

If you have a wire with resistance of 5 ohms and a potential difference of 75 volts, you can calculate the current by:

$$I = 75 \text{ volts} / 5 \text{ ohms}$$
$$I = 15 \text{ amperes}$$

A current of 10 or more amperes will cause a wire to get hot. 22 amperes is about the maximum for a house circuit. Anything above 25 amperes can start a fire.

Electrostatics is the study of stationary electric charges. A plastic rod that is rubbed with fur or a glass rod that is rubbed with silk will become electrically charged and will attract small pieces of paper. The charge on the plastic rod rubbed with fur is negative and the charge on glass rod rubbed with silk is positive.

Electrically charged objects share these characteristics:

1. Like charges repel one another.
2. Opposite charges attract each other.
3. Charge is conserved. A neutral object has no net change. If the plastic rod and fur are initially neutral, when the rod becomes charged by the fur, a negative charge is transferred from the fur to the rod. The net negative charge on the rod is equal to the net positive charge on the fur.

Materials through which electric charges can easily flow are called **conductors**. Metals which are good conductors include silicon and boron. On the other hand, an **insulator** is a material through which electric charges do not move easily, if at all. Examples of insulators would be the nonmetal elements of the periodic table. A simple device used to indicate the existence of a positive or negative charge is called an **electroscope**. An electroscope is made up of a conducting knob and attached to it are very lightweight conducting leaves usually made of foil (gold or aluminum). When a charged object touches the knob, the leaves push away from each other because like charges repel. It is not possible to tell whether the charge is positive or negative.

Charging by induction:

Touch the knob with a finger while a charged rod is nearby. The electrons will be repulsed and flow out of the electroscope through the hand. If the hand is removed while the charged rod remains close, the electroscope will retain the charge.

When an object is rubbed with a charged rod, the object will take on the same charge as the rod. However, charging by induction gives the object the opposite charge as that of the charged rod.

Grounding charge:

Charge can be removed from an object by connecting it to the earth through a conductor. The removal of static electricity by conduction is called **grounding**.

Skill 13.2 Recognize the nature and properties of mechanical and electromagnetic waves (e.g., frequency, source, medium, spectrum, wave-particle duality).

A mechanical wave can be defined as a disturbance that travels through a medium, moving energy from one place to another. This disturbance is also called an electrical force field. The wave is not capable of transporting energy without a medium, as in vacuum conditions. The medium is the material through which the disturbance is moving and can be thought of as a series of interacting particles. The example of a slinky wave is often used to illustrate the nature of a wave, where pressure exerted on the first coil moves through the remaining coils. A sound wave is also a mechanical wave. The frequency of a wave refers to how often the particles of the medium vibrate when a wave passes through the medium. Frequency is measured in units of cycles/second, waves/second, vibrations/second, or something/second. Another unit for frequency is the Hertz (abbreviated Hz) where 1 Hz is equivalent to 1 cycle/second. The period of a wave is the time required for a particle on a medium to make one complete vibrational cycle. Wave period is measured in units of time such as seconds, hours, days or years, and is NOT synonymous with frequency. Electromagnetic waves are both electric and magnetic in nature and are capable of traveling through a vacuum. They do not require a medium in order to transport their energy. Light, microwaves, x-rays, and TV and radio transmissions are all kinds of electromagnetic waves. They are all a wavy disturbance that repeats itself over a distance called the wavelength. Electromagnetic waves come in varying sizes and properties, by which they are organized in the electromagnetic spectrum. The electromagnetic spectrum is measured as frequency (f) in hertz and wavelength (λ) in meters. The frequency times the wavelength of every electromagnetic wave equals the speed of light (3.0×10^9 meters/second).

Roughly, the range of wavelengths of the electromagnetic spectrum is:

	f		λ	
Radio waves	$10^{5} - 10^{-1}$	hertz	$10^{3} - 10^{9}$	meters
Microwaves	$10^{-1} - 10^{-3}$	hertz	$10^{9} - 10^{11}$	meters
Infrared radiation	$10^{-3} - 10^{-6}$	hertz	$10^{11.2} - 10^{14.3}$	meters
Visible light	$10^{-6.2} - 10^{-6.9}$	hertz	$10^{14.3} - 10^{15}$	meters
Ultraviolet radiation	$10^{-7} - 10^{-9}$	hertz	$10^{15} - 10^{17.2}$	meters
X-Rays	$10^{-9} - 10^{-11}$	hertz	$10^{17.2} - 10^{19}$	meters
Gamma Rays	$10^{-11} - 10^{-15}$	hertz	$10^{19} - 10^{23.25}$	meters

Radio waves are used for transmitting data. Common examples are television, cell phones, and wireless computer networks. Microwaves are used to heat food and deliver Wi-Fi service. Infrared waves are utilized in night vision goggles. Visible light we are all familiar with as the human eye is most sensitive to this wavelength range. UV light causes sunburns and would be even more harmful if most of it were not captured in the Earth's ozone layer. X-rays aid us in the medical field and gamma rays are most useful in the field of astronomy.

Skill 13.3   Describe the effects and applications of electromagnetic forces in real-life situations, including electric power generation, circuit breakers, and brownouts.

Electricity can be used to change the chemical composition of a material. For instance, when electricity is passed through water, it breaks the water down into hydrogen gas and oxygen gas.

Circuit breakers in a home monitor the electric current. If there is an overload, the circuit breaker will create an open circuit, stopping the flow of electricity.

Computers can be made small enough to fit inside a plastic credit card by creating what is known as a solid state device. In this device, electrons flow through solid material such as silicon.

Resistors are used to regulate volume on a television or radio or through a dimmer switch for lights.

A bird can sit on an electrical wire without being electrocuted because the bird and the wire have about the same potential. However, if that same bird would touch two wires at the same time he would not have to worry about flying south next year.

When caught in an electrical storm, a car is a relatively safe place from lightning because of the resistance of the rubber tires. A metal building would not be safe unless there was a lightning rod that would attract the lightning and conduct it into the ground.

A brown-out occurs when there exists a condition of lower than normal power line voltage. This may be short term (minutes to hours) or long term (1/2 day or more). A power line voltage reduction of 8 - 12% is usually considered a Brown-out. Electric utilities may reduce line voltage to Brown-out levels in an effort to manage power generation and distribution. This is most likely to occur on very hot days, when most air conditioning and refrigeration equipment would be operating almost continuously. Even without purposeful intervention from the local utility company, extreme overloads (spikes) could tax the electrical system to the point where a permanent brown-out state could exist over much of the company's distribution network.

Skill 13.4   Analyze and predict the behavior of mechanical and electromagnetic waves under varying physical conditions, including basic optics, color, ray diagrams, and shadows.

The place where one medium ends and another begins is called a **boundary**, and the manner in which a wave behaves when it reaches that boundary is called **boundary behavior**. The following principles apply to boundary behavior in waves:

1) wave speed is always greater in the less dense medium
2) wavelength is always greater in the less dense medium
3) wave frequency is not changed by crossing a boundary
4) the reflected pulse becomes inverted when a wave in a less dense medium is heading toward a boundary with a more dense medium
5) the amplitude of the incident pulse is always greater than the amplitude of the reflected pulse.

For an example, we will use a rope whose left side is less dense, or thinner, than the right side of the rope.

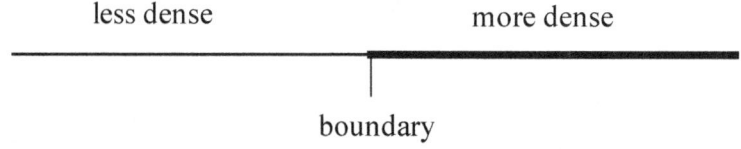

A pulse is introduced on the left end of the rope. This **incident pulse** travels right along the rope towards the boundary between the two thicknesses of rope. When the incident pulse reaches the boundary, two behaviors will occur:

1) Some of the energy will be reflected back to the left side of the boundary. This energy is known as the **reflected pulse**.
2) The rest of the energy will travel into the thicker end of the rope. This energy is referred to as the **transmitted pulse**.

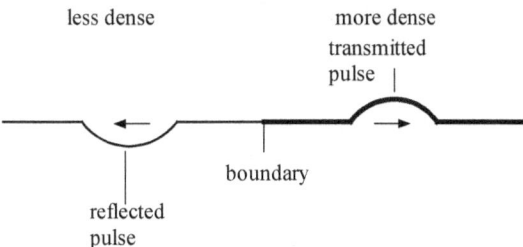

When the incident pulse travels from a denser medium to a less dense medium, the reflected pulse is not inverted.

Reflection occurs when waves bounce off a barrier. The **law of reflection** states that when a ray of light reflects off a surface, the angle of incidence is equal to the angle of reflection.

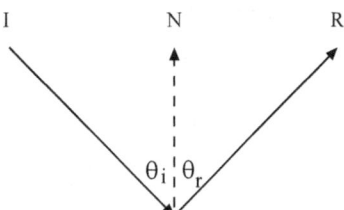

Line I represents the **incident ray**, the ray of light striking the surface. Line R is the **reflected ray**, the ray of light reflected off the surface. Line N is known as the **normal line**. It is a perpendicular line at the point of incidence that divides the angle between the incident ray and the reflected ray into two equal rays. The angle between the incident ray and the normal line is called the **angle of incidence**; the angle between the reflected ray and the normal line is called the **angle of reflection**.

Waves passing from one medium into another will undergo **refraction**, or bending. Accompanying this bending are a change in both speed and the wavelength of the waves.

In this example, light waves traveling through the air will pass through glass.

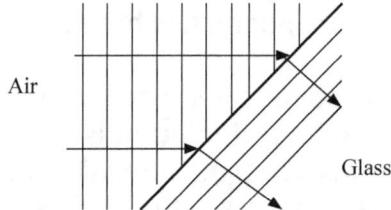

Refraction occurs only at the boundary. Once the wavefront passes across the boundary, it travels in a straight line.

Diffraction involves a change in direction of waves as they pass through an opening or around an obstacle in their path.

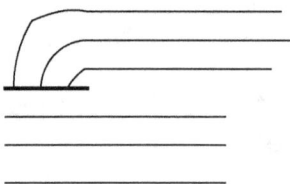

The amount of diffraction depends upon the wavelength. The amount of diffraction increases with increasing wavelength and decreases with decreasing wavelength. Sound and water waves exhibit this ability.

When we refer to light, we are usually talking about a type of electromagnetic wave that stimulates the retina of the eye, or visible light. Each individual wavelength within the spectrum of visible light represents a particular **color**. When a particular wavelength strikes the retina, we perceive that color. Visible light is sometimes referred to as ROYGBIV (red, orange, yellow, green, blue, indigo, violet). The visible light spectrum ranges from red (the longest wavelength) to violet (the shortest wavelength) with a range of wavelengths in between. If all the wavelengths strike your eye at the same time, you will see white. Conversely, when no wavelengths strike your eye, you perceive black.

A **shadow** results from the inability of light waves to diffract as sound and water waves can. An obstacle in the way of the light waves blocks the light waves, thereby creating a shadow.

SUBAREA IV.   **EARTH SYSTEMS AND THE UNIVERSE**

COMPETENCY 0014   **UNDERSTAND AND APPLY KNOWLEDGE OF EARTH'S LAND, WATER, AND ATMOSPHERIC SYSTEMS AND THE HISTORY OF EARTH.**

Skill 14.1   **Identify the structure and composition of Earth's land, water, and atmospheric systems and how they affect weather, erosion, fresh water, and soil.**

Water is recycled throughout ecosystems. Just two percent of all the available water is fixed and held in ice or the bodies of organisms. Available water includes surface water (lakes, ocean, and rivers) and ground water (aquifers, wells). 96% of all available water is from ground water. Water is recycled through the processes of evaporation and precipitation. The water present now is the water that has been here since our atmosphere formed.

When water falls from the atmosphere it can have an erosive property. This can happen from impact alone but also from acid rain. Erosion is known for its destructive properties, but in an indirect way, it also builds by bringing materials to new locations. **Erosion** is the inclusion and transportation of surface materials by another moveable material, usually water, wind, or ice. The most important cause of erosion is running water. Streams, rivers, and tides are constantly at work removing weathered fragments of bedrock and carrying them away from their original location. A stream erodes bedrock by the grinding action of the sand, pebbles and other rock fragments. This grinding against each other is called abrasion. Streams also erode rocks by dissolving or absorbing their minerals. Limestone and marble are readily dissolved by streams.

The breaking down of rocks at or near to the earth's surface is known as **weathering**. Weathering breaks down these rocks into smaller and smaller pieces. There are two types of weathering: physical weathering and chemical weathering.

Physical weathering is the process by which rocks are broken down into smaller fragments without undergoing any change in chemical composition. Physical weathering is mainly caused by the freezing of water, the expansion of rock, and the activities of plants and animals.

Frost wedging is the cycle of daytime thawing and refreezing at night. This cycle causes large rock masses, especially the rocks exposed on mountain tops, to be broken into smaller pieces.

The peeling away of the outer layers from a rock is called exfoliation. Rounded mountain tops are called exfoliation domes and have been formed in this way.

Chemical weathering is the breaking down of rocks through changes in their chemical composition. An example would be the change of feldspar in granite into clay. Water, oxygen, and carbon dioxide are the main agents of chemical weathering. When water and carbon dioxide combine chemically, they produce a weak acid that breaks down rocks. In addition, acidic substances from factories and car exhausts dissolve in rain water forming **acid rain.** Acid rain forms predominantly from pollutant oxides in the air (usually nitrogen-based NO_x or sulfur-based SO_x), which become hydrated into their acids (nitric or sulfuric acid). When the rain falls into stone, the acids can react with metallic compounds and gradually wear the stone away.

Skill 14.2   Recognize the scope of geologic time and the continuing physical changes of Earth through time.

Geological time is divided into periods depending on the kind of life that existed at that time. These periods are grouped together into eras. The history of the Earth is calculated by studying the ages of the various layers of sedimentary rock.

Era	Period	Time	Characteristics
Cenozoic	Quaternary	1.6 million years ago to the present.	The Ice Age occurred, and human beings evolved.
	Tertiary	65-1.64 million years ago.	Mammals and birds evolved to replace the great reptiles and dinosaurs that had just become extinct. Forests gave way to grasslands, and the climate become cooler.
Mesozoic	Cretaceous	135-65 million years ago.	Reptiles and dinosaurs roamed the Earth. Most of the modern continents had split away from the large landmass, Pangaea, and many were flooded by shallow chalk seas.
	Jurassic / Triassic	350-135 million years ago.	Reptiles were beginning to evolve. Pangaea started to break up. Deserts gave way to forests and swamps.
Paleozoic	Permian / Carboniferous	355-250 million years ago.	Continents came together to form one big landmass, Pangaea. Forests (that formed today's coal) grew on deltas around the new mountains, and deserts formed.
	Devonian	410-355 million years ago.	Continents started moving toward each other. The first land animals, such as insects and amphibians, existed. Many fish swam in the seas.
	Silurian / Ordovician	510-410 million years ago.	Sea life flourished, and the first fish evolved. The earliest land plants began to grow around shorelines and estuaries.
	Cambrian	570-510 million years ago.	No life on land, but all kinds of sea animals existed.
Precambrian	Proterozoic	Beginning of the Earth to 570 million years ago (seven-eighths of the Earth's history).	Some sort of life existed.
	Archaean		No life.

Skill 14.3 Evaluate scientific theories about Earth's origin and history and how these theories explain contemporary living systems

The dominant scientific theory about the origin of the Universe, and consequently the Earth, is the **Big Bang Theory**. According to this theory, an atom exploded about 10 to 20 billion years ago throwing matter in all directions. Although this theory has never been proven, and probably never will be, it is supported by the fact that distant galaxies in every direction are moving away from us at great speeds.

Earth, itself, is believed to have been created 4.5 billion years ago as a solidified cloud of gases and dust left over from the creation of the sun. As millions of years passed, radioactive decay released energy that melted some of Earth's components. Over time, the heavier components sank into the center of the Earth and accumulated into at the core. As the Earth cooled, a crust formed with natural depressions. Water rising from the interior of the Earth filled these depressions and formed the oceans. Slowly, the Earth acquired the appearance it has today.

The **Heterotroph Hypothesis** supposes that life on Earth evolved from **heterotrophs**, the first cells. According to this hypothesis, life began on Earth about 3.5 billion years ago. Scientists have shown that the basic molecules of life formed from lightning, ultraviolet light, and radioactivity. Over time, these molecules became more complex and developed metabolic processes, thereby becoming heterotrophs. Heterotrophs could not produce their own food and fed off organic materials. However, they released carbon dioxide which allowed for the evolution of **autotrophs**, which could produce their own food through photosynthesis. The autotrophs and heterotrophs became the dominant life forms and evolved into the diverse forms of life we see today.

Proponents of **creationism** believe that the species we currently have were created as recounted in the book of Genesis in the Bible. This retelling asserts that God created all life about 6,000 years ago in one mass creation event. However, scientific evidence casts doubt on creationism.

Evolution

The most significant evidence to support the history of evolution is fossils, which have been used to construct a fossil record. Fossils give clues as to the structure of organisms and the times at which they existed. However, there are limitations to the study of fossils, which leave huge gaps in the fossil record.

Scientists also try to relate two organisms by comparing their internal and external structures. This is called **comparative anatomy**. Comparative anatomy categorizes anatomical structures as **homologous** (features in different species that point to a common ancestor), **analogous** (structures that have superficial similarities because of similar functions, but do not point to a common ancestor), and **vestigial** (structures that have no modern function, indicating that different species diverged and evolved). Through the study of **comparative embryology**, homologous structures that do not appear in mature organisms may be found between different species in their embryological development.

There have been two basic **theories of evolution: Lamarck's and Darwin's**. Lamarck's theory that proposed that an organism can change its structure through use or disuse and that acquired traits can be inherited has been disproved.

Darwin's theory of **natural selection** is the basis of all evolutionary theory. His theory has four basic points:

1. Each species produces more offspring than can survive.
2. The individual organisms that make up a larger population are born with certain variations.
3. The overabundance of offspring creates competition for survival among individual organisms (**survival of the fittest**).
4. Variations are passed down from parent to offspring.

Points 2 and 4 form the genetic basis for evolution.

New species develop from two types of evolution: divergent and convergent. **Divergent evolution**, also known as **speciation**, is the divergence of a new species from a previous form of that species. There are two main ways in which speciation may occur: **allopatric speciation** (resulting from geographical isolation so that species cannot interbreed) and **adaptive radiation** (creation of several new species from a single parent species). **Convergent evolution** is a process whereby different species develop similar traits from inhabiting similar environments, facing similar selection pressures, and/or use parts of their bodies for similar functions. This type of evolution is only superficial. It can never result in two species being able to interbreed.

Skill 14.4 Recognize the interrelationships between living organisms and Earth's resources and evaluate the uses of Earth's resources

The region of the Earth and its atmosphere in which living things are found is known as the **biosphere**. The biosphere is made up of distinct areas called **ecosystems**, each of which has its own characteristic climate, soils, and communities of plants and animals.

The most important nonliving factors affecting an ecosystem are the chemical cycles, the water cycle, oxygen, sunlight, and the soil. The two basic chemical cycles are the carbon cycle and the nitrogen cycle. They involve the passage of these elements between the organisms and the environment.

In the **carbon cycle**, animals and plants use carbon dioxide from the air to produce glucose, which they use in respiration and other life processes. Animals consume plants, use what they can of the carbon matter and excrete the rest as waste. This waste decays into carbon dioxide. During respiration, plants and animals release carbon dioxide back into the air. The carbon used by plants and animals stays in their bodies until death, after which decay sends the organic compounds back into the Earth and carbon dioxide back into the air.

Nitrogen found in the atmosphere is generally unusable by living organisms. In the **nitrogen cycle,** nitrogen-fixing bacteria in the soil and/or the roots of legumes transform the inert nitrogen into compounds. Plants take these compounds, synthesize the twenty amino acids found in nature, and turn them into plant proteins. Animals can only synthesize eight of the amino acids. They eat the plants to produce protein from the plant's materials. Animals and plants give off nitrogen waste and death products in the form of ammonia. The ammonia will either be transformed into nitrites and nitrates by bacteria and reenter the cycle when they are taken up by plants, or be broken down by bacteria to produce inert nitrogen to be released back into the air.

Most of the Earth's water is found in the oceans and lakes. Through the **water cycle**, water evaporates into the atmosphere and condenses into clouds. Water then falls to the Earth in the form of precipitation, returning to the oceans and lakes on falling on land. Water on the land may return to the oceans and lakes as runoff or seep from the soil as groundwater.

The amount of **oxygen** available in a particular location may create competition. Oxygen is readily available to animals on land; but in order for it to be available to aquatic organisms, it must be dissolved in water.

Sunlight is also important to most organisms. Organisms on land compete for sunlight, but sunlight does not reach into the lowest depths of the ocean. Organisms in these regions must find another means of producing food.

The type of **soil** found in a particular ecosystem determines what species can live in that ecosystem.

The ecosystems of the Earth consist of: temperate forests, deserts, wetlands, tropical rain forests, oceans, grasslands, rivers and lakes, mountains, towns and cities, seashores, and polar and tundra lands.

TEACHER CERTIFICATION STUDY GUIDE

COMPETENCY 0015 UNDERSTAND AND APPLY KNOWLEDGE OF THE DYNAMIC NATURE OF EARTH.

Skill 15.1 Analyze and explain large-scale dynamic forces, events, and processes that affect Earth's land, water, and atmospheric systems, including conceptual questions about plate tectonics, El Nino, drought, and climatic shifts.

El Niño refers to a sequence of changes in the ocean and atmospheric circulation across the Pacific Ocean. The water around the equator is unusually hot every two to seven years. Trade winds normally blowing east to west across the equatorial latitudes, piling warm water into the western Pacific. A huge mass of heavy thunderstorms usually forms in the area and produce vast currents of rising air that displace heat poleward. This helps create the strong mid-latitude jet streams. The world's climate patterns are disrupted by this change in location of the massive cluster of thunderstorms. The West coast of America experienced a wet winter. Sacramento, California recorded 103 days of rain.

Air masses moving toward or away from the Earth's surface are called air currents. Air moving parallel to Earth's surface is called **wind**. Weather conditions are generated by winds and air currents carrying large amounts of heat and moisture from one part of the atmosphere to another. Wind speeds are measured by instruments called anemometers.

The wind belts in each hemisphere consist of convection cells that encircle Earth like belts. There are three major wind belts on Earth (1) trade winds (2) prevailing westerlies, and (3) polar easterlies. Wind belt formation depends on the differences in air pressures that develop in the doldrums, the horse latitudes, and the polar regions. The Doldrums surround the equator. Within this belt heated air usually rises straight up into Earth's atmosphere. The Horse latitudes are regions of high barometric pressure with calm and light winds and the Polar regions contain cold dense air that sinks to the earth's surface

Winds caused by local temperature changes include sea breezes, and land breezes.

Sea breezes are caused by the unequal heating of the land and an adjacent, large body of water. Land heats up faster than water. The movement of cool ocean air toward the land is called a sea breeze. Sea breezes usually begin blowing about mid-morning; ending about sunset.

A breeze that blows from the land to the ocean or a large lake is called a **land breeze**.

SCIENCE: BIOLOGY

Monsoons are huge wind systems that cover large geographic areas and that reverse direction seasonally. The monsoons of India and Asia are examples of these seasonal winds. They alternate wet and dry seasons. As denser cooler air over the ocean moves inland, a steady seasonal wind called a summer or wet monsoon is produced.

Cloud types:

Cirrus clouds - White and feathery high in sky

Cumulus – thick, white, fluffy

Stratus – layers of clouds cover most of the sky

Nimbus – heavy, dark clouds that represent thunderstorm clouds

Variation on the clouds mentioned above:

Cumulo-nimbus

Strato-nimbus

The air temperature at which water vapor begins to condense is called the **dew point**.

Relative humidity is the actual amount of water vapor in a certain volume of air compared to the maximum amount of water vapor this air could hold at a given temperature.

Skill 15.2   Identify and explain Earth processes and cycles and cite examples in real-life situations, including conceptual questions on rock cycles, volcanism, and plate tectonics.

Data obtained from many sources led scientists to develop the theory of plate tectonics. This theory is the most current model that explains not only the movement of the continents, but also the changes in the earth's crust caused by internal forces.

Plates are rigid blocks of earth's crust and upper mantle. These solid blocks make up the lithosphere. The earth's lithosphere is broken into nine large sections and several smaller ones. These moving slabs are called plates. The major plates are named after the continents they are "transporting."

The plates float on and move with a layer of hot, plastic-like rock in the upper mantle. Geologists believe that the heat currents circulating within the mantle cause this plastic zone of rock to slowly flow, carrying along the overlying crustal plates.

Movement of these crustal plates creates areas where the plates diverge as well as areas where the plates converge. A major area of divergence is located in the Mid-Atlantic. Currents of hot mantle rock rise and separate at this point of divergence creating new oceanic crust at the rate of 2 to 10 centimeters per year. Convergence is when the oceanic crust collides with either another oceanic plate or a continental plate. The oceanic crust sinks forming an enormous trench and generating volcanic activity. Convergence also includes continent to continent plate collisions. When two plates slide past one another a transform fault is created.

These movements produce many major features of the earth's surface, such as mountain ranges, volcanoes, and earthquake zones. Most of these features are located at plate boundaries, where the plates interact by spreading apart, pressing together, or sliding past each other. These movements are very slow, averaging only a few centimeters each year.

Boundaries form between spreading plates where the crust is forced apart in a process called rifting. Rifting generally occurs at mid-ocean ridges. Rifting can also take place within a continent, splitting the continent into smaller landmasses that drift away from each other, thereby forming an ocean basin between them. The Red Sea is a product of rifting. As the seafloor spreading takes place, new material is added to the inner edges of the separating plates. In this way the plates grow larger, and the ocean basin widens. This is the process that broke up the super continent Pangaea and created the Atlantic Ocean.

Boundaries between plates that are colliding are zones of intense crustal activity. When a plate of ocean crust collides with a plate of continental crust, the more dense oceanic plate slides under the lighter continental plate and plunges into the mantle. This process is called **subduction**, and the site where it takes place is called a subduction zone. A subduction zone is usually seen on the sea-floor as a deep depression called a trench.

The crustal movement that is identified by plates sliding sideways past each other produces a plate boundary characterized by major faults that are capable of unleashing powerful earth-quakes. The San Andreas Fault forms such a boundary between the Pacific Plate and the North American Plate.

Orogeny is the term given to natural mountain building.

A mountain is terrain that has been raised high above the surrounding landscape by volcanic action, or some form of tectonic plate collisions. The plate collisions could be intercontinental or ocean floor collisions with a continental crust (subduction). The physical composition of mountains would include igneous, metamorphic, or sedimentary rocks; some may have rock layers that are tilted or distorted by plate collision forces.

There are many different types of mountains. The physical attributes of a mountain range depends upon the angle at which plate movement thrust layers of rock to the surface. Many mountains (Adirondacks, Southern Rockies) were formed along high angle faults.

Folded mountains (Alps, Himalayas) are produced by the folding of rock layers during their formation. The Himalayas are the highest mountains in the world and contain Mount Everest, which rises almost 9 km above sea level. The Himalayas were formed when India collided with Asia. The movement that created this collision is still in process at the rate of a few centimeters per year.

Fault-block mountains (Utah, Arizona, and New Mexico) are created when plate movement produces tension forces instead of compression forces. The area under tension produces normal faults and rock along these faults is displaced upward.

Dome mountains are formed as magma tries to push up through the crust but fails to break the surface. Dome mountains resemble a huge blister on the earth's surface.

Upwarped mountains (Black Hills of South Dakota) are created in association with a broad arching of the crust. They can also be formed by rock thrust upward along high angle faults.

Faults are categorized on the basis of the relative movement between the blocks on both sides of the fault plane. The movement can be horizontal, vertical or oblique.

A dip-slip fault occurs when the movement of the plates is vertical and opposite. The displacement is in the direction of the inclination, or dip, of the fault. Dip-slip faults are classified as normal faults when the rock above the fault plane moves down relative to the rock below.

Reverse faults are created when the rock above the fault plane moves up relative to the rock below. Reverse faults having a very low angle to the horizontal are also referred to as thrust faults.

Faults in which the dominant displacement is horizontal movement along the trend or strike (length) of the fault are called **strike-slip faults**. When a large strike-slip fault is associated with plate boundaries it is called a **transform fault**. The San Andreas Fault in California is a well-known transform fault.

Faults that have both vertical and horizontal movement are called **oblique-slip faults.**

Volcanism is the term given to the movement of magma through the crust and its emergence as lava onto the earth's surface. Volcanic mountains are built up by successive deposits of volcanic materials.

An active volcano is one that is presently erupting or building to an eruption. A dormant volcano is one that is between eruptions but still shows signs of internal activity that might lead to an eruption in the future. An extinct volcano is said to be no longer capable of erupting. Most of the world's active volcanoes are found along the rim of the Pacific Ocean, which is also a major earthquake zone. This curving belt of active faults and volcanoes is often called the Ring of Fire. The world's best known volcanic mountains include: Mount Etna in Italy and Mount Kilimanjaro in Africa. The Hawaiian Islands are actually the tops of a chain of volcanic mountains that rise from the ocean floor.

There are three types of volcanic mountains: shield volcanoes, cinder cones, and composite volcanoes.

Shield Volcanoes are associated with quiet eruptions. Lava emerges from the vent or opening in the crater and flows freely out over the earth's surface until it cools and hardens into a layer of igneous rock. A repeated lava flow builds this type of volcano into the largest volcanic mountain. Mauna Loa found in Hawaii, is the largest volcano on earth.

Cinder Cone Volcanoes are associated with explosive eruptions as lava is hurled high into the air in a spray of droplets of various sizes. These droplets cool and harden into cinders and particles of ash before falling to the ground. The ash and cinder pile up around the vent to form a steep, cone-shaped hill called the cinder cone. Cinder cone volcanoes are relatively small but may form quite rapidly.

Composite Volcanoes are described as being built by both lava flows and layers of ash and cinders. Mount Fuji in Japan, Mount St. Helens in Washington, USA, and Mount Vesuvius in Italy are all famous composite volcanoes.

When lava cools, **igneous rock** is formed. This formation can occur either above ground or below ground.

Intrusive rock includes any igneous rock that was formed below the earth's surface. Batholiths are the largest structures of intrusive type rock and are composed of near granite materials; they are at the core of the Sierra Nevada Mountains.

Extrusive rock includes any igneous rock that was formed at the earth's surface.

Dikes are old lava tubes formed when magma entered a vertical fracture and hardened. Sometimes magma squeezes between two rock layers and hardens into a thin horizontal sheet called a **sill**. A **laccolith** is formed in much the same way as a sill, but the magma that creates a laccolith is very thick and does not flow easily. It pools and forces the overlying strata up, creating an obvious surface dome.

A **caldera** is normally formed by the collapse of the top of a volcano. This collapse can be caused by a massive explosion that destroys the cone and empties most, if not all, of the magma chamber below the volcano. The cone collapses into the empty magma chamber forming a caldera.

An inactive volcano may have magma solidified in its pipe. This structure, called a volcanic neck, is resistant to erosion and today may be the only visible evidence of the past presence of an active volcano.

Skill 15.3 **Analyze the transfer of energy within and among Earth's land, water, and atmospheric systems, including the identification of energy sources of volcanoes, hurricanes, thunderstorms, and tornadoes.**

A **thunderstorm** is a brief, local storm produced by the rapid upward movement of warm, moist air within a cumulo-nimbus cloud. Thunderstorms always produce lightning and thunder, accompanied by strong wind gusts and heavy rain or hail.

A severe storm with swirling winds that may reach speeds of hundreds of km per hour is called a **tornado**. Such a storm is also referred to as a "twister". The sky is covered by large cumulo-nimbus clouds and violent thunderstorms; a funnel-shaped swirling cloud may extend downward from a cumulonimbus cloud and reach the ground. Tornadoes are narrow storms that leave a narrow path of destruction on the ground.

A swirling, funnel-shaped cloud that **extends** downward and touches a body of water is called a **waterspout**.

Hurricanes are storms that develop when warm, moist air carried by trade winds rotates around a low-pressure "eye". A large, rotating, low-pressure system accompanied by heavy precipitation and strong winds is called a tropical cyclone or is better known as a hurricane. In the Pacific region, a hurricane is called a typhoon.

Storms that occur only in the winter are known as blizzards or ice storms. A **blizzard** is a storm with strong winds, blowing snow and frigid temperatures. An **ice storm** consists of falling rain that freezes when it strikes the ground, covering everything with a layer of ice.

Skill 15.4 Explain the functions and applications of the instruments and technologies used to study the earth sciences, including seismographs, barometers, and satellite systems.

Satellites have improved our ability to communicate and transmit radio and television signals. Navigational abilities have been greatly improved through the use of satellite signals. Sonar uses sound waves to locate objects and is especially useful underwater. The sound waves bounce off the object and are used to assist in location. **Seismographs** record vibrations in the earth and allow us to measure earthquake activity. Common instruments for forecasting weather include the **aneroid barometer** and the **mercury barometer,** which both measure air pressure. In the aneroid barometer, the air exerts varying pressures on a metal diaphragm that will then read air pressure. The mercury barometer operates when atmospheric pressure pushes on a pool of mercury in a glass tube. The higher the pressure, the higher up the tube mercury will rise.

Relative humidity is measured by two kinds of additional weather instruments, the psychrometer and the hair gygrometer.

TEACHER CERTIFICATION STUDY GUIDE

COMPETENCY 0016 UNDERSTAND AND APPLY KNOWLEDGE OF OBJECTS IN THE UNIVERSE AND THEIR DYNAMIC INTERACTIONS.

Skill 16.1 Describe and explain the relative and apparent motions of the sun, the moon, stars, and planets in the sky.

Until the summer of 2006, there were nine recognized planets in our solar system: Mercury, Venus, Earth, Mars, Jupiter, Saturn, Uranus, Neptune, and Pluto. These nine planets are divided into two groups based on distance from the sun. The inner planets include: Mercury, Venus, Earth, and Mars. The outer planets include: Jupiter, Saturn, Uranus, Neptune and Pluto. Pluto's status as a planet is being reconsidered.

Mercury -- the closest planet to the sun. Its surface has craters and rocks. The atmosphere is composed of hydrogen, helium and sodium. Mercury was named after the Roman messenger god.

Venus -- has a slow rotation when compared to Earth. Venus and Uranus rotate in opposite directions from the other planets. This opposite rotation is called retrograde rotation. The surface of Venus is not visible due to the extensive cloud cover. The atmosphere is composed mostly of carbon dioxide. Sulfuric acid droplets in the dense cloud cover gives Venus a yellow appearance. Venus has a greater greenhouse effect than observed on Earth. The dense clouds combined with carbon dioxide trap heat. Venus was named after the Roman goddess of love.

Earth -- considered a water planet with 70% of its surface covered with water. Gravity holds the masses of water in place. The different temperatures observed on earth allows for the different states of water to exist; solid, liquid or gas. The atmosphere is composed mainly of oxygen and nitrogen. Earth is the only planet that is known to support life.

Mars -- the surface of Mars contains numerous craters, active and extinct volcanoes, ridges and valleys with extremely deep fractures. Iron oxide found in the dusty soil makes the surface seem rust colored and the skies seem pink in color. The atmosphere is composed of carbon dioxide, nitrogen, argon, oxygen and water vapor. Mars has polar regions with ice caps composed of water. Mars has two satellites. Mars was named after the Roman war god.

Jupiter – is the largest planet in the solar system. Jupiter has 16 moons. The atmosphere is composed of hydrogen, helium, methane and ammonia. There are white colored bands of clouds indicating rising gas and dark colored bands of clouds indicating descending gases, caused by heat resulting from the energy of Jupiter's core. Jupiter has a Great Red Spot that is thought to be a hurricane type cloud. Jupiter has a strong magnetic field.

SCIENCE: BIOLOGY

Saturn – is the second largest planet in the solar system. Saturn has beautiful rings of ice and rock and dust particles circling it. Saturn's atmosphere is composed of hydrogen, helium, methane, and ammonia. Saturn has 20 plus satellites. Saturn was named after the Roman god of agriculture.

Uranus -- is the second largest planet in the solar system with retrograde revolution. Uranus a gaseous planet and it has 10 dark rings and 15 satellites. Its atmosphere is composed of hydrogen, helium, and methane. Uranus was named after the Greek god of the heavens.

Neptune -- is another gaseous planet with an atmosphere consisting of hydrogen, helium, and methane. Neptune has 3 rings and 2 satellites. Neptune was named after the Roman sea god that its atmosphere has the same color of the seas.

Pluto -- is considered the smallest planet in the solar system. Pluto's atmosphere probably contains methane, ammonia, and frozen water. Pluto has 1 satellite. Pluto revolves around the sun every 250 years. Pluto was named after the Roman god of the underworld.

Skill 16.2   Recognize properties of objects (e.g., comets, asteroids) within the solar system and their dynamic interactions.

Astronomers believe that asteroids are the rocky fragments that may have been the remains of the birth of the solar system that never formed into a planet. **Asteroids** are found in the region between Mars and Jupiter.

Comets are masses of frozen gases, cosmic dust, and small rocky particles. Astronomers think that most comets originate in a dense comet cloud beyond Pluto. Comet consists of a nucleus, a comma, and a tail. A comet's tail always points away from the sun. The most famous comet, **Halley's Comet,** is named after the person whom first discovered it in 240 B.C. It returns to the skies near earth every 75 to 76 years.

Meteoroids are composed of particles of rock and metal of various sizes. When a meteoroid travels through the earth's atmosphere, friction causes its surface to heat up and it begins to burn. The burning meteoroid falling through the earth's atmosphere is now called a **meteor,** also known as a "shooting star." **Meteorites** are meteors that strike the earth's surface. A physical example of the impact of the meteorite on the earth's surface can be seen in Arizona, The Barringer Crater is a huge Meteor Crater. There many other such meteor craters found throughout the world.

Skill 16.3 Recognize the types, properties, and dynamics of objects external to the solar system (e.g., black holes, supernovas, galaxies).

Astronomers use groups or patterns of stars called **constellations** as reference points to locate other stars in the sky. Familiar constellations include: Ursa Major (also known as the big bear) and Ursa Minor (known as the little bear). Within the Ursa Major, the smaller constellation, The Big Dipper is found. Within the Ursa Minor, the smaller constellation, The Little Dipper is found.

Different constellations appear as the earth continues its revolution around the sun with the seasonable changes.

First Magnitude stars are 21 of the brightest stars that can be seen from earth, these are the first stars noticed at night. In the Northern Hemisphere there are 15 commonly observed first magnitude stars.

A vast collection of stars is defined as **galaxies**. Galaxies are classified as irregular, elliptical, and spiral. An irregular galaxy has no real structured appearance; most are in their early stages of life. An elliptical galaxy is smooth ellipses, containing little dust and gas, but composed of millions or trillions of stars. Spiral galaxies are disk-shaped and have extending arms that rotate around its dense center. Earth's galaxy is found in the Milky Way and it is a spiral galaxy.

A **pulsar** is defined as a variable radio source that emits signals in very short, regular bursts; believed to be a rotating neutron star.

A **quasar** is defined as an object that photographs like a star but has an extremely large redshift and a variable energy output; believed to be the active core of a very distant galaxy.

Black holes are defined as an object that has collapsed to such a degree that light can not escape from its surface; light is trapped by the intense gravitational field.

TEACHER CERTIFICATION STUDY GUIDE

COMPETENCY 0017 UNDERSTAND AND APPLY KNOWLEDGE OF THE ORIGINS OF AND CHANGES IN THE UNIVERSE.

Skill 17.1 Identify scientific theories dealing with the origin of the universe (e.g., big bang).

Two main theories to explain the origins of the universe include: (1) **The Big Bang Theory** and (2) **The Steady-State Theory.**

The Big Bang Theory has been widely accepted by many astronomers. It states that the universe originated from a magnificent explosion spreading mass, matter and energy into space. The galaxies formed from this material as it cooled during the next half-billion years.

The Steady-State Theory is the least accepted theory. It states that the universe is a continuously being renewed. Galaxies move outward and new galaxies replace the older galaxies. Astronomers have not found any evidence to prove this theory.

The future of the universe is hypothesized with the Oscillating Universe Hypothesis. It states that the universe will oscillate or expand and contract. Galaxies will move away from one another and will in time slow down and stop. Then a gradual moving toward each other will again activate the explosion or The Big Bang theory.

Skill 17.2 Analyze evidence relating to the origin and physical evolution of the universe (e.g., microwave background radiation, expansion).

Cosmic microwave background radiation (CMBR) is the oldest light we can see. It is a snapshot of how the universe looked in its early beginnings. First discovered in 1964, CMBR is composed of photons which we can see because of the atoms that formed when the universe cooled to 3000 K. Prior to that, after the Big Bang, the universe was so hot that the photons were scattered all over the universe, making the universe opaque. The atoms caused the photons to scatter less and the universe to become transparent to radiation. Since cooling to 3000K, the universe has continued to expand and cool.

COBE, launched in 1989, was the first mission to explore slight fluctuations in the background. WMAP, launched in 2001, took a clearer picture of the universe, providing evidence to support the Big Bang Theory and add details to the early conditions of the universe. Based upon this more recent data, scientists believe the universe is about 13.7 billion years old and that there was a period of rapid expansion right after the Big Bang. They have also learned that there were early variations in the density of matter resulting in the formation of the galaxies, the geometry of the universe is flat, and the universe will continue to expand forever.

Skill 17.3   Compare the physical and chemical processes involved in the life cycles of objects within galaxies.

Scientists believe that **stars** form when compression waves traveling through clouds of gas create knots of gas in the clouds. The force of gravity within these denser areas then attracts gas particles. As the knot grows, the force increases and attracts more gas particles, eventually forming a large sphere of compressed gas with internal temperatures reaching a few million degrees C. At these temperatures, the gases in the knot become so hot that nuclear fusion of hydrogen to form helium takes place, creating large amounts of nuclear energy and forming a new star. Pressure from the radiation of these new stars causes more knots to form in the gas cloud, initiating the process of creating more stars.

Scientists theorize that **planets** form from gas and dust surrounding young stars. As the density of the forming star increases, this gas and dust slowly condenses into a spinning disk. The denser areas of the disk develop a gravitational force which attracts more dust and gas as the disk orbits the star. Over millions of years, these dense areas consolidate and grow, forming planets. In the case of the Sun, the larger icy fragments surrounding it attracted more gas and dust forming the more massive planets such as Jupiter and Saturn. These larger planets developed gravitational forces great enough to attract hydrogen and helium atoms, turning them into gas giants. The smaller planets, such as Earth, could not attract these atoms and became mainly rocky.

It is believed that **black holes** form as stars evolve. As the nuclear fuels are used up in the core of a star, the pressure associated with the production of these fuels no longer exists to resist contraction of the core. Two new types of pressure, electron and neutron, arise. However, if the star is more than about five times as massive as the Sun, neither pressure will prevent the star from collapsing into a black hole.

When the universe was forming, most of the material became concentrated in the planets and moons. There were, however, many small, rocky objects called **planetesimals** that also formed from the gas and dust. These planetesimals include **comets** and **asteroids**. A large cloud of comets, known as the Oort cloud, exists beyond Pluto. A change in the gravitational pull of our galaxy may disturb the orbit of a comet causing it to fall toward the Sun. The ice in the comet turns into vapor, releasing dust from the body. Gas and dust then form the tail of the comet.

In the early life of the solar system, some of the planetesimals came together more toward the center of the solar system. The gravitational pull of Jupiter prevented these planetesimals from developing into full planets. They broke up into thousands of minor planets, known as asteroids.

It is believed that **black holes** form as stars evolve. As the nuclear fuels are used up in the core of a star, the pressure associated with the production of these fuels no longer exists to resist contraction of the core. Two new types of pressure, electron and neutron, arise. However, if the star is more than about five times as massive as the Sun, neither pressure will prevent the star from collapsing into a black hole.

When the universe was forming, most of the material became concentrated in the planets and moons. There were however many small, rocky objects called **planetesimals** that also formed from the gas and dust. These planetesimals include **comets** and **asteroids**. A large cloud of comets, known as the Oort cloud, exists beyond Pluto. A change in the gravitational pull of our galaxy may disturb the orbit of a comet causing it to fall toward the Sun. The ice in the comet turns into vapor, releasing dust from the body. Gas and dust then form the tail of the comet.

In the early life of the solar system, some of the planetesimals came together more toward the center of the solar system. The gravitational pull of Jupiter prevented these planetesimals from developing into full planets. They broke up into thousands of minor planets, known as asteroids.

Skill 17.4　Explain the functions and applications of the instruments, technologies, and tools used in the study of the space sciences, including the relative advantages and disadvantages of earth-based versus space-based instruments and optical versus non-optical instruments.

Types of **telescopes** used in the study of the space sciences include optical, radio, infrared, ultraviolet, x-ray, and gamma-ray. Optical telescopes work by collecting and magnifying visible light that is given off by stars or reflected from the surfaces of the planets. However, stars also give off other types of electromagnetic radiation, including radio waves, microwaves, infrared light, ultraviolet light, X rays, and gamma rays. Therefore, specific types of non-optical instruments have been developed to collect information about the universe through these other types of electromagnetic waves.

Many of the telescopes used by astronomers are earth-based, located in observatories around the world. However, only radio waves, visible light, and some infrared radiation can penetrate our atmosphere to reach the earth's surface. Therefore, scientists have launched telescopes into space, where the instruments can collect other types of electromagnetic waves. Space probes are also able to gather information from distant parts of the solar system.

In addition to telescopes, scientists construct mathematical models and computer simulations to form a scientific account of events in the universe. These models and simulations are built using evidence from many sources, including the information gathered through telescopes and space probes.

SUBAREA V.   **CELL BIOLOGY, HEREDITY, AND EVOLUTION**

COMPETENCY 0018   **UNDERSTAND AND APPLY KNOWLEDGE OF THE CONCEPTS OF CELL BIOLOGY.**

Skill 18.1   Demonstrate an understanding of the structural and functional aspects of nucleic acids, proteins (including enzyme activity), carbohydrates, and lipids.

A compound consists of two or more elements. There are four major chemical compounds found in the cells and bodies of living things. These include carbohydrates, lipids, proteins and nucleic acids.

Monomers are the simplest unit of structure. **Monomers** can be combined to form **polymers**, or long chains, making a large variety of molecules possible. Monomers combine through the process of condensation reaction (also called dehydration synthesis). In this process, one molecule of water is removed between each of the adjoining molecules. In order to break the molecules apart in a polymer, water molecules are added between monomers, thus breaking the bonds between them. This is called hydrolysis.

Carbohydrates contain a ratio of two hydrogen atoms for each carbon and oxygen $(CH_2O)_n$. Carbohydrates include sugars and starches. They function in the release of energy. **Monosaccharides** are the simplest sugars and include glucose, fructose, and galactose. They are major nutrients for cells. In cellular respiration, the cells extract the energy in glucose molecules. **Disaccharides** are made by joining two monosaccharides by condensation to form a glycosidic linkage (covalent bond between two monosaccharides). Maltose is formed from the combination of two glucose molecules, lactose is formed from joining glucose and galactose, and sucrose is formed from the combination of glucose and fructose. **Polysaccharides** consist of many monomers joined. They are storage material hydrolyzed as needed to provide sugar for cells or building material for structures protecting the cell. Examples of polysaccharides include starch, glycogen, cellulose and chitin.

    Starch - major energy storage molecule in plants. It is a polymer consisting of glucose monomers.
    Glycogen - major energy storage molecule in animals. It is made up of many glucose molecules.
    Cellulose - found in plant cell walls, its function is structural. Many animals lack the enzymes necessary to hydrolyze cellulose, so it simply adds bulk (fiber) to the diet.
    Chitin - found in the exoskeleton of arthropods and fungi. Chitin contains an amino sugar (glycoprotein).

Lipids are composed of glycerol (an alcohol) and three fatty acids. Lipids are **hydrophobic** (water fearing) and will not mix with water. There are three important families of lipids, fats, phospholipids and steroids.

Fats consist of glycerol (alcohol) and three fatty acids. Fatty acids are long carbon skeletons. The nonpolar carbon-hydrogen bonds in the tails of fatty acids are why they are hydrophobic. Fats are solids at room temperature and come from animal sources (butter, lard).

Phospholipids are a vital component in cell membranes. In a phospholipid, one or two fatty acids are replaced by a phosphate group linked to a nitrogen group. They consist of a **polar** (charged) head that is hydrophilic or water loving and a **nonpolar** (uncharged) tail which is hydrophobic or water fearing. This allows the membrane to orient itself with the polar heads facing the interstitial fluid found outside the cell and the internal fluid of the cell.

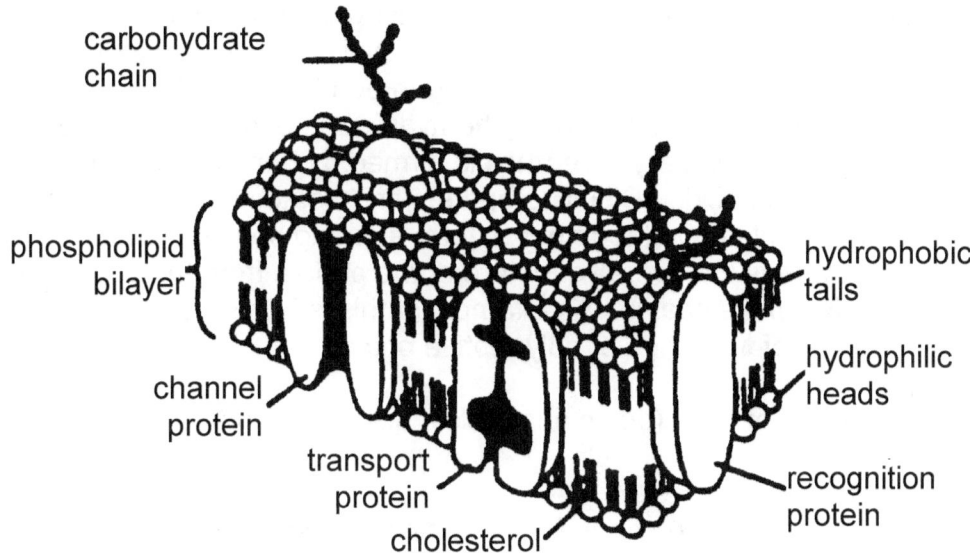

Steroids are insoluble and are composed of a carbon skeleton consisting of four inter-connected rings. An important steroid is cholesterol, which is the precursor from which other steroids are synthesized. Hormones, including cortisone, testosterone, estrogen, and progesterone, are steroids. Their insolubility keeps them from dissolving in body fluids.

Proteins compose about fifty percent of the dry weight of animals and bacteria. Proteins function in structure and aid in support (connective tissue, hair, feathers, quills), storage of amino acids (albumin in eggs, casein in milk), transport of substances (hemoglobin), hormonal to coordinate body activities (insulin), membrane receptor proteins, contraction (muscles, cilia, flagella), body defense (antibodies), and as enzymes to speed up chemical reactions.

All proteins are made of twenty **amino acids**. An amino acid contains an amino group and an acid group. The radical group varies and defines the amino acid. Amino acids form through condensation reactions with the removal of water. The bond that is formed between two amino acids is called a peptide bond. Polymers of amino acids are called polypeptide chains. An analogy can be drawn between the twenty amino acids and the alphabet. Millions of words can be formed using an alphabet of only twenty-six letters. This diversity is also possible using only twenty amino acids. This results in the formation of many different proteins, whose structure defines their function.

There are four levels of protein structure: primary, secondary, tertiary, and quaternary.

Primary structure is the protein's unique sequence of amino acids. A slight change in primary structure can affect a protein's conformation and its ability to function. **Secondary structure** is the coils and folds of polypeptide chains. The coils and folds are the result of hydrogen bonds along the polypeptide backbone. The secondary structure is either in the form of an alpha helix or a pleated sheet. The alpha helix is a coil held together by hydrogen bonds. A pleated sheet is the polypeptide chain folding back and forth. The hydrogen bonds between parallel regions hold it together. **Tertiary structure** is formed by bonding between the side chains of the amino acids. Disulfide bridges are created when two sulfhydryl groups on the amino acids bond together to form a strong covalent bond. **Quaternary structure** is the overall structure of the protein from the aggregation of two or more polypeptide chains. An example of this is hemoglobin. Hemoglobin consists of two kinds of polypeptide chains.

Nucleic acids consist of DNA (deoxyribonucleic acid) and RNA (ribonucleic acid).

Nucleic acids contain the instructions for the amino acid sequence of proteins and the instructions for replicating. The monomer of nucleic acids is called a nucleotide. A nucleotide consists of a 5 carbon sugar, (deoxyribose in DNA, ribose in RNA), a phosphate group, and a nitrogenous base. The base sequence codes for the instructions. There are five bases: adenine, thymine, cytosine, guanine, and uracil. Uracil is found only in RNA and replaces the thymine. A summary of nucleic acid structure can be seen in the table below:

	SUGAR	PHOSPHATE	BASES
DNA	deoxyribose	present	adenine, thymine, cytosine, guanine
RNA	ribose	present	adenine, uracil, cytosine, guanine

Due to the molecular structure, adenine will always pair with thymine in DNA or uracil in RNA. Cytosine always pairs with guanine in both DNA and RNA. This allows for the symmetry of the DNA molecule seen below.

RNA
(single-stranded)

DNA
(double-stranded)

Adenine and thymine (or uracil) are linked by two covalent bonds and cytosine and guanine are linked by three covalent bonds. The guanine and cytosine bonds are harder to break apart than thymine (uracil) and adenine because of the greater number of these bonds. The DNA molecule is called a double helix due to its twisted ladder shape.

Enzymes act as biological catalysts to speed up reactions. Enzymes are the most diverse of all types of proteins. They are not used up in a reaction and are recyclable. Each enzyme is specific for a single reaction. Enzymes act on a substrate. The substrate is the material to be broken down or put back together. Most enzymes end in the suffix -ase (lipase, amylase). The prefix is the substrate being acted on (lipids, sugars).

$$\text{Substrate} \xrightarrow{\text{Enzyme}} \text{Product}$$

SCIENCE: BIOLOGY

The active site is the region of the enzyme that binds to the substrate. There are two theories for how the active site functions. The **lock and key theory** states that the shape of the enzyme is specific because it fits into the substrate like a key fits into a lock. It aids in holding molecules close together so reactions can easily occur.

The **Induced fit theory** states that an enzyme can stretch and bend to fit the substrate. This is the most accepted theory.

Many factors can affect enzyme activity. Temperature and pH are two of those factors. The temperature can affect the rate of reaction of an enzyme. The optimal pH for enzymes is between 6 and 8, with a few enzymes whose optimal pH falls out of this range.

Cofactors aid in the enzyme's function. Cofactors may be inorganic or organic. Organic cofactors are known as coenzymes. An example of a coenzyme is vitamins. Some chemicals can inhibit an enzyme's function. **Competitive inhibitors** block the substrate from entering the active site of the enzyme to reduce productivity. **Noncompetitive inhibitors** bind to the enzyme in a location not in the active site but still interrupt substrate binding. In most cases, noncompetitive inhibitors alter the shape of the enzyme. An **allosteric enzyme** can exist in two shapes; they are active in one form and inactive in the other. Overactive enzymes may cause metabolic diseases.

Skill 18.2   Analyze, at the cellular level, the chemical processes by which organic materials are synthesized and used and relate these processes to energy production and utilization in living systems (e.g., photosynthesis, respiration).

Cellular respiration is the metabolic pathway in which food (glucose, etc.) is broken down to produce energy in the form of ATP. Both plants and animals utilize respiration to create energy for metabolism. In respiration, energy is released by the transfer of electrons in a process known as an **oxidation-reduction (redox)** reaction. The oxidation phase of this reaction is the loss of an electron and the reduction phase is the gain of an electron. Redox reactions are important for the stages of respiration.

Glycolysis is the first step in respiration. It occurs in the cytoplasm of the cell and does not require oxygen. Each of the ten stages of glycolysis is catalyzed by a specific enzyme. The following is a summary of those stages.

In the first stage the reactant is glucose. For energy to be released from glucose, it must be converted to a reactive compound. This conversion occurs through the phosphorylation of a molecule of glucose by the use of two molecules of ATP. This is an investment of energy by the cell. The six carbon product, called fructose -1,6- bisphosphate, breaks into two 3-carbon molecules of sugar. A phosphate group is added to each sugar molecule and hydrogen atoms are removed. Hydrogen is picked up by NAD^+ (a vitamin). Since there are two sugar molecules, two molecules of NADH are formed. The reduction (adding of hydrogen) of NAD allows the potential of energy transfer. As the phosphate bonds are broken, ATP is made. Two ATP molecules are generated as each original 3 carbon sugar molecule is converted to pyruvic acid (pyruvate). A total of four ATP molecules are made in the four stages. Since two molecules of ATP were needed to start the reaction in stage 1, there is a net gain of two ATP molecules at the end of glycolysis. This accounts for only two percent of the total energy in a molecule of glucose.

Beginning with pyruvate, which was the end product of glycolysis, the following steps occur before entering the **Krebs cycle**.

1. Pyruvic acid is changed to acetyl-CoA (coenzyme A). This is a three carbon pyruvic acid molecule which has lost one molecule of carbon dioxide (CO_2) to become a two carbon acetyl group. Pyruvic acid loses a hydrogen to NAD^+ which is reduced to NADH.

2. Acetyl CoA enters the Krebs cycle. For each molecule of glucose it started with, two molecules of Acetyl CoA enter the Krebs cycle (one for each molecule of pyruvic acid formed in glycolysis).

The **Krebs cycle** (also known as the citric acid cycle), occurs in four major steps. First, the two-carbon acetyl CoA combines with a four-carbon molecule to form a six-carbon molecule of citric acid. Next, two carbons are lost as carbon dioxide (CO_2) and a four-carbon molecule is formed to become available to join with CoA to form citric acid again. Since we started with two molecules of CoA, two turns of the Krebs cycle are necessary to process the original molecule of glucose. In the third step, eight hydrogen atoms are released and picked up by FAD and NAD (vitamins and electron carriers).
Lastly, for each molecule of CoA (remember there were two to start with) you get:

        3 molecules of NADH x 2 cycles
        1 molecule of $FADH_2$ x 2 cycles
        1 molecule of ATP x 2 cycles

Therefore, this completes the breakdown of glucose. At this point, a total of four molecules of ATP have been made; two from glycolysis and one from each of the two turns of the Krebs cycle. Six molecules of carbon dioxide have been released; two prior to entering the Krebs cycle, and two for each of the two turns of the Krebs cycle. Twelve carrier molecules have been made; ten NADH and two $FADH_2$. These carrier molecules will carry electrons to the electron transport chain. ATP is made by substrate level phosphorylation in the Krebs cycle. Notice that the Krebs cycle in itself does not produce much ATP, but functions mostly in the transfer of electrons to be used in the electron transport chain where the most ATP is made.

In the **Electron Transport Chain,** NADH transfers electrons from glycolysis and the Kreb's cycle to the first molecule in the chain of molecules embedded in the inner membrane of the mitochondrion. Most of the molecules in the electron transport chain are proteins. Nonprotein molecules are also part of the chain and are essential for the catalytic functions of certain enzymes. The electron transport chain does not make ATP directly. Instead, it breaks up a large free energy drop into a more manageable amount. The chain uses electrons to pump H^+ across the mitochondrion membrane. The H^+ gradient is used to form ATP synthesis in a process called **chemiosmosis** (oxidative phosphorylation). ATP synthetase and energy generated by the movement of hydrogen ions coming off of NADH and $FADH_2$ builds ATP from ADP on the inner membrane of the mitochondria. Each NADH yields three molecules of ATP (10 x 3) and each $FADH_2$ yields two molecules of ATP (2 x 2). Thus, the electron transport chain and oxidative phosphorylation produces 34 ATP.

The net gain from the whole process of respiration is 36 molecules of ATP:

    Glycolysis - 4 ATP made, 2 ATP spent = net gain of 2 ATP
    Acetyl CoA- 2 ATP used
    Krebs cycle - 1 ATP made for each turn of the cycle = net gain of 2 ATP
    Electron transport chain - 34 ATP gained

Photosynthesis is an anabolic process that stores energy in the form of a three carbon sugar. We will use glucose as an example for this section. Photosynthesis is done only by organisms that contain chloroplasts (plants, some bacteria, some protists). There are a few terms to be familiar with when discussing photosynthesis.

An **autotroph** (self feeder) is an organism that makes its own food from the energy of the sun or other elements. Autotrophs include:

1. **photoautotrophs** - make food from light and carbon dioxide releasing oxygen that can be used for respiration.
2. **chemoautotrophs** - oxidize sulfur and ammonia; this is done by some bacteria.

Heterotrophs (other feeder) are organisms that must eat other living things for their energy. **Consumers** are the same as heterotrophs; all animals are heterotrophs. **Decomposers** break down once living things. Bacteria and fungi are examples of decomposers. **Scavengers** eat dead things. Examples of scavengers are bacteria, fungi and some animals.

The **chloroplast** is the site of photosynthesis. It is similar to the mitochondria due to the increased surface area of the thylakoid membrane. It also contains a fluid called stroma between the stacks of thylakoids. The thylakoid membrane contains pigments (chlorophyll) that are capable of capturing light energy.

Photosynthesis reverses the electron flow. Water is split by the chloroplast into hydrogen and oxygen. The oxygen is given off as a waste product as carbon dioxide is reduced to sugar (glucose). This requires the input of energy, which comes from the sun.

Photosynthesis occurs in two stages: the light reactions and the Calvin cycle (dark reactions). The conversion of solar energy to chemical energy occurs in the light reactions. Electrons are transferred by the absorption of light by chlorophyll and cause the water to split, releasing oxygen as a waste product. The chemical energy that is created in the light reaction is in the form of NADPH. ATP is also produced by a process called photophosphorylation. These forms of energy are produced in the thylakoids and are used in the Calvin cycle to produce sugar.

The second stage of photosynthesis is the **Calvin cycle**. Carbon dioxide in the air is incorporated into organic molecules already in the chloroplast. The NADPH produced in the light reaction is used as reducing power for the reduction of the carbon to carbohydrate. ATP from the light reaction is also needed to convert carbon dioxide to carbohydrate (sugar).

The process of photosynthesis is made possible by the presence of the sun. Visible light ranges in wavelengths of 750 nanometers (red light) to 380 nanometers (violet light). As wavelength decreases, the amount of energy available increases. Light is carried as photons, which is a fixed quantity of energy. Light is reflected (what we see), transmitted, or absorbed (what the plant uses). The plant's pigments capture light of specific wavelengths. Remember that the light that is reflected is what we see as color. Plant pigments include:

> Chlorophyll *a* - reflects green/blue light; absorbs red light
> Chlorophyll *b* - reflects yellow/green light; absorbs red light
> Carotenoids - reflects yellow/orange; absorbs violet/blue

The pigments absorb photons. The energy from the light excites electrons in the chlorophyll that jump to orbitals with more potential energy and reach an "excited" or unstable state.

The formula for photosynthesis is:

$$CO_2 + H_2O + \text{energy (from sunlight)} \rightarrow C_6H_{12}O_6 + O_2$$

The high energy electrons are trapped by primary electron acceptors which are located on the thylakoid membrane. These electron acceptors and the pigments form reaction centers called photosystems that are capable of capturing light energy. Photosystems contain a reaction-center chlorophyll that releases an electron to the primary electron acceptor. This transfer is the first step of the light reactions. There are two photosystems, named according to their date of discovery, not their order of occurrence.

Photosystem I is composed of a pair of chlorophyll *a* molecules. Photosystem I is also called P700 because it absorbs light of 700 nanometers. Photosystem I makes ATP whose energy is needed to build glucose.

Photosystem II - this is also called P680 because it absorbs light of 680 nanometers. Photosystem II produces ATP + $NADPH_2$ and the waste gas oxygen.

Both photosystems are bound to the **thylakoid membrane**, close to the electron acceptors.

The production of ATP is termed **photophosphorylation** due to the use of light. Photosystem I uses cyclic photophosphorylation because the pathway occurs in a cycle. It can also use noncyclic photophosphorylation which starts with light and ends with glucose. Photosystem II uses noncyclic photophosphorylation only.

Below is a diagram of the relationship between cellular respiration and photosynthesis.

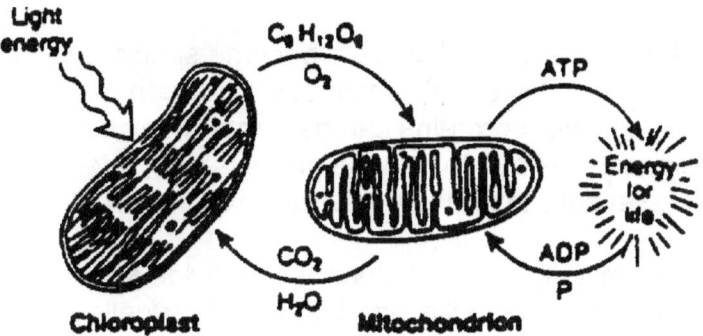

Glycolysis generates ATP with oxygen (aerobic) or without oxygen (anaerobic). Aerobic respiration has already been discussed. Anaerobic respiration can occur by fermentation. ATP can be generated by fermentation by substrate level phosphorylation if there is enough NAD^+ present to accept electrons during oxidation. In anaerobic respiration, NAD^+ is regenerated by transferring electrons to pyruvate. There are two common types of fermentation.

In **alcoholic fermentation**, pyruvate is converted to ethanol in two steps. In the first step, carbon dioxide is released from the pyruvate. In the second step, ethanol is produced by the reduction of acetaldehyde by NADH. This results in the regeneration of NAD^+ for glycolysis. Alcohol fermentation is carried out by yeast and some bacteria.

Pyruvate is reduced to form lactate as a waste product by NADH in the process of **lactic acid fermentation.** Animal cells and some bacteria that do not use oxygen utilize lactic acid fermentation to make ATP. Lactic acid forms when pyruvic acid accepts hydrogen from NADH. A buildup of lactic acid is what causes muscle soreness following exercise.

Energy remains stored in the lactic acid or alcohol until needed. This is not an efficient type of respiration. When oxygen is present, aerobic respiration occurs after glycolysis.

Both aerobic and anaerobic pathways oxidize glucose to pyruvate by glycolysis and both pathways have NAD^+ as the oxidizing agent. A substantial difference between the two pathways is that in fermentation, an organic molecule such as pyruvate or acetaldehyde is the final electron acceptor. In respiration, the final electron acceptor is oxygen. Another key difference is that respiration yields much more energy from a sugar molecule than fermentation does. Respiration can produce up to 18 times more ATP than fermentation.

Skill 18.3   Demonstrate knowledge of the mechanisms and genetics of cellular differentiation in forming specialized tissues, organs, and complete organisms.

Differentiation is the process in which cells become specialized in structure and function. The fate of the cell is usually maintained through many subsequent generations. Gene regulatory proteins can generate many cell types during development. Scientists believe that these proteins are passed down to the next generation of cells to ensure that the specialized expression of the genes occurs.

Stem cells are not terminally differentiated. It can divide for as long as the animal is alive. When the stem cell divides, its daughter cells can either remain a stem cell or can go forth with terminal differentiation. There are many types of stem cells. They are specialized for different classes of terminally differentiated cells.

Embryonic stem cells give rise to all the tissues and cell types in the body. In culture, these cells have led to the creation of animal tissue that can replace damaged tissues. It is hopeful that with continued research, embryonic stem cells can be cultured to replace muscles, tissues, and organs of individuals whose own are damaged.

COMPETENCY 0019 UNDERSTAND AND APPLY KNOWLEDGE OF THE MOLECULAR BASIS OF HEREDITY AND THE ASSOCIATED MATHEMATICAL PROBABILITIES.

Skill 19.1 Explain the structure and function of genes.

Chromosomes are the physical structures found in every cell that carry the genetic information of an organism and function in the transmission of hereditary information. The gene is the fundamental unit of heredity. Each chromosome contains a sequence of genes each with a specific locus. A locus is the position a given gene occupies on a chromosome. Each gene consists of a sequence of DNA that dictates a particular characteristic of an organism. Separating the genes on a chromosome are regions of DNA that do not code for proteins or other cellular products, but may function in the regulation of coding regions.

Skill 19.2 Analyze the molecular basis of DNA replication, transcription, translation, and gene expression.

DNA replicates semiconservatively. This means the two original strands are conserved and serve as a template for the new strand.

In DNA replication, the first step is to separate the two strands. As they separate, they need to unwind the supercoils to reduce tension. An enzyme called **helicase** unwinds the DNA as the replication fork proceeds and **topoisomerases** relieve the tension by nicking one strand and letting the supercoil relax. Once the strands have been separated, they need to be stabilized. Single stranded binding proteins (SSBs) bind to the single strands until the DNA is replicated.

An RNA polymerase called primase adds ribonucleotides to the DNA template to initiate DNA synthesis. This short RNA-DNA hybrid is called a **primer**. Once the DNA is single stranded, **DNA polymerases** add nucleotides in the 5' ⑧ 3' direction.

As DNA synthesis proceeds along the replication fork, it becomes obvious that replication is semi-discontinuous; meaning one strand is synthesized in the direction the replication fork is moving and the other is synthesizing in the opposite direction. The strand that is continuously synthesized is the **leading strand** and the discontinuously synthesized strand is the **lagging strand**. As the replication fork proceeds, new primer is added to the lagging strand and it is synthesized discontinuously in fragments called **Okazaki fragments**.

The RNA primers that remain need to be removed and replaced with deoxyribonucleotides. DNA polymerase has 5' ® 3' polymerase activity and has 3' ® 5' exonuclease activity. This enzyme binds to the nick between the Okazaki fragment and the RNA primer. It removes the primer and adds deoxyribonucleotides in the 5' ® 3' direction. The nick still remains until **DNA ligase** seals it with the final product being a double stranded segment of DNA.

Once the double stranded segment is replicated, there is a proofreading system by DNA replication enzymes. In eukaryotes, DNA polymerases have 3' ® 5' exonuclease activity—they move backwards and remove nucleotides where the enzyme recognizes an error, then it adds the correct nucleotide in the 5' ® 3' direction. In E. coli, DNA polymerase II synthesizes DNA during repair of DNA damage.

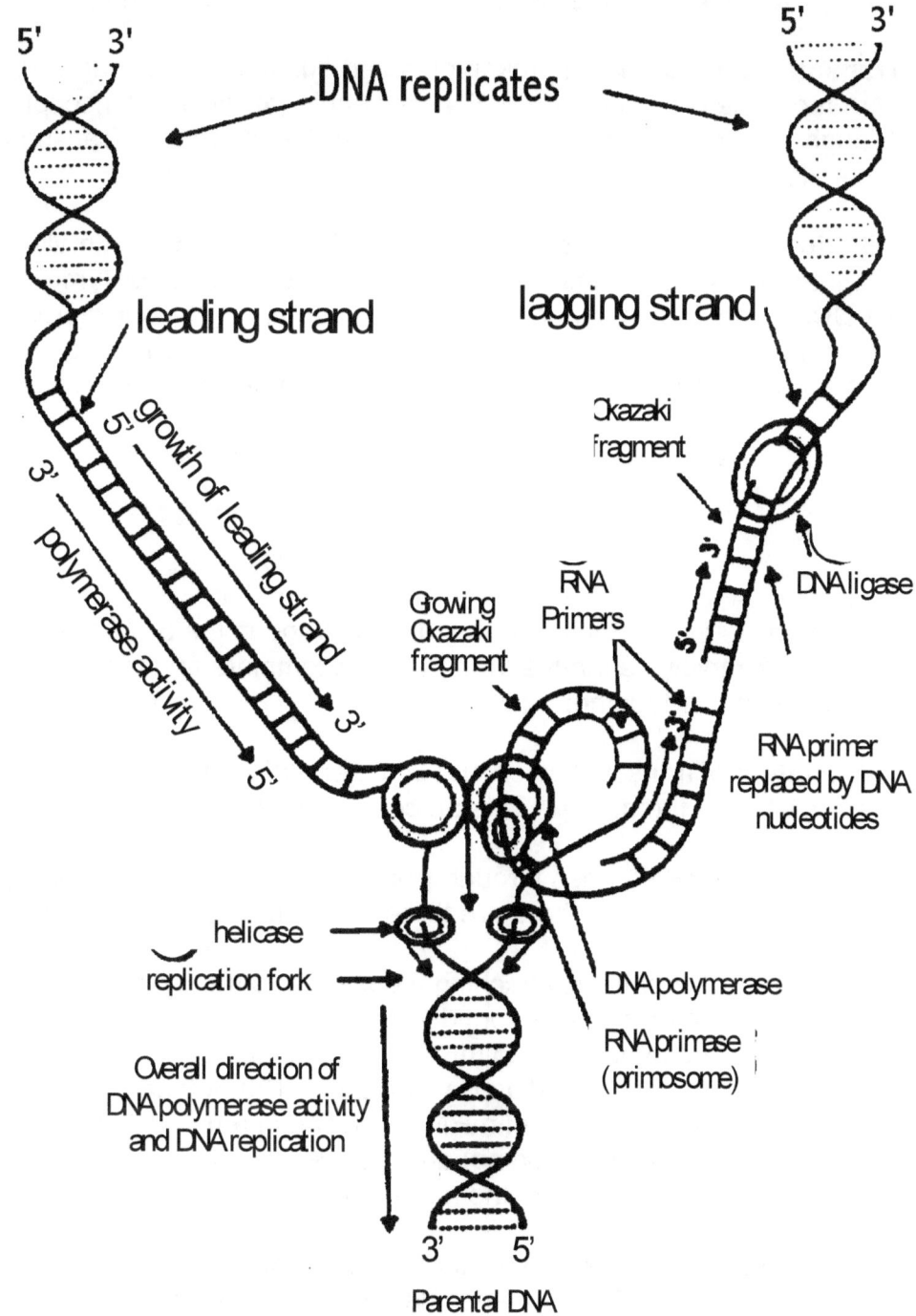

Figure 13

Proteins are synthesized through the processes of transcription and translation. Three major classes of RNA are needed to carry out these processes. The first is **messenger RNA (mRNA)**, which contains information for translation.

Ribosomal RNA (rRNA) is a structural component of the ribosome and **transfer RNA (tRNA)** carries amino acids to the ribosome for protein synthesis.

Transcription is similar in prokaryotes and eukaryotes. During transcription, the DNA molecule is copied into an RNA molecule (mRNA). Transcription occurs through the steps of initiation, elongation, and termination. Transcription also occurs for rRNA and tRNA, but the focus here is on mRNA.

Initiation begins at the promoter of the double stranded DNA molecule. The promoter is a specific region of DNA that directs the **RNA polymerase** to bind to the DNA. The double stranded DNA opens up and RNA polymerase begins transcription in the 5' ⊗ 3' direction by pairing ribonucleotides to the deoxyribonucleotides as follows to get a complementary mRNA segment:

Deoxyribonucleotide		Ribonucleotide
A	⊗	U
G	⊗	C

Elongation is the synthesis on the mRNA strand in the 5' ⊗ 3' direction. The new mRNA rapidly separates from the DNA template and the complementary DNA strands pair together again.

Termination of transcription occurs at the end of a gene. Cleavage occurs at specific sites on the mRNA. This process is aided by termination factors.

In eukaryotes, mRNA goes through **posttranscriptional processing** before going on to translation. There are three basic steps of processing:

1. 5' capping is attaching a base with a methyl attached to it that protects 5' end from degradation and serves as the site where ribosome binds to mRNA for translation.
2. 3' polyadenylation is when about 100-300 adenines are added to the free 3' end of mRNA resulting in a poly-A-tail.
3. Introns (non-coding) are removed and the coding exons are spliced together to form the mature mRNA.

Translation is the process in which the mRNA sequence becomes a polypeptide. The mRNA sequence determines the amino acid sequence of a protein by following a pattern called the genetic code. The **genetic code** consists of triplet nucleotide combinations called **amino acids**. There are 20 amino acids mRNA codes for. Amino acids are the building blocks of protein. They are attached together by peptide bonds to form a polypeptide chain. There are 64 triplet combinations called codons. Three codons are termination codons and the remaining 61 code for amino acids.

Ribosomes are the site of translation. They contain rRNA and many proteins. Translation occurs in three steps: initiation, elongation, and termination. Initiation occurs when the methylated tRNA binds to the ribosome to form a complex. This complex then binds to the 5' cap of the mRNA. In elongation, tRNAs carry the amino acid to the ribosome and place it in order according to the mRNA sequence. tRNA is very specific – it only accepts one of the 20 amino acids that corresponds to the anticodon. The anticodon is complementary to the codon. For example, using the codon sequence below:

the mRNA reads A U G / G A G / C A U / G C U
the anticodons are U A C / C U C / G U A / C G A

Termination occurs when the ribosome reaches any one of the stop codons : UAA, UAG, or UGA. The newly formed polypeptide then undergoes posttranslational modification to alter or remove portions of the polypeptide.

Skill 19.3   Analyze the mechanisms and impacts of mutations.

Inheritable changes in DNA are called mutations. **Mutations** may be errors in replication or a spontaneous rearrangement of one or more segments by factors like radioactivity, drugs, or chemicals. The severity of the change is not as critical as where the change occurs. DNA contains large segments of non-coding areas called introns. The important coding areas are called exons. If an error occurs on an intron, there is no effect. If the error occurs on an exon, it may be minor to lethal depending on the severity of the mistake. Mutations may occur on somatic or sex cells. Usually the mutations on sex cells are more dangerous since they contain the basis of all information for the developing offspring. But mutations are not always bad. They are the basis of evolution and if they make a more favorable variation that enhances the organism's survival, then they are beneficial. But mutations may also lead to abnormalities and birth defects and even death. There are several types of mutations.

A **point mutation** is a mutation involving a single nucleotide or a few adjacent nucleotides. Let's suppose a normal sequence was as follows:

Normal: A B C D E F
Duplication - one gene is repeated   A B **C C** D E F
Inversion - a segment of the sequence is flipped around   A **E D C B** F
Deletion - a gene is left out   A B C E F   (D is lost)
Insertion or Translocation - a segment from another
place on the DNA is stuck in the wrong place   A B C **R S** D E F
Breakage - a piece is lost   A B C   (DEF is lost)

Deletion and insertion mutations that shift the reading frame are **frame shift mutations**. A **silent mutation** makes no change in the amino acid sequence, therefore it does not alter the protein function. A **missense mutation** results in an alteration in the amino acid sequence.

A mutation's effect on protein function depends on which amino acid is involved and how many are involved. The structure of a protein usually determines its function. A mutation that does not alter the structure will probably have little or no effect on the protein's function. However, a mutation that does alter the structure of a protein can severely affect protein activity is called **loss-of-function mutation**. Sickle-cell anemia and cystic fibrosis are examples of loss-of-function mutations.

Sickle-cell anemia is characterized by weakness, heart failure, joint and muscular impairment, fatigue, abdominal pain and dysfunction, impaired mental function, and eventual death. The mutation that causes this genetic disorder is a point mutation in the sixth amino acid. A normal hemoglobin molecule has glutamic acid as the sixth amino acid and the sickle-cell hemoglobin has valine at the sixth position. This causes the chemical properties of hemoglobin to change. The hemoglobin of a sickle-cell person has a lower affinity for oxygen, and that causes red blood cells to have a sickle shape. The sickle shape of the red blood cell does not allow the cells to pass through capillaries well, forming clogs.

Cystic fibrosis is the most common genetic disorder of people with European ancestry. This disorder affects the exocrine system. A fibrous cyst is formed on the pancreas that blocks the pancreatic ducts. This causes sweat glands to release high levels of salt. A thick mucus is secreted from mucous glands that accumulates in the lungs. This accumulation of mucus causes bacterial infections and possibly death. Cystic fibrosis cannot be cured but can be treated for a short while. Most children with the disorder die before adulthood. Scientists identified a protein that transports chloride ions across cell membranes. Those with cystic fibrosis have a mutation in the gene coding for the protein. The majority of the mutant alleles have a deletion of the three nucleotides coding for phenylalanine at position 508. The other people with the disorder have mutant alleles caused by substitution, deletion, and frameshift mutations.

Skill 19.4   Demonstrate an understanding of genetic and mathematical explanations associated with probabilities of the transmission of traits and heritable defects in organisms (e.g., pedigrees, Punnett squares).

The same techniques of pedigree analysis apply when tracing inherited disorders. Thousands of genetic disorders are the result of inheriting a recessive trait. These disorders range from nonlethal traits (such as albinism) to life-threatening (such as cystic fibrosis).

Most people with recessive disorders are born to parents with normal phenotypes. The mating of heterozygous parents would result in an offspring genotypic ratio of 1:2:1; thus 1 out of 4 offspring would express this recessive trait. The heterozygous parents are called carriers because they do not express the trait phenotypically but pass the trait on to their offspring.

Lethal dominant alleles are much less common than lethal recessives. This is because lethal dominant alleles are not masked in heterozygotes. Mutations in a gene of the sperm or egg can result in a lethal dominant allele, usually killing the developing offspring.

Sex linked traits - the Y chromosome found only in males (XY) carries very little genetic information, whereas the X chromosome found in females (XX) carries very important information. Since men have no second X chromosome to cover up a recessive gene, the recessive trait is expressed more often in men. Women need the recessive gene on both X chromosomes to show the trait. Examples of sex linked traits include hemophilia and color-blindness.

Sex influenced traits - traits are influenced by the sex hormones. Male pattern baldness is an example of a sex influenced trait. Testosterone influences the expression of the gene. Mostly men lose their hair due to this.

Nondisjunction - during meiosis, chromosomes fail to separate properly. One sex cell may get both chromosomes and another may get none. Depending on the chromosomes involved this may or may not be serious. Offspring end up with either an extra chromosome or are missing one. An example of nondisjunction is Down Syndrome, where three #21 chromosomes are present.

Chromosome Theory - Noted by Walter Sutton in the early 1900's. In the late 1800's, the processes of mitosis and meiosis were now understood. Sutton saw how this explanation confirmed Mendel's "factors". The chromosome theory basically states that genes are located on chromosomes. The chromosomes undergo independent assortment and segregation.

Skill 19.5 Demonstrate knowledge of the concepts and consequences associated with recombinant DNA applications.

In its simplest form, genetic engineering requires enzymes to cut DNA, a vector, and a host organism for the recombinant DNA. A **restriction enzyme** is a bacterial enzyme that cuts foreign DNA in specific locations. The restriction fragment that results can be inserted into a bacterial plasmid (**vector**). Other vectors that may be used include viruses and bacteriophages. The splicing of restriction fragments into a plasmid results in a recombinant plasmid. This recombinant plasmid can now be placed in a host cell, usually a bacterial cell, and replicate.

The use of recombinant DNA provides a means to transplant genes among species. This opens the door for cloning specific genes of interest. Hybridization can be used to find a gene of interest. A probe is a molecule complementary in sequence to the gene of interest. The probe, once it has bonded to the gene, can be detected by labeling with a radioactive isotope or a fluorescent tag.

TEACHER CERTIFICATION STUDY GUIDE

COMPETENCY 0020 UNDERSTAND AND APPLY KNOWLEDGE OF THE HISTORICAL PROGRESSION OF CELLULAR BIOLOGY AND GENETICS AND THE BASIC RESEARCH METHODS AND TECHNOLOGIES USED IN THESE AREAS.

Skill 20.1 Analyze the historical progression of cellular biology and biotechnology, including the changes in knowledge due to advances in technology and the resulting societal implications.

Genetic engineering has made enormous contributions to medicine. Genetic engineering has opened the door to DNA technology. The use of DNA probes and polymerase chain reaction (PCR) has enabled scientists to identify and detect elusive pathogens. Diagnosis of genetic diseases is now possible before the onset of symptoms.

Genetic engineering has allowed for the treatment of some genetic disorders. **Gene therapy** is the introduction of a normal allele to the somatic cells to replace the defective allele. The medical field has had success in treating patients with a single enzyme deficiency disease. Gene therapy has allowed doctors and scientists to introduce a normal allele that would provide the missing enzyme.

Insulin and mammalian growth hormones have been produced in bacteria by gene-splicing techniques. Insulin treatment helps control diabetes for millions of people who suffer from the disease. The insulin produced in genetically engineered bacteria is chemically identical to that made in the pancreas. Human grown hormone (HGH) has been genetically engineered for treatment of dwarfism caused by insufficient amounts of HGH. HGH is being further researched for treatment of broken bones and severe burns.

Biotechnology has advanced the techniques used to create vaccines. Genetic engineering allows for the modification of a pathogen in order to attenuate it for vaccine use. In fact, vaccines created by a pathogen attenuated by gene-splicing may be safer than using the traditional mutants.

Forensic scientists regularly use DNA technology to solve crimes. DNA testing can determine a person's guilt or innocence. A suspect's DNA fingerprint is compared to the DNA found at the crime scene. If the fingerprints match, guilt can then be established.

Many microorganisms are used to detoxify toxic chemicals and to recycle waste. Sewage treatment plants use microbes to degrade organic compounds. Some compounds, like chlorinated hydrocarbons, cannot be easily degraded. Scientists are working on genetically modifying microbes to be able to degrade the harmful compounds that the current microbes cannot.

SCIENCE: BIOLOGY

Genetic engineering has benefited agriculture also. For example, many dairy cows are given bovine growth hormone to increase milk production. Commercially grown plants are often genetically modified for optimal growth.

Strains of wheat, cotton, and soybeans have been developed to resist herbicides used to control weeds. This allows for the successful growth of the plants while destroying the weeds. Crop plants are also being engineered to resist infections and pests. Scientists can genetically modify crops to contain a viral gene that does not affect the plant and will "vaccinate" the plant from a virus attack. Crop plants are now being modified to resist insect attacks. This allows for farmers to reduce the amount of pesticide used on plants.

Genetic engineering has drastically advanced the biotechnology. With these advancements come concerns for safety and ethical questions. Many safety concerns have answered by strict government regulations. The FDA, USDA, EPA, and National Institutes of Health are just a few of the government agencies that regulate pharmaceutical, food, and environmental technology advancements.

Several ethical questions arise when discussing biotechnology. Should embryonic stem cell research be allowed? Is animal testing humane? These are just a couple of ethical questions that every person wonders. There are strong arguments for both sides of the issues and there are some government regulations in place to monitor these issues.

Skill 20.2   Demonstrate knowledge of the basic methods, processes, and tools used in cellular and molecular biology research (e.g., electrophoresis, transformation, polymerase chain reaction).

Gel electrophoresis is another method for analyzing DNA. Electrophoresis separates DNA or protein by size or electrical charge. The DNA runs towards the positive charge as it separates the DNA fragments by size. The gel is treated with a DNA-binding dye that fluoresces under ultraviolet light. A picture of the gel can be taken and used for analysis.

One of the most widely used genetic engineering techniques is **polymerase chain reaction (PCR)**. PCR is a technique in which a piece of DNA can be amplified into billions of copies within a few hours. This process requires primer to specify the segment to be copied, and an enzyme (usually taq polymerase) to amplify the DNA. PCR has allowed scientists to perform several procedures on the smallest amount of DNA.

COMPETENCY 0021 UNDERSTAND AND APPLY KNOWLEDGE OF BIOLOGICAL EVOLUTION AND DIVERSITY.

Skill 21.1 Demonstrate an understanding of biological diversity, with an emphasis on the evolutionary relationships among the major groups of organisms.

The hypothesis that life developed on Earth from nonliving materials is the most widely accepted theory on the origin of life. The transformation from nonliving materials to life had four stages. The first stage was the nonliving (abiotic) synthesis of small monomers such as amino acids and nucleotides. In the second stage, these monomers combine to form polymers, such as proteins and nucleic acids. The third stage is the accumulation of these polymers into droplets called protobionts. The last stage is the origin of heredity, with RNA as the first genetic material.

The first stage of this theory was hypothesized in the 1920s. A. I. Oparin and J. B. S. Haldane were the first to theorize that the primitive atmosphere was a reducing atmosphere with no oxygen present. The gases were rich in hydrogen, methane, water and ammonia. In the 1950s, Stanley Miller proved Oparin's theory in the laboratory by combining the above gases. When given an electrical spark, he was able to synthesize simple amino acids. It is commonly accepted that amino acids appeared before DNA. Other laboratory experiments have supported the other stages in the origin of life theory could have happened.

Other scientists believe simpler hereditary systems originated before nucleic acids. In 1991, Julius Rebek was able to synthesize a simple organic molecule that replicates itself. According to his theory, this simple molecule may be the precursor of RNA.

Prokaryotes are the simplest life form. Their small genome size limits the number of genes that control metabolic activities. Over time, some prokaryotic groups became multicellular organisms for this reason. Prokaryotes then evolved to form complex bacterial communities where species benefit from one another.

The **endosymbiotic theory** of the origin of eukaryotes states that eukaryotes arose from symbiotic groups of prokaryotic cells. According to this theory, smaller prokaryotes lived within larger prokaryotic cells, eventually evolving into chloroplasts and mitochondria. Chloroplasts are the descendants of photosynthetic prokaryotes and mitochondria are likely to be the descendants of bacteria that were aerobic heterotrophs. Serial endosymbiosis is a sequence of endosymbiotic events. Serial endosymbiosis may also play a role in the progression of life forms to become eukaryotes.

Skill 21.2 Demonstrate an understanding of the processes of natural selection and speciation.

Natural selection is based on the survival of certain traits in a population through the course of time. The phrase "survival of the fittest," is often associated with natural selection. Fitness is the contribution an individual makes to the gene pool of the next generation.

Natural selection acts on phenotypes. An organism's phenotype is constantly exposed to its environment. Based on an organism's phenotype, selection indirectly adapts a population to its environment by maintaining favorable genotypes in the gene pool.

There are three modes of natural selection. Stabilizing selection favors the more common phenotypes, directional selection shifts the frequency of phenotypes in one direction, and diversifying selection occurs when individuals on both extremes of the phenotypic range are favored.

Sexual selection leads to the secondary sex characteristics between male and females. Animals that use mating behaviors may be successful or unsuccessful. An animal that lacks attractive plumage or has a weak mating call will not attract the female, thereby eventually limiting that gene in the gene pool. Mechanical isolation, where sex organs do not fit the female, has an obvious disadvantage.

The most commonly used species concept is the **Biological Species Concept (BSC)**. This states that a species is a reproductive community of populations that occupy a specific niche in nature. It focuses on reproductive isolation of populations as the primary criterion for recognition of species status. The biological species concept does not apply to organisms that are completely asexual in their reproduction, fossil organisms, or distinctive populations that hybridize.

Reproductive isolation is caused by any factor that impedes two species from producing viable, fertile hybrids. Reproductive barriers can be categorized as **prezygotic** (premating) or **postzygotic** (postmating).

The prezygotic barriers are as follows:

1. Habitat isolation – species occupy different habitats in the same territory.
2. Temporal isolation – populations reaching sexual maturity/flowering at different times of the year.
3. Ethological isolation – behavioral differences that reduce or prevent interbreeding between individuals of different species (including pheromones and other attractants).
4. Mechanical isolation – structural differences that make gamete transfer difficult or impossible.
5. Gametic isolation – male and female gametes do not attract each other; no fertilization.

The postzygotic barriers are as follows:

1. Hybrid inviability – hybrids die before sexual maturity.
2. Hybrid sterility – disrupts gamete formation; no normal sex cells.
3. Hybrid breakdown – reduces viability or fertility in progeny of the F_2 backcross.

Geographical isolation can also lead to the origin of species. **Allopatric speciation** is speciation without geographic overlap. It is the accumulation of genetic differences through division of a species' range, either through a physical barrier separating the population or through expansion by dispersal such that gene flow is cut. In **sympatric speciation**, new species arise within the range of parent populations. Populations are sympatric if their geographical range overlaps. This usually involves the rapid accumulation of genetic differences (usually chromosomal rearrangements) that prevent interbreeding with adjacent populations.

Skill 21.3   Describe evidence (e.g., comparative anatomy, paleontology, genetics) supporting the theory of evolution and evolutionary relationships.

Fossils are the key to understanding biological history. They are the preserved remnants left by an organism that lived in the past. Scientists have established the geological time scale to determine the age of a fossil. The geological time scale is broken down into four eras: the Precambrian, Paleozoic, Mesozoic, and Cenozoic. The eras are further broken down into periods that represent a distinct age in the history of Earth and its life. Scientists use rock layers called strata to date fossils. The older layers of rock are at the bottom. This allows scientists to correlate the rock layers with the era they date back to. Radiometric dating is a more precise method of dating fossils. Rocks and fossils contain isotopes of elements accumulated over time. The isotope's half-life is used to date older fossils by determining the amount of isotope remaining and comparing it to the half-life.

Dating fossils is helpful to construct an evolutionary tree. Scientists can arrange the succession of animals based on their fossil record. The fossils of an animal's ancestors can be dated and placed on its evolutionary tree. For example, the branched evolution of horses shows the progression of the modern horse's ancestors to be larger, to have a reduced number of toes, and have teeth modified for grazing.

Skill 21.4 Evaluate recent findings or research that are associated with the testing of the theory of evolution and its mechanisms.

Evidence from fossils. Based on a myriad of similarities and differences between living species, evolutionary biology makes predictions about the features of ancestral forms. For example, numerous features indicate that birds are derived from reptilian ancestors. By contrast, these data reject the possibility that birds were derived from other groups, such as flying insects. Scientists have discovered fossil birds with feathers and legs like modern birds, but which also have teeth, clawed digits on their forelimbs, and a tailbone like their reptilian ancestors. Fossils are especially important evidence for evolution because, with little effort, each of us can use our eyes and minds to observe and interpret the dinosaur and other ancient fossils in public museums.

Evidence from genetics. The genomes of all organisms contain overwhelming evidence for evolution. All living species share the same basic mechanism of heredity using DNA (or RNA in some viruses) to encode genes that are passed from parent to offspring, and which are transcribed and translated into proteins during each organism's life. Using DNA sequences, biologists quantify the genetic similarities and differences among species, in order to determine which species are more closely related to one another and which are more distantly related. In doing so, biologists use essentially the same evidence and logic used to determine paternity in lawsuits. The pattern of genetic relatedness between all species indicates a branching tree that implies divergence from a common ancestor. Within this tree of life, there are also occasional reticulations where two branches fuse, rather than separate. (For example, mitochondria are organelles found in the cells of plants and animals. Mitochondria have their own genes, which are more similar to genes in bacteria than to genes on the chromosomes in the cell nucleus. Thus, one of our distant ancestors arose from a symbiosis of two different cell types). The genetic similarity between species, which exists by virtue of evolution from the same ancestral form, is an essential fact that underlies biomedical research. This similarity allows us to begin to understand the effects of our own genes by conducting research on genes from other species. For example, genes that control the process of DNA repair in bacteria, flies, and mice have been discovered to influence certain cancers in humans. These findings also suggest strategies for intervention that can be explored in other species before testing on humans.

Evolution in action. Evolutionary change continues to this day, and it will proceed so long as life itself exists. In recent years, many bacterial pathogens have evolved resistance to antibiotics used to cure infections, thereby requiring the development of new and more costly treatments. In some frightening cases, bacteria have evolved resistance to every available antibiotic, so there is no longer any effective treatment. In the case of HIV, which causes AIDS, significant viral evolution occurs within the course of infection of a single patient, and this rapid evolution enables the virus to evade the immune system. Many agricultural pests have evolved resistance to chemicals that farmers have used for only a few decades. As we work to control diseases and pests, the responsible organisms have been evolving to escape our controls. Moreover, scientists can perform experiments to study evolution in real time, just as experiments are used to observe dynamic processes in physics, chemistry, and other branches of biology. To study evolution in action, scientists use organisms like bacteria and fruit flies that reproduce quickly, so they can see changes that require many generations.

Ongoing research and findings result in scientists re-examining and reinterpreting previous evolutionary understandings. One recent re-examination is the evolution of aquatic fish to terrestrial tetrapods. Until the 1980's the fossil record of tetrapods was limited and was based on fragmentary remains. This resulted in a one-sided view of the evolution of fish to land animal. The finding of new fossils in the early 1900's in East Greenland greatly expanded the tetrapod record, providing the evidence needed to re-evaluate the evolution of tetrapods. The first tetrapods are now seen as fish with legs. Further, instead of thinking of a transition between aquatic fishes and terrestrial tetrapods, the new understanding considers both the transition between fish and tetrapod and the transition between aquatic and terrestrial.

The unexpected characteristics that were found on the newly discovered fossils have led to reinterpretations of the previously held beliefs. Some were found to be less adept on land, while others were found to be less aquatic than earlier fossils. The multitude of newly available specimens has allowed scientists to enhance their understanding of early tetrapod anatomy. As late as 2006, the discovery of another tetrapod-like fish, *Tiktaalik*, has substantially enriched the understanding of the transition of lobe-fins to tetrapods. Advancements in technology and research will allow scientists to continue to further their understanding of the evolution of tetrapods as more specimens are discovered. This same re-evalution and reinterpretation is taking place in many species.

Skill 21.5 Analyze the historical progression of the study of biological evolution, including the changes in knowledge due to advances in technology and the resulting societal implications.

There are two theories on the rate of evolution. **Gradualism** is the theory that minor evolutionary changes occur at a regular rate. Darwin's book, "On the Origin of Species," is based on this theory of gradualism. Charles Darwin was born in 1809 and spent 5 years in his twenties on a ship called the *Beagle*. Of all the locations the *Beagle* sailed to, it was the Galapagos Islands that infatuated Darwin. There he collected 13 species of finches that were quite similar. He could not accurately determine whether these finches were of the same species. He later learned these finches were in fact separate species. Darwin began to hypothesize that new species arose from its ancestors by the gradual collection of adaptations to a different environment. Darwin's most popular hypothesis is on the beak size of Galapagos finches. He theorized that the finches' beak sizes evolved to accommodate different food sources. Many people did not believe in Darwin's theories until recent field studies proved successful.

Although Darwin believed the origin of species was gradual, he was bewildered by the gaps in fossil records of living organisms. **Punctuated equilibrium** is the model of evolution that states that organismal form diverges and species form rapidly over relatively short periods of geological history, and then progress through long stages of stasis with little or no change. Punctuationalists use fossil records to support their claim. It is probable that both theories are correct, depending on the particular lineage studied.

TEACHER CERTIFICATION STUDY GUIDE

SUBAREA VI.   **ORGANISMAL BIOLOGY AND ECOLOGY**

COMPETENCY 0022   **UNDERSTAND AND APPLY KNOWLEDGE OF ORGANISMAL BIOLOGY, USING EXAMPLES FROM EACH KINGDOM.**

Skill 22.1   **Recognize the basic physiological needs and requirements (e.g., energy, nutrients, oxygen) of organisms.**

All living organisms, from simple bacteria to complex mammals, conduct the following processes: reproduction, growth and development, metabolism, and homeostasis/response to the environment. To undertake these tasks, an organism needs adequate energy, nutrients, oxygen (unless anaerobic), and shelter. Energy is required by an animal to conduct most metabolic processes. To reproduce and grow, an organism must use energy, so a lack of it would result in a failure to thrive and eventual death. Nutrients help to sustain life by providing essential building blocks to the organism. We all know the old adage, an apple a day keeps the doctor away. Apples are full of fiber and vitamins helpful in maintaining good health. More significant contributions from nutrients to physical structure include the consumption of carbohydrates, carbon, calcium, and phosphorous. Humans and other mammals require oxygen to breathe. These same organisms release carbon dioxide as a waste product that is then recycled by plants. Plants use the carbon dioxide to create their own energy via photosynthesis. Some organisms are cold blooded and can adjust their own internal temperature. Mammals are warm blooded and shelter from extreme temperatures becomes important for survival. Aside from temperature regulation, shelter from predators is also important for obvious reasons.

Skill 22.2   **Demonstrate knowledge of the biochemical and molecular biology of processes fundamental to metabolic function of various systems of living organisms.**

Metabolism is the sum of all the chemical changes in a cell that convert nutrients to energy and macromolecules, the complex chemical molecules important to cell structure and function. The four main classes of macromolecules are polysaccharides (carbohydrates), nucleic acids, proteins, and lipids. Metabolism consists of two contrasting processes, anabolism and catabolism. Anabolism is biosynthesis, the formation of complex macromolecules from simple precursors. Anabolic reactions require the input of energy to proceed. Catabolism is the breaking down of macromolecules obtained from the environment or cellular reserves to produce energy in the form of ATP and basic precursor molecules. The energy produced by catabolic reactions drives the anabolic pathways of the cell.

Anabolism

The anabolic pathways of a cell diverge, synthesizing a large variety of macromolecules. All anabolic reactions produce complex molecules by linking small subunits, called monomers, together to form a large unit, or polymer. The main mechanism of anabolism is condensation reactions that covalently link monomer units and release water.

Polysaccharides (carbohydrates) consist of monosaccharide units (e.g. glucose) linked together by glycosidic linkages, covalent bonds formed through condensation reactions. Glycogen is the principle storage form of glucose in animal and human cells. Cells produce glycogen by linking glucose monomers to form polymer chains.

Nucleic acids are large polymers of nucleotides. Cells link nucleotides, consisting of a five-carbon sugar, a phosphate group, and a nitrogenous base, through condensation reactions. During DNA and RNA synthesis, the template molecule dictates the sequence of nucleotides by complementary base pairing.

Proteins are large polymers of amino acid subunits called polypeptides. Cells synthesize proteins by linking amino acids, forming peptide linkages through condensation reactions. RNA sequences direct the synthesis of proteins.

Lipids are a diverse group of molecules that are hydrophobic and insoluble in water. Cells synthesize lipids from fatty acid chains formed by the addition of two-carbon units derived from a molecule called acetyl coenzyme A (acetyl-CoA). The reactions involved in lipid synthesis include condensation, oxidation/reduction, and alkylation.

Catabolism

The catabolic pathways of a cell break down macromolecules and produce energy to drive the anabolic pathways. In addition, catabolic pathways release precursor molecules (e.g. amino acids, nucleotides) used in biosynthesis. The basic reaction of catabolism is hydrolysis, the addition of a water molecule across a covalent bond.

Cells break the glycosidic linkages of stored or consumed polysaccharides, releasing glucose or other sugars that can be converted to glucose. The cells further degrade glucose to basic chemical end products, producing energy in the form of ATP. Glycolysis is the process by which cells oxidize one glucose molecule to form two pyruvate molecules. Glycolysis also produces a small amount of ATP. Next, in organisms that utilize oxygen, the citric acid cycle completely oxidizes the pyruvate molecules to carbon dioxide and water, producing more ATP. Finally, the other products of the citric acid cycle, high-energy electron carriers (NADH and FADH) donate electrons to the electron transfer chain. The high-energy electrons move to lower energy levels, producing energy that pumps hydrogen atoms across the cell membrane to generate a concentration gradient. Diffusion of hydrogen atoms back across the membrane is coupled to ATP synthesis (see section below: Chemiosmosis). One molecule of glucose completely oxidized aerobically yields 38 ATP.

Hydrolysis of lipids releases fatty acids that are a rich energy source. Fatty acids contain more than twice as much potential energy as do carbohydrates or proteins. The breakdown of fatty acids produces basic chemical compounds and energy in the form of ATP.

Cells break down consumed proteins into amino acid units and other simple derivatives. Cells then use the amino acids to form new peptide chains or convert the derivative units into new amino acids. Cells can also acquire energy from the degradation of proteins, but the energy yield is not as high as that of polysaccharides and fatty acids.

Finally, hydrolysis of nucleic acids by enzymes produces oligonucleotides (short strings of DNA or RNA) that are further degraded to produce free nucleosides (sugar-nitrogenous base units). Cells further digest nucleosides, separating the nitrogenous base from the sugar. Digestion of nucleosides ultimately results in the production of nitrogenous bases, simple sugars, and basic precursor compounds used in the synthesis of new DNA or RNA.

ATP PRODUCTION THROUGH CHEMIOSMOSIS

Chemiosmosis is the coupling of the diffusion of molecules across a membrane for adenosine triphosphate (ATP) synthesis. In both photosynthesis and respiration, cells use the energy from the transfer of electrons to pump hydrogen ions across the membranes of mitochondria and chloroplasts. This process establishes an electrochemical concentration gradient, where the concentration of hydrogen ions outside of the cellular organelles is much higher than the concentration within the cell. Thus, diffusion of ions back across the membrane yields energy. Mitochondria and chloroplasts use this energy to create the high-energy molecule ATP by adding a phosphate group to adenosine diphosphate (ADP).

Cellular respiration is the complete breakdown of glucose to produce energy. The final steps of the respiration process occur in the mitochondria. Cells create the electrochemical concentration gradient across the mitochondrial membrane, using the energy from the transport of electrons to pump ions out of the mitochondria. Hydrogen ions diffuse back into mitochondria, toward the area of lower concentration, through an enzyme called ATP synthase. This energy yielding process drives the phosphorylation of ADP to form ATP.

Skill 22.3 Analyze interrelationships of the functions of various organismal systems.

Groups of related organs are organ systems. Organ systems consist of organs working together to perform a common function. The commonly recognized organ systems of animals include the reproductive system, nervous system, circulatory system, respiratory system, lymphatic system (immune system), endocrine system, urinary system, muscular system, digestive system, integumentary system, and skeletal system. In addition, organ systems are interconnected and a single system rarely works alone to complete a task.

One obvious example of the interconnectedness of organ systems is the relationship between the circulatory and respiratory systems. As blood circulates through the organs of the circulatory systems, it is re-oxygenated in the lungs of the respiratory system. Another example is the influence of the endocrine system on other organ systems. Hormones released by the endocrine system greatly influence processes of many organ systems including the nervous and reproductive systems.

In addition, bodily response to infection is a coordinated effort of the lymphatic (immune system) and circulatory systems. The lymphatic system produces specialized immune cells, filters out disease-causing organisms, and removes fluid waste from in and around tissue. The lymphatic system utilizes capillary structures of the circulatory system and interacts with blood cells in a coordinated response to infection.

Finally, the muscular and skeletal systems are closely related. Skeletal muscles attach to the bones of the skeleton and drive movement of the body.

Skill 22.4 Analyze how organisms recognize and localize various internal and external signals to maintain homeostasis.

The molecular composition of the immediate environment outside of the organism is not the same as it is inside and the temperature outside may not be optimal for metabolic activity within the organism. **Homeostasis** is the control of these differences between internal and external environments. There are three homeostatic systems to regulate these differences.

Osmoregulation deals with maintenance of the appropriate level of water and salts in body fluids for optimum cellular functions. **Excretion** is the elimination of metabolic waste products from the body including excess water. **Thermoregulation** maintains the internal, or core, body temperature of the organism within a tolerable range for metabolic and cellular processes.

Skill 22.5 Demonstrate knowledge of various instruments and technologies that enhance the study of organisms on the microscopic and macroscopic levels.

Biologists use various instruments to study organisms on the microscopic and macroscopic level. These instruments include computerized tracking devices, microscopes, PCR equipment, DNA sequencers, and dissection tools.

Computerized tracking devices – Biologists use computerized tracking devices to study the behavior of animals in an ecosystem. Biologists can implant computer chips on animals to track movement and migration, population changes, and general behavioral characteristics.

Microscopes – Biologists use different types of microscopes to study microscopic organisms and microscopic characteristics of larger organisms. Biologists use phase contrast microscopes to study colorless specimens, such as body tissue. Transmission electron microscopes can visualize very small cellular components, almost down to the atomic level.

PCR equipment – The polymerase chain reaction (PCR) is an invaluable tool for the rapid amplification of DNA. PCR allows for the study of genetic characteristics of organisms when only small amounts of organismal DNA are present. PCR equipment includes gel electrophoresis, thermal cyclers, and DNA primers.

DNA sequencers – DNA sequencing machines allow scientists to determine the nucleotide sequence of organismal DNA. Biologists use DNA sequences to study genetic characteristics of organisms. For example, many diseases have characteristic genetic markers.

Dissection tools – Biologists dissect organisms to study organismal anatomy. Dissection allows biologists to better understand body structure and characteristics of disease.

COMPETENCY 0023   UNDERSTAND AND APPLY KNOWLEDGE OF BIOLOGICAL DIVERSITY IN TERMS OF THE STRUCTURE, FUNCTION, AND NOMENCLATURE OF THE MAJOR GROUPS OF ORGANISMS.

Skill 23.1   Analyze the relationships between structure and function in various organisms.

Structure correlates with function in living organisms: structure follows function. By analyzing a biological structure you can postulate its function. For example, the bones in a bird's wings have a strong, light honeycomb structure. One can theorize that this structure contributes to the flight of the bird. Another example is the incisors of meat eating animals. These sharp teeth allow for ease in tearing off flesh from their prey. At the subcellular level, the extensive folding of the inner membrane of the mitochondria allows for a greater amount of this membrane to fit into the very small organelle.

Skill 23.2   Distinguish among organisms from different major taxonomic groups based on their characteristics.

Porifera - the sponges; they contain spicules for support. They possess flagella for movement in the larval stage but later become sessile and attach to a firm object. They may reproduce sexually (either by cross or self fertilization) or asexually (by budding). They are filter feeders and digest food by phagocytosis. They are mostly marine and always live in water due to the need of a hydroskeleton for support.

Cnidaria (Coelenterata) - the jellyfish; these animals possess stinging cells called the nematocyst. They may be found in a sessile polyp form with the tentacles at the top of the animals or in a moving medusa form with the tentacles floating below. They have a hydroskeleton that uses water for support. They have no true muscles. They may reproduce asexually (by budding) or sexually. They are the first to possess a primitive nervous system.

Platyhelminthes - the flatworms; the flat shape of these animals aid in the diffusion of gases. They are the first group with true muscles. They can reproduce asexually (by regeneration) or sexually. They may be hermaphroditic and possess both sex organs but cannot fertilize themselves. These worms are parasites because they have no true nervous system.

Nematoda - the roundworms; the first animal with a true digestive system with a separate mouth and anus. They may be parasites or simple consumers. They reproduce sexually with male and female worms. They possess longitudinal muscles and thrash about when they move.

Mollusca - clams, octopus; the soft bodied animals. These animals have a muscular foot for movement. They breathe through gills and most are able to make a shell for protection from predators. They have an open circulatory system with sinuses bathing the body regions.

Annelida - the segmented worms; the first with specialized tissue. The circulatory system is more advanced in these worms and is a closed system with blood vessels. The nephridia are their excretory organs. They are hermaphroditic and each worm fertilizes the other upon mating. They support themselves with a hydrostatic skeleton and have circular and longitudinal muscles for movement.

Arthropoda - insects, crustaceans and spiders; this is the largest group of the animal kingdom. Phylum arthropoda accounts for about 85% of all the animal species. Animals possess an exoskeleton made of chitin. They must molt to grow. They breathe through gills, trachea, or book lungs. Movement varies with members being able to swim, fly, and crawl. There is a division of labor among the appendages (legs, antennae, etc). This is an extremely successful phylum with members occupying diverse habitats.

Echinodermata - sea urchins and starfish; these animals have spiny skin. Their habitat is marine. They have tube feet for locomotion and feeding

Chordata - all animals with a notocord or a backbone. The classes in this phylum include Agnatha (jawless fish), Chondrichthyes (cartilage fish), Osteichthyes (bony fish), Amphibia (frogs and toads; gills which are replaced by lungs during development), Reptilia (snakes, lizards; the first to lay eggs with a protective covering), Aves (birds; warm-blooded), and Mammalia (animals with body hair that bear their young alive, possess mammary glands that produce milk, and are warm-blooded).

Skill 23.3 **Demonstrate knowledge of the historical development of biological classification systems.**

It is believed that there are probably over ten million different species of living things. Of these, 1.5 million have been named and classified. Systems of classification show similarities and also assist scientists with a world wide system of organization.

Carolus Linnaeus is termed the father of taxonomy. **Taxonomy** is the science of classification. Linnaeus based his system on morphology (study of structure). Later on, evolutionary relationships (phylogeny) were also used to sort and group species. The modern classification system uses binomial nomenclature. This consists of a two word name for every species. The genus is the first part of the name and the species is the second part. Notice in the levels explained below that Homo sapiens is the scientific name for humans. Starting with the kingdom, the groups get smaller and more alike as one moves down the levels in the classification of humans:

Kingdom: Animalia, Phylum: Chordata, Subphylum: Vertebrata, Class: Mammalia, Order: Primate, Family: Hominidae, Genus: Homo, Species: sapiens

The current five kingdom system separates prokaryotes from eukaryotes. The prokaryotes belong to the kingdom monera while the eukaryotes belong to either kingdom protista, plantae, fungi, or animalia. Recent comparisons of nucleic acids and proteins between different groups of organisms have led to problems concerning the five kingdom system. Based on these comparisons, alternative kingdom systems have emerged. Six and eight kingdoms as well as a three domain system have been proposed as a more accurate classification system. It is important to note that classification systems evolve as more information regarding characteristics and evolutionary histories of organisms arise.

Species are defined by the ability to successfully reproduce with members of their own kind.

Several different morphological criteria are used to classify organisms:

1. **Ancestral characters** - characteristics that are unchanged after evolution (ie: 5 digits on the hand of an ape).

2. **Derived characters** - characteristics that have evolved more recently (ie: the absence of a tail on an ape).

3. **Conservative characters** - traits that change slowly.

4. **Homologous characters** - characteristics with the same genetic basis but used for a different function. (ie: wing of a bat, arm of a human. The bone structure is the same, but the limbs are used for different purposes).

5. **Analogous characters** – structures that differ, but are used for similar purposes (ie- the wing of a bird and the wing of a butterfly).

6. **Convergent evolution** - development of similar adaptations by organisms that are unrelated.

Biological characteristics are also used to classify organisms. Protein comparison, DNA comparison, and analysis of fossilized DNA are powerful comparative methods used to measure evolutionary relationships between species. Taxonomists consider the organism's life history, biochemical (DNA) makeup, behavior, and how the organisms are distributed geographically. The fossil record is also used to show evolutionary relationships.

Skill 23.4   Apply methods of biological classification and nomenclature.

Taxonomy is the science of classification, the laws and principles covering the classification of objects. It is also interchangeably used with the term systematics, although the latter is more often thought of as including related disciplines like biogeography and evolutionary biology.

Aristotle in the 7th century BCE was considered as the first taxonomist. The next taxonomist was Theophrastus who wrote, *De Plantes*, which covered medicinal plants only. Carolus Linnaeus (1707-1778) collated descriptive catalogues, *Species Plantarum* of 1753 and *Systema Naturae* of 1758, in which plants and animals were classified, described, named, numbered and provided with means of identification.

The four main things in taxonomy are –

1. Classification (hierarchical arrangement of taxa)
2. Descriptions (for each level)
3. Nomenclature (internationally accepted binomial system in Latin)
4. Identification aids (keys, pictures, collections etc.,)

Classification: There are two main types of classification:

1. Artificial classification – based on a few arbitrarily selected characters, e.g., healing properties of plants. Linnaeus used the number of stamens and pistils in his so called sexual system of classification. Linnaeus's system came under criticism in the 19th century.

2. Natural classification – In the 19th century, two Parisian biologists, de Jussieu and Adanson used a greater number of characteristics selected from a wide range of homologous (shared due to common ancestors) characters. At that time, those characters were based on morphology, but they are extended to include whatever characters including DNA sequences and behavior.

Descriptions: The hierarchical classification provides a structure for recording information at any level. Each taxon has both a name and description. These descriptions are unique to that particular taxon.

Nomenclature; Each taxon has one scientific name. This name is of absolutely essential function in communication and retrieval of biological information. They are in Latinized form, often with endings (-formes, -idae, -ceae). By international agreement, taxonomists who name taxa follow the codes of nomenclature: International Code of Zoological Nomenclature for animals, International Code of Botanical Nomenclature for plants and fungi, and International Code of Nomenclature for bacteria for bacteria and actinomycetes.

The names of genera are single words with capital initial letters, usually underlined in hand writing and italicized in print, e.g., *Drosophila, Quercus*

The names of species are binomials, the first genus name and specific name or epithet, e.g., Passiflora edulis, Felix tigris.

Subdivisions below species have trinomials, e.g., Cervus elaphus maral, Vicia faba anatolica.

The relationship between taxonomy and history of evolution: Evolutionary taxonomy classifies groups according to the course of evolution. It states that the process of evolution produces the natural groups of natural classification. The similarities of the natural groups are due to common ancestry, which can only be inferred, not observed. It is inferred by sharing of the characters, not only due to common ancestry but also due to convergence. The evolutionary taxonomists have to differentiate between these two. They have to identify homologies (ancestral) and exclude analogies (convergent characters). The techniques of evolutionary taxonomy are imperfect. Evolutionary biologists are aware of this and in such a situation, they prefer to classify according to phenotypic divergence.

Dichotomous Key:

A dichotomous key is a biological tool for identifying unknown organisms to some taxonomic level. It is constructed of a series of couplets, each consisting of two statements describing characteristics of a particular organism or group of organisms.

A choice between the statements is made that bet fits the organism in question. The statements typically begin with broad characteristics and become narrower as more choices are needed.

Example A – Numerical key

1. Seeds round – soybeans
1. Seeds oblong – 2
2. Seeds white – northern beans
2. Seeds black – black beans

Example B - Alphabetical key

A. Seeds oblong – B
   B. Seeds white – northern beans
   B. Seeds black – black beans
A. Seeds round - soybeans

Competency 0024   **Understand and apply knowledge of ecological concepts.**

Skill 24.1   **Explain the interactions and interdependence of organisms in various ecosystems, including the environmental influences and limiting factors that affect them.**

There are many interactions that may occur between different species living together. Predation, parasitism, competition, commensalisms, and mutualism are the different types of relationships populations have amongst each other.

Predation and **parasitism** result in a benefit for one species and a detriment for the other. Predation is when a predator eats its prey. The common conception of predation is of a carnivore consuming other animals. This is one form of predation. Although not always resulting in the death of the plant, herbivory is a form of predation. Some animals eat enough of a plant to cause death. Parasitism involves a predator that lives on or in their hosts, causing detrimental effects to the host. Insects and viruses living off and reproducing in their hosts is an example of parasitism. Many plants and animals have defenses against predators. Some plants have poisonous chemicals that will harm the predator if ingested and some animals are camouflaged so they are harder to detect.

Competition is when two or more species in a community use the same resources. Competition is usually detrimental to both populations. Competition is often difficult to find in nature because competition between two populations is not continuous. Either the weaker population will no longer exist, or one population will evolve to utilize other available resources.

Symbiosis is when two species live close together. Parasitism is one example of symbiosis described above. Another example of symbiosis is commensalisms. **Commensalism** occurs when one species benefits from the other without harmful effects. **Mutualism** is when both species benefit from the other. Species involved in mutualistic relationships must coevolve to survive. As one species evolves, the other must as well if it is to be successful in life. The grouper and a species of shrimp live in a mutualistic relationship. The shrimp feed off parasites living on the grouper; thus the shrimp are fed and the grouper stays healthy. Many microorganisms are in mutualistic relationships.

Skill 24.2   Demonstrate an understanding of the concepts of population dynamics and the effects of population dynamics on environments and communities.

A **population** is a group of individuals of one species that live in the same general area. Many factors can affect the population size and its growth rate. Population size can depend on the total amount of life a habitat can support. This is the carrying capacity of the environment. Once the habitat runs out of food, water, shelter, or space, the carrying capacity decreases, and then stabilizes.

Limiting factors can affect population growth. As a population increases, the competition for resources is more intense, and the growth rate declines. This is a **density-dependent** growth factor. The carrying capacity can be determined by the density-dependent factor. **Density-independent factors** affect the individuals regardless of population size. The weather and climate are good examples. Too hot or too cold temperatures may kill many individuals from a population that has not reached its carrying capacity.

Zero population growth rate occurs when the birth and death rates are equal in a population. Exponential growth rate occurs when there is and abundance of resources and the growth rate is at its maximum, called the intrinsic rate of increase. This relationship can be understood in a growth curve.

An exponentially growing population starts off with a little change, then rapidly increases.

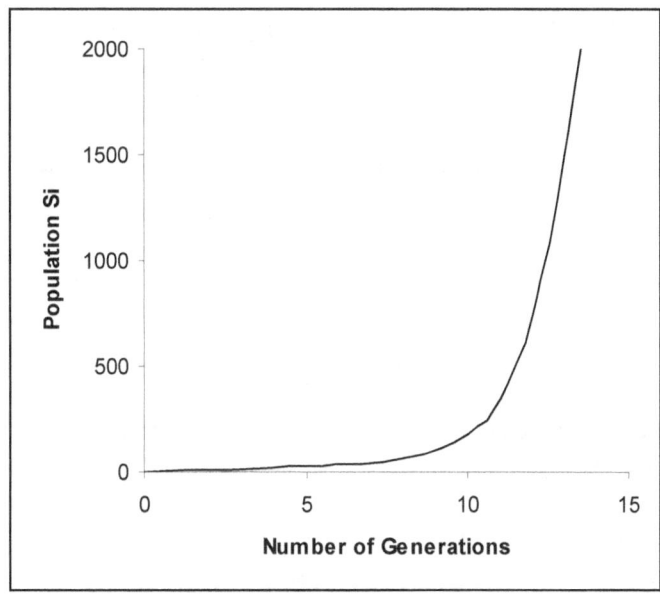

Logistic population growth incorporates the carrying capacity into the growth rate. As a population reaches the carrying capacity, the growth rate begins to slow down and level off.

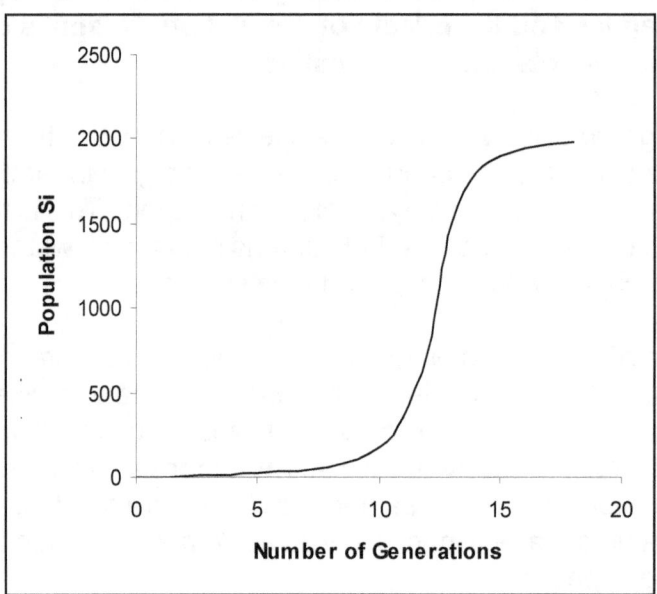

Many populations follow this model of population growth. Humans, however, are an exponentially growing population. Eventually, the carrying capacity of the Earth will be reached, and the growth rate will level off. How and when this will occur remains a mystery.

Population density is the number of individuals per unit area or volume. The spacing pattern of individuals in an area is dispersion. Dispersion patterns can be clumped, with individuals grouped in patches; uniformed, where individuals are approximately equidistant from each other; or random.

Population densities are usually estimated based on a few representative plots. Aggregation of a population in a relatively small geographic area can have detrimental effects to the environment. Food, water, and other resources will be rapidly consumed, resulting in an unstable environment. A low population density is less harmful to the environment. The use of natural resources will be more widespread, allowing for the environment to recover and continue growth.

Skill 24.3   Analyze ways in which humans influence and are influenced by the environment.

The human population has been growing exponentially for centuries. People are living longer and healthier lives than ever before. Better health care and nutrition practices have helped in the survival of the population.

Human activity affects parts of the nutrient cycles by removing nutrients from one part of the biosphere and adding them to another. This results in nutrient depletion in one area and nutrient excess in another. This affects water systems, crops, wildlife, and humans.

Humans are responsible for the depletion of the ozone layer. This depletion is due to chemicals used for refrigeration and aerosols. The consequences of ozone depletion will be severe. Ozone protects the Earth from the majority of UV radiation. An increase of UV will promote skin cancer and unknown effects on wildlife and plants.

Humans have a tremendous impact on the world's natural resources. The world's natural water supplies are affected by human use. Waterways are major sources for recreation and freight transportation. Oil and wastes from boats and cargo ships pollute the aquatic environment. The aquatic plant and animal life is affected by this contamination.

Deforestation for urban development has resulted in the extinction or relocation of several species of plants and animals. Animals are forced to leave their forest homes or perish amongst the destruction. The number of plant and animal species that have become extinct due to deforestation is unknown. Scientists have only identified a fraction of the species on Earth. It is known that if the destruction of natural resources continues, there may be no plants or animals successfully reproducing in the wild.

Skill 24.4 Explain the functions and applications of the methods, instruments, and technologies used in the research of ecology.

A holistic view of nature is stressed in ecology and therefore impacts the ways an ecologist might approach studying the life of a particular species. The behavioral relationship between individuals of a species is **behavioral ecology** — for example, the study of the queen bee, and how she relates to the worker bees and the drones. The organized activity of a species is **community ecology**; for example, the activity of bees assures the pollination of flowering plants. Bee hives additionally produce honey which is consumed by still other species, such as bears. The relationship between the environment and a species is **environmental ecology** — for example, the consequences of environmental change on bee activity. Bees may die out due to environmental changes. The environment simultaneously affects and is a consequence of this activity and is thus intertwined with the survival of the species.

The instruments and technologies used in the research of ecological topics will vary depending on the specific ecological discipline. Physiological ecology (or ecophysiology) and behavioral ecology examine adaptations of the individual to its environment. Population ecology (or autecology) studies the dynamics of populations of a single species. Community ecology (or synecology) focuses on the interactions between species within an ecological community. Ecosystem ecology studies the flows of energy and matter through the biotic and abiotic components of ecosystems. Landscape ecology examines processes and relationships across multiple ecosystems or very large geographic areas.

Concentrated contact with diverse animals operating in nature, combined with on-the-spot discussions of the often profound evolutionary principles germane to understanding their behavior and related morphological and physiological design are often the basis of ecological research. It is only via thorough, determined digestion of evolutionary concepts and direct involvement in designing and implementing rigorous research methodologies, that one develops an understanding of the power of evolutionary biological thinking for elucidating the structure and functional significance of animals' bodies and minds.

Three basic modes of investigation are often used: the comparative method, measurement of fitness differentials among behavioral variants, and analysis of functional design. These methods and their associated problems and controversies will be introduced with the aid of recent papers from the primary literature. Attentive observation coupled with evolutionary thinking will be the foundation for everything we do in the course.

Technology is having a paramount impact on the present and future of ecological research. The basic scheme of the approach is to utilize the latest advances in technology and ecology to mimic the ecological environment under laboratory conditions, which will then elevate researchers' ability to study and manipulate the actual environment. For example, experiments with a variety of wavelengths of light are now possible with the use of gallium nitride in the production of light-emitting sources. Research using these devices can be applied to the study of the effects of light on fish. Researchers are now able to carry out various experiments to investigate a fish's vision, its sensitivity to light of different wavelengths and how fish respond to visual cues.

Another example is the use of Geographic Information Systems technology to provide information about land cover, wetlands, public land, and natural divisions in the form of maps, tables, and analyses. The collection of computer hardware, software, and geographic data for capturing, managing, analyzing, and displaying all forms of geographically referenced information allow ecologists to find features, identify patterns, and then map and analyze data, changes and specific densities within areas. This technology is particularly helpful in population, community, and environmental ecology.

An older and often used method for studying organisms within their own habitat is tracking. In this method a harmless device is attached to an animal. Scientists are able to follow the animal and learn about its eating, movement, and mating habitats. This is extremely useful in migratory species. GPS technology has improved these devices.

Skill 24.5 Analyze the risk/cost/benefit factors in environmental impact studies.

Environmental impact studies are detailed reports on the potential effect of proposed construction, development, and design products on the local environment. Such studies consider the risks to the environment, the potential costs (both monetary and otherwise) of development, and the potential benefits of development.

When planning development and construction, decision makers must consider potential environmental risks. Potential environmental risks of development include groundwater contamination, destruction of habitats and natural resources, and pollution of air and soil. For example, certain types of development and industrial practices may put the health of local residents at risk due to contamination of the air or water supply.

Environmental impact studies also analyze the costs of development and the costs of environmental protection. The costs of development and protection include monetary costs, human health costs, aesthetic costs, and ecological costs. For example, environmental protection has a direct monetary cost. In addition, development can endanger human health and destroy natural beauty. Finally, environmental law requires that developers pay close attention to the impact of development on critical habitats and endangered and threatened species. Decision makers must balance the costs of development against the costs of environmental protection.

Environmental impact studies also assess the potential benefits of development and protection. For example, a study may assess how a proposed development will benefit the local economy and analyze how environmental protection will benefit the local community and ecology. Such thorough reporting allows for an in depth cost-benefit analysis of the proposed development and environmental protection initiatives.

COMPETENCY 0025 UNDERSTAND AND APPLY KNOWLEDGE OF MATTER, ENERGY, AND ORGANIZATION IN LIVING SYSTEMS.

Skill 25.1 Analyze energy flow between biological systems and the physical environment.

Energy is lost as the trophic levels progress from producer to tertiary consumer. The amount of energy that is transferred between trophic levels is called the ecological efficiency. The visual of this energy flow is represented in a **pyramid of productivity**.

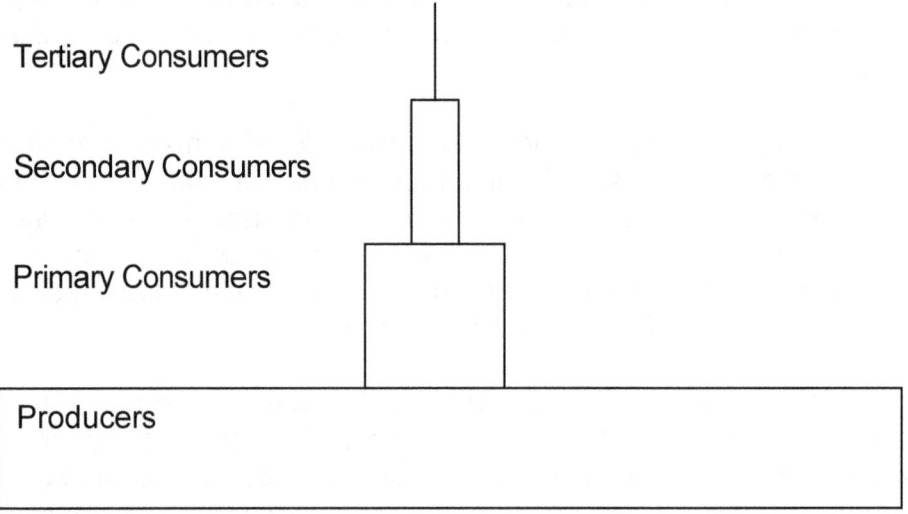

The **biomass pyramid** represents the total dry weight of organisms in each trophic level. A **pyramid of numbers** is a representation of the population size of each trophic level. The producers, being the most populous, are on the bottom of this pyramid with the tertiary consumers on the top with the fewest numbers.

Skill 25.2 Analyze the effects of limited availability of resources on the distribution and abundance of organisms and populations.

A limiting factor is the component of a biological process that determines how quickly or slowly the process proceeds. Photosynthesis is the main biological process determining the rate of ecosystem productivity, the rate at which an ecosystem creates biomass. Thus, in evaluating the productivity of an ecosystem, potential limiting factors are light intensity, gas concentrations, and mineral availability. The Law of the Minimum states that the required factor in a given process that is most scarce controls the rate of the process.

One potential limiting factor of ecosystem productivity is light intensity because photosynthesis requires light energy. Light intensity can limit productivity in two ways. First, too little light limits the rate of photosynthesis because the required energy is not available. Second, too much light can damage the photosynthetic system of plants and microorganisms thus slowing the rate of photosynthesis. Decreased photosynthesis equals decreased productivity.

Another potential limiting factor of ecosystem productivity is gas concentrations. Photosynthesis requires carbon dioxide. Thus, increased concentration of carbon dioxide often results in increased productivity. While carbon dioxide is often not the ultimate limiting factor of productivity, increased concentration can indirectly increase rates of photosynthesis in several ways. First, increased carbon dioxide concentration often increases the rate of nitrogen fixation (available nitrogen is another limiting factor of productivity). Second, increased carbon dioxide concentration can decrease the pH of rain, improving the water source of photosynthetic organisms.

Finally, mineral availability also limits ecosystem productivity. Plants require adequate amounts of nitrogen and phosphorus to build many cellular structures. The availability of the inorganic minerals phosphorus and nitrogen often is the main limiting factor of plant biomass production. In other words, in a natural environment, phosphorus and nitrogen availability most often limits ecosystem productivity, rather than carbon dioxide concentration or light intensity.

The above limiting factors all affect the productivity of ecosystems on a large scale. Individual organisms can be affected as well. Distribution and abundance of organisms can change in response to environment, including the availability of resources. A poor nutrient year can cause death to large populations, or, at the very least, cause the weakest to perish as individuals fight for scarce food. Even if a year is considered normal as far as food availability, seasons change. The distribution of animals changes to follow their ideal food source. Excellent examples include migratory animals. The abundance of migratory animals does not change, but their distribution does. Migratory animals are expected to move. What about the animals who have experienced a shift in their ecosystem? Their abundance may be affected by lack of food, and then their distribution may change as they move outward from their original homes in search of better resources.

Skill 25.3 Demonstrate an understanding of the transfer and transformation of energy in various biological reactions.

Biogeochemical cycles are nutrient cycles that involve both biotic and abiotic factors.

Water cycle - 2% of all the available water is fixed and unavailable in ice or the bodies of organisms. Available water includes surface water (lakes, ocean, rivers) and ground water (aquifers, wells) 96% of all available water is from ground water. The water cycle is driven by solar energy. Water is recycled through the processes of evaporation and precipitation. The water present now is the water that has been here since our atmosphere formed.

Carbon cycle - Ten percent of all available carbon in the air (from carbon dioxide gas) is fixed by photosynthesis. Plants fix carbon in the form of glucose, animals eat the plants and are able to obtain their source of carbon. When animals release carbon dioxide through respiration, the plants again have a source of carbon to fix again.

Nitrogen cycle - Eighty percent of the atmosphere is in the form of nitrogen gas. Nitrogen must be fixed and taken out of the gaseous form to be incorporated into an organism. Only a few genera of bacteria have the correct enzymes to break the triple bond between nitrogen atoms in a process called nitrogen fixation. These bacteria live within the roots of legumes (peas, beans, alfalfa) and add nitrogen to the soil so it may be taken up by the plant. Nitrogen is necessary to make amino acids and the nitrogenous bases of DNA.

Phosphorus cycle - Phosphorus exists as a mineral and is not found in the atmosphere. Fungi and plant roots have a structure called mycorrhizae that are able to fix insoluble phosphates into useable phosphorus. Urine and decayed matter return phosphorus to the earth where it can be fixed in the plant. Phosphorus is needed for the backbone of DNA and for ATP manufacturing.

In the carbon cycle, decomposers recycle the carbon accumulated in durable organic material that does not immediately proceed to the carbon cycle. Ammonification is the decomposition of organic nitrogen back to ammonia. This process in the nitrogen cycle is carried out by aerobic and anaerobic bacterial and fungal decomposers. Decomposers add phosphorous back to the soil by decomposing the excretion of animals.

Skill 25.4 Analyze food webs, including the roles of and relationships among producers, consumers, and decomposers.

Trophic levels are based on the feeding relationships that determine energy flow and chemical cycling.

Autotrophs are the primary producers of the ecosystem. **Producers** mainly consist of plants. **Primary consumers** are the next trophic level. The primary consumers are the herbivores that eat plants or algae. **Secondary consumers** are the carnivores that eat the primary consumers. **Tertiary consumers** eat the secondary consumer. These trophic levels may go higher depending on the ecosystem. **Decomposers** are consumers that feed off animal waste and dead organisms. This pathway of food transfer is known as the food chain.

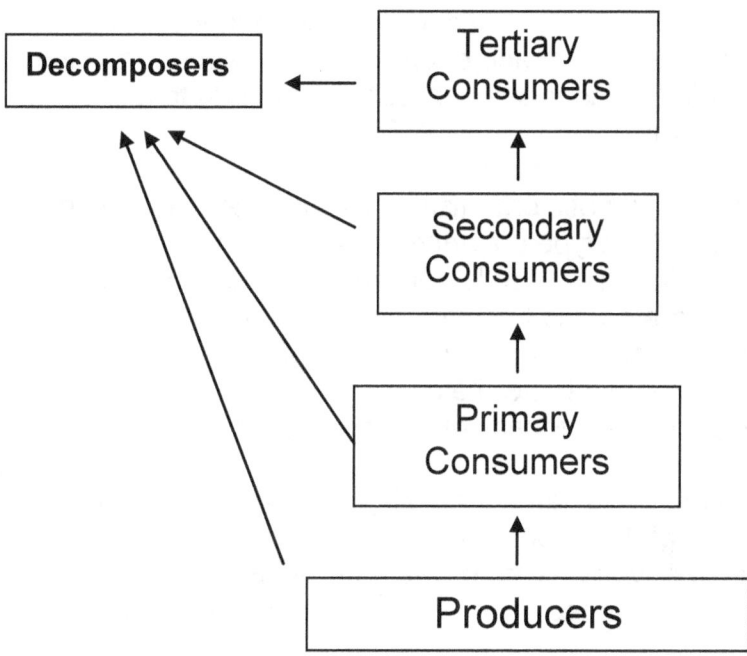

Most food chains are more elaborate, becoming food webs. As we move up the food web, the organization and complexity of organisms increases. For example, tertiary consumers are generally more complex than primary producers. Producers obtain energy from only one source (usually sun light) and convert it to a more durable form. Because many producers are small in size, their transport and release systems are relatively basic. Some large producers (e.g. plants and trees) have more complex transport and release systems. Consumers, on the other hand, must obtain and transform energy and matter from many sources. This diversity requires greater complexity and organization. Humans, for example, obtain energy and matter from plants and animals and transform the matter into various cellular components. Humans also possess complex systems of transport and release to facilitate the flow of energy and matter through the body.

Skill 25.5 Relate the varying complexity and organization of organisms to the means by which they obtain, transform, transport, and release matter and energy.

Members of the five different kingdoms of the classification system of living organisms often differ in their basic life functions. Here we compare and analyze the five kingdoms with regards to obtaining nutrients, converting it to energy, and excreting waste.

Bacteria are prokaryotic, single-celled organisms that lack cell nuclei. The different types of bacteria obtain nutrients in a variety of ways. Most bacteria absorb nutrients from the environment through small channels in their cell walls and membranes (chemotrophs) while some perform photosynthesis (phototrophs). Chemoorganotrophs use organic compounds as energy sources while chemolithotrophs can use inorganic chemicals as energy sources. Depending on the type of metabolism and energy source, bacteria release a variety of waste products (e.g. alcohols, acids, carbon dioxide) to the environment through diffusion.

Animals are multicellular, eukaryotic organisms. All animals obtain nutrients by eating food (ingestion). Different types of animals derive nutrients from eating plants, other animals, or both. Animal cells perform respiration that converts food molecules, mainly carbohydrates and fats, into energy. The excretory systems of animals, like animals themselves, vary in complexity. Simple invertebrates eliminate waste through a single tube, while complex vertebrates have a specialized system of organs that process and excrete waste.

Plants, like animals, are multi-cellular, eukaryotic organisms. Plants obtain nutrients from the soil through their root systems and convert sunlight into energy through photosynthesis. Many plants store waste products in vacuoles or organs (e.g. leaves, bark) that are discarded. Some plants also excrete waste through their roots.

Fungi are eukaryotic, mostly multi-cellular organisms. All fungi are heterotrophs, obtaining nutrients from other organisms. More specifically, most fungi obtain nutrients by digesting and absorbing nutrients from dead organisms. Fungi secrete enzymes outside of their body to digest organic material and then absorb the nutrients through their cell walls.

Protists are eukaryotic, single-celled organisms. Most protists are heterotrophic, obtaining nutrients by ingesting small molecules and cells and digesting them in vacuoles.

Sample Test

Directions: Read each item and select the best response.

1. A student designed a science project testing the effects of light and water on plant growth. You would recommend that she:

   A. manipulate the temperature as well.

   B. also alter the pH of the water as another variable.

   C. omit either water or light as a variable.

   D. also alter the light concentration as another variable.

2. Identify the control in the following experiment. A student had four plants grown under the following conditions and was measuring photosynthetic rate by measuring mass. 2 plants in 50% light and 2 plants in 100% light.

   A. plants grown with no added nutrients

   B. plants grown in the dark

   C plants in 100% light

   D. plants in 50% light

3. In an experiment measuring the growth of bacteria at different temperatures, identify the independent variable.

   A. growth of number of colonies

   B. temperature

   C. type of bacteria used

   D. light intensity

4. A scientific theory:

   A. proves scientific accuracy.
   B. is never rejected.
   C. results in a medical breakthrough.
   D. may be altered at a later time.

5. Which is the correct order of methodology? 1) testing revised explanation, 2) setting up a controlled experiment to test explanation, 3) drawing a conclusion, 4) suggesting an explanation for observations, and 5) compare observed results to hypothesized results

   A. 4, 2, 3, 1, 5

   B. 3, 1, 4, 2, 5

   C. 4, 2, 5, 1, 3

   D. 2, 5, 4, 1, 3

6. Given a choice, which is the most desirable method of heating a substance in the lab?

   A. alcohol burner

   B. gas burner

   C. bunsen burner

   D. hot plate

7. Biological waste should be disposed of:

   A. in the trash can.

   B. under a fume hood.

   C. in the broken glass box.

   D. in an autoclavable biohazard bag.

8. Chemicals should be stored:

   A. in a cool dark room.

   B. in a dark room.

   C. according to their reactivity with other substances.

   D. in a double locked room.

9. Given the choice of lab activities, which would you omit?

   A. a genetics experiment tracking the fur color of mice

   B. dissecting a preserved fetal pig

   C. a lab relating temperature to respiration rate using live goldfish.

   D. pithing a frog to see the action of circulation

10. Who should be notified in the case of a serious chemical spill?

    I. the custodian
    II. The fire department
    III. the chemistry teacher
    IV. the administration

    A. I

    B. II

    C. II and III

    D. II and IV

11. The "Right to Know" law states:

    A. the inventory of toxic chemicals checked against the "Substance List" be available.

    B. that students are to be informed on alternatives to dissection.

    C. that science teachers are to be informed of student allergies.

    D. that students are to be informed of infectious microorganisms used in lab.

12. In which situation would a science teacher be liable?

    A. a teacher leaves to receive an emergency phone call and a student slips and falls.

    B. a student removes their goggles and gets dissection fluid in their eye.

    C. a faulty gas line results in a fire.

    D. a students cuts themselves with a scalpel.

13. Which statement best defines negligence?

    A. failure to give oral instructions for those with reading disabilities

    B. failure to exercise ordinary care

    C. inability to supervise a large group of students.

    D. reasonable anticipation that an event may occur

14. Which item should always be used when using chemicals with noxious vapors?

    A. eye protection

    B. face shield

    C. fume hood

    D. lab apron

15. Identify the correct sequence of organization of living things.

    A. cell – organelle – organ – tissue – organ system – organism

    B. cell – tissue – organ – organelle – organ system – organism

    C. organelle – cell – tissue – organ – organ system – organism

    D. organ system – tissue – organelle – cell – organism – organ

16. Which is not a characteristic of living things?

    A. movement

    B. cellular structure

    C. metabolism

    D. reproduction

17. Which kingdom is comprised of organisms made of one cell with no nuclear membrane?

    A. Monera

    B. Protista

    C. Fungi

    D. Algae

18. Potassium chloride is an example of a(n):

    A. non polar covalent bond

    B. polar covalent bond

    C. ionic bond

    D. hydrogen bond

19. Which of the following is a monomer?

    A. RNA

    B. glycogen

    C. DNA

    D. amino acid

20. Which of the following are properties of water?

    I. High specific heat
    II. Strong ionic bonds
    III. Good solvent
    IV. High freezing point

    A. I, III, IV

    B. II and III

    C. I and II

    D. II, III, IV

21. Which does not affect enzyme rate?

    A. increase of temperature

    B. amount of substrate

    C. pH

    D. size of the cell

22. Sulfur oxides and nitrogen oxides in the environment react with water to cause:

    A. ammonia

    B. acidic precipitation

    C. sulfuric acid

    D. global warming

23. The loss of an electron is _____ and the gain of an electron is _____.

    A. oxidation, reduction

    B. reduction, oxidation

    C. glycolysis, photosynthesis

    D. photosynthesis, glycolysis

24. The product of anaerobic respiration in animals is:

    A. carbon dioxide

    B. lactic acid

    C. pyruvate

    D. ethyl alcohol

25. In the comparison of respiration to photosynthesis, which statement is true?

    A. oxygen is a waste product in photosynthesis but not in respiration

    B. glucose is produced in respiration but not in photosynthesis

    C. carbon dioxide is formed in photosynthesis but not in respiration

    D. water is formed in respiration but not in photosynthesis

26. Carbon dioxide is fixed in the form of glucose in:

    A. Krebs cycle

    B. the light reactions

    C. the dark reactions (Calvin cycle)

    D. glycolysis

27. During the Kreb's cycle, 8 carrier molecules are formed. What are they?

   A. 3 NADH, 3 FADH, 2 ATP

   B. 6 NADH and 2 ATP

   C. 4 FADH$_2$ and 4 ATP

   D. 6 NADH and 2 FADH$_2$

28. Which of the following is not posttranscriptional processing?

   A. 5' capping

   B. intron splicing

   C. polypeptide splicing

   D. 3' polyadenylation

29. Polymerase chain reaction:

   A. is a group of polymerases

   B. technique for amplifying DNA

   C. primer for DNA synthesis

   D. synthesis of polymerase

30. Homozygous individuals:

   A. have two different alleles

   B. are of the same species

   C. have the same features

   D. have a pair of identical alleles

31. The two major ways to determine taxonomic classification are:

   A. evolution and phylogeny

   B. reproductive success and evolution

   C. phylogeny and morphology

   D. size and color

32. Man's scientific name is Homo sapiens. Choose the proper classification beginning with kingdom and ending with order.

   A. Animalia, Vertebrata, Mammalia, Primate, Hominidae

   B. Animalia, Vertebrata, Chordata, Mammalia, Primate

   C. Animalia, Chordata, Vertebrata, Mammalia, Primate

   D. Chordata, Vertebrata, Primate, Homo, sapiens

33. The scientific name Canis familiaris refers to the animal's

   A. kingdom and phylum names

   B. genus and species names

   C. class and species names

   D. order and family names

34. Members of the same species

    A. look identical

    B. never change

    C. reproduce successfully among their group

    D. live in the same geographic location

35. What is necessary for diffusion to occur?

    A. carrier proteins

    B. energy

    C. a concentration gradient

    D. a membrane

36. Which is an example of the use of energy to move a substance through a membrane from areas of low concentration to areas of high concentration?

    A. osmosis

    B. active transport

    C. exocytosis

    D. phagocytosis

37. A plant cell is placed in salt water. The resulting movement of water out of the cell is called:

    A. facilitated diffusion

    B. diffusion

    C. transpiration

    D. osmosis

38. As the amount of waste production increases in a cell, the rate of excretion:

    A. slowly decreases

    B. remains the same

    C. increases

    D. stops due to cell death

39. A type of molecule not found in the membrane of an animal cell is:

    A. phospholipid

    B. protein

    C. cellulose

    D. cholesterol

40. Which type of cell would contain the most mitochondria?

   A. muscle cell
   B. nerve cell
   C. epithelium
   D. blood cell

41. The first cells that evolved on earth were probably of which type?

   A. autotrophs
   B. eukaryotes
   C. heterotrophs
   D. prokaryotes

42. According to the fluid-mosaic model of the cell membrane, membranes are composed of:

   A. phospholipid bilayers with proteins embedded in the layers
   B. one layer of phospholipids with cholesterol embedded in the layer
   C. two layers of protein with lipids embedded the layers
   D. DNA and fluid proteins

43. All the following statements regarding both a mitochondria and a chloroplast are correct except:

   A. they both produce energy over a gradient
   B. they both have DNA and are capable of reproduction
   C. they both transfer light energy to chemical energy
   D. they both make ATP

44. This stage of mitosis includes cytokinesis or division of the cytoplasm and its organelles:

   A. anaphase
   B. interphase
   C. prophase
   D. telophase

45. Replication of chromosomes occurs during which phase of the cell cycle?

   A. prophase
   B. interphase
   C. metaphase
   D. anaphase

46. Which statement regarding mitosis is correct?

   A. diploid cells produce haploid cells for sexual reproduction

   B. sperm and egg cells are produced

   C. diploid cells produce diploid cells for growth and repair

   D. it allows for greater genetic diversity

47. In a plant cell, telophase is described as:

   A. the time of chromosome doubling

   B. cell plate formation

   C. the time when crossing over occurs

   D. cleavage furrow formation

48. Identify this stage of mitosis:

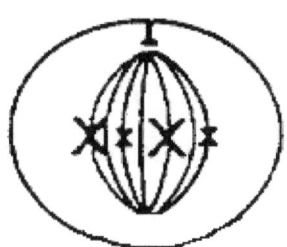

   A. anaphase

   B. metaphase

   C. telophase

   D. prophase

49. Identify this stage of mitosis:

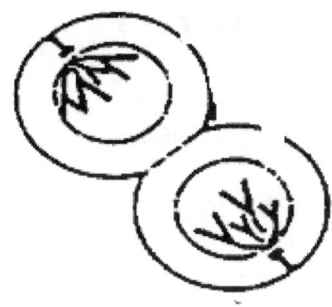

   A. prophase

   B. telophase

   C. anaphase

   D. metaphase

50. Identify this stage of mitosis:

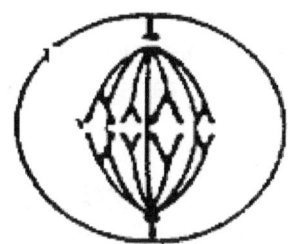

   A. anaphase

   B. metaphase

   C. prophase

   D. telophase

51. Oxygen is given off in the:

   A. light reactions of photosynthesis

   B. dark reactions of photosynthesis

   C. Kreb's cycle

   D. reduction of NAD+ to NADH

52. In the electron transport chain, all the following are true except:

   A. it occurs in the mitochondrion

   B. it does not make ATP directly

   C. the net gain of energy is 30 ATP

   D. most molecules in the electron transport chain are proteins.

53. The area of a DNA nucleotide that varies is the:

   A. deoxyribose

   B. phosphate group

   C. nitrogen base

   D. sugar

54. A DNA strand has the base sequence of TCAGTA. Its DNA complement would have the following sequence:

   A. ATGACT

   B. TCAGTA

   C. AGUCAU

   D. AGTCAT

55. Genes function in specifying the structure of which molecule?

   A. carbohydrates

   B. lipids

   C. nucleic acids

   D. proteins

56. What is the correct order of steps in protein synthesis?

   A. transcription, then replication

   B. transcription, then translation

   C. translation, then transcription

   D. replication, then translation

57. This carries amino acids to the ribosome in protein synthesis:

    A. messenger RNA

    B. ribosomal RNA

    C. transfer RNA

    D. DNA

58. A protein is sixty amino acids in length. This requires a coded DNA sequence of how many nucleotides?

    A. 20

    B. 30

    C. 120

    D. 180

59. A DNA molecule has the sequence of ACTATG. What is the anticodon of this molecule?

    A. UGAUAC

    B. ACUAUG

    C. TGATAC

    D. ACTATG

60. The term "phenotype" refers to which of the following?

    A. a condition which is heterozygous

    B. the genetic makeup of an individual

    C. a condition which is homozygous

    D. how the genotype is expressed

61. The ratio of brown-eyed to blue-eyed children from the mating of a blue-eyed male to a heterozygous brown-eyed female would be expected to be which of the following?

    A. 2:1

    B. 1:1

    C. 1:0

    D. 1:2

62. The Law of Segregation defined by Mendel states that:

A. when sex cells form, the two alleles that determine a trait will end up on different gametes

B. only one of two alleles is expressed in a heterozygous organism

C. the allele expressed is the dominant allele

D. alleles of one trait do not affect the inheritance of alleles on another chromosome

63. When a white flower is crossed with a red flower, incomplete dominance can be seen by the production of which of the following?

A. pink flowers

B. red flowers

C. white flowers

D. red and white flowers

64. Sutton observed that genes and chromosomes behaved the same. This led him to his theory which stated:

A. that meiosis causes chromosome separation

B. that linked genes are able to separate

C. that genes and chromosomes have the same function

D. that genes are found on chromosomes

65. Amniocentesis is:

A. a non-invasive technique for detecting genetic disorders

B. a bacterial infection

C. extraction of amniotic fluid

D. removal of fetal tissue

66. A child with type O blood has a father with type A blood and a mother with type B blood. The genotypes of the parents respectively would be which of the following?

A. AA and BO

B. AO and BO

C. AA and BB

D. AO and OO

67. Any change that affects the sequence of bases in a gene is called a (n):

   A. deletion

   B. polyploid

   C. mutation

   D. duplication

68. The *lac* operon:

   I. contains the *lac Z, lac Y, lac A* genes
   II. converts glucose to lactose
   III. contains a repressor
   IV. is on when the repressor is activated

   A. I

   B. II

   C. III and IV

   D. I and III

69. Which of the following factors will affect the Hardy-Weinberg law of equilibrium, leading to evolutionary change?

   A. no mutations

   B. non-random mating

   C. no immigration or emigration

   D. Large population

70. If a population is in Hardy-Weinberg equilibrium and the frequency of the recessive allele is .3, what percentage of the population would be expected to be heterozygous?

   A. 9%

   B. 49%

   C. 42%

   D. 21%

71. Crossing over, which increases genetic diversity, occurs during which stage(s)?

   A. telophase II in meiosis

   B. metaphase in mitosis

   C. interphase in both mitosis and meiosis

   D. prophase I in meiosis

72. Cancer cells divide extensively and invade other tissues. This continuous cell division is due to:

   A. density dependent inhibition

   B. density independent inhibition

   C. chromosome replication

   D. Growth factors

73. Which process(es) results in a haploid chromosome number?

    A. both meiosis and mitosis

    B. mitosis

    C. meiosis

    D. replication and division

74. Segments of DNA can be transferred from the DNA of one organism to another through the use of which of the following?

    A. bacterial plasmids

    B. viruses

    C. chromosomes from frogs

    D. plant DNA

75. Which of the following is not true regarding restriction enzymes?

    A. they do not aid in recombination procedures

    B. they are used in genetic engineering

    C. they are named after the bacteria in which they naturally occur

    D. they identify and splice certain base sequences on DNA

76. A virus that can remain dormant until a certain environmental condition causes its rapid increase is said to be:

    A. lytic

    B. benign

    C. saprophytic

    D. lysogenic

77. Which is not considered to be a morphological type of bacteria?

    A. obligate

    B. coccus

    C. spirillum

    D. bacillus

78. Antibiotics are effective in fighting bacterial infections due to their ability to:

    A. interfere with DNA replication in the bacteria

    B. prevent the formation of new cell walls in the bacteria

    C. disrupt the ribosome of the bacteria

    D. All of the above.

79. Bacteria commonly reproduce by a process called binary fission. Which of the following best defines this process?

   A. viral vectors carry DNA to new bacteria

   B. DNA from one bacterium enters another

   C. DNA doubles and the bacterial cell divides

   D. DNA from dead cells is absorbed into bacteria

80. All of the following are examples of a member of Kingdom Fungi except:

   A. mold

   B. algae

   C. mildew

   D. mushrooms

81. Protists are classified into major groups according to:

   A. their method of obtaining nutrition

   B. reproduction

   C. metabolism

   D. their form and function

82. In comparison to protist cells, moneran cells:

   I. are usually smaller
   II. evolved later
   III. are more complex
   IV. contain more organelles

   A. I

   B. I and II

   C. II and III

   D. I and IV

83. Spores characterize the reproduction mode for which of the following group of plants?

   A. algae

   B. flowering plants

   C. conifers

   D. ferns

84. Water movement to the top of a twenty foot tree is most likely due to which principle?

   A. osmotic pressure

   B. xylem pressure

   C. capillarity

   D. transpiration

85. What are the stages of development from the egg to the plant?

    A. morphogenesis, growth, and cellular differentiation

    B. cell differentiation, growth, and morphogenesis

    C. growth, morphogenesis, and cellular differentiation

    D. growth, cellular differentiation, and morphogenesis

86. In angiosperms, the food for the developing plant is found in which of the following structures?

    A. ovule

    B. endosperm

    C. male gametophyte

    D. cotyledon

87. The process in which pollen grains are released from the anthers is called:

    A. pollination

    B. fertilization

    C. blooming

    D. dispersal

88. Which of the following is not a characteristic of a monocot?

    A. parallel veins in leaves

    B. petals of flowers occur in multiples of 4 or 5

    C. one seed leaf

    D. vascular tissue scattered throughout the stem

89. What controls gas exchange on the bottom of a plant leaf?

    A. stomata

    B. epidermis

    C. collenchyma and schlerenchyma

    D. palisade mesophyll

90. How are angiosperms different from other groups of plants?

    A. presence of flowers and fruits

    B. production of spores for reproduction

    C. true roots and stems

    D. seed production

91. Generations of plants alternate between:

    A. angiosperms and bryophytes

    B. flowering and nonflowering stages

    C. seed bearing and spore bearing plants

    D. haploid and diploid stages

92. Double fertilization refers to which choice of the following?

    A. two sperm fertilizing one egg

    B. fertilization of a plant by gametes from two separate plants

    C. two sperm enter the plant embryo sac; one sperm fertilizes the egg, the other forms the endosperm

    D. the production of non-identical twins through fertilization of two separate eggs

93. Characteristics of coelomates include:

    I. no true digestive system
    II. two germ layers
    III. true fluid filled cavity
    IV. three germ layers

    A. I

    B. II and IV

    C. IV

    D. III and IV

94. Which phylum accounts for 85% of all animal species?

    A. Nematoda

    B. Chordata

    C. Arthropoda

    D. Cnidaria

95. Which is the correct statement regarding the human nervous system and the human endocrine system?

    A. the nervous system maintains homeostasis whereas the endocrine system does not

    B. endocrine glands produce neurotransmitters whereas nerves produce hormones

    C. nerve signals travel on neurons whereas hormones travel through the blood

    D. he nervous system involves chemical transmission whereas the endocrine system does not

96. A muscular adaptation to move food through the digestive system is called:

    A. peristalsis

    B. passive transport

    C. voluntary action

    D. bulk transport

97. The role of neurotransmitters in nerve action is to:

   A. turn off sodium pump

   B. turn off calcium pump

   C. send impulse to neuron

   D. send impulse to the body

98. Fats are broken down by which substance?

   A. bile produced in the gall bladder

   B. lipase produced in the gall bladder

   C. glucagons produced in the liver

   D. bile produced in the liver

99. Fertilization in humans usually occurs in the:

   A. uterus

   B. ovary

   C. fallopian tubes

   D. vagina

100. All of the following are found in the dermis layer of skin except:

   A. sweat glands

   B. keratin

   C. hair follicles

   D. blood vessels

101. Which is the correct sequence of embryonic development in a frog?

   A. cleavage – blastula – gastrula

   B. cleavage – gastrula – blastula

   C. blastula – cleavage – gastrula

   D. gastrula – blastula – cleavage

102. Food is carried through the digestive tract by a series of wave-like contractions. This process is called:

   A. peristalsis

   B. chyme

   C. digestion

   D. absorption

103. Movement is possible by the action of muscles pulling on:

A. skin

B. bones

C. joints

D. ligaments

104. All of the following are functions of the skin except:

A. storage

B. protection

C. sensation

D. regulation of temperature

105. Hormones are essential to the regulation of reproduction. What organ is responsible for the release of hormones for sexual maturity?

A. pituitary gland

B. hypothalamus

C. pancreas

D. thyroid gland

106. A bicyclist has a heart rate of 110 beats per minute and a stroke volume of 85 mL per beat. What is the cardiac output?

A. 9.35 L/min

B. 1.29 L/min

C. 0.772 L/min

D. 129 L/min

107. After sea turtles are hatched on the beach, they start the journey to the ocean. This is due to

A. innate behavior

B. territoriality

C. the tide

D. learned behavior

108. A school age boy had the chicken pox as a baby. He will most likely not get this disease again because of:

A. passive immunity

B. vaccination

C. antibiotics

D. active immunity

109. High humidity and temperature stability are present in which of the following biomes?

   A. taiga

   B. deciduous forest

   C. desert

   D. tropical rain forest

110. The biological species concept applies to:

   A. asexual organisms

   B. extinct organisms

   C. sexual organisms

   D. fossil organisms

111. Which term is not associated with the water cycle?

   A. precipitation

   B. transpiration

   C. fixation

   D. evaporation

112. All of the following are density independent factors that affect a population except:

   A. temperature

   B. rainfall

   C. predation

   D. soil nutrients

113. In the growth of a population, the increase is exponential until carrying capacity is reached. This is represented by a (n)

   A. S curve

   B. J curve

   C. M curve

   D. L curve

114. Primary succession occurs after:

   A. nutrient enrichment

   B. a forest fire

   C. bare rock is exposed after a water table recedes

   D. a housing development is built

115. Crabgrass – grasshopper – frog – snake – eagle If DDT were present in an ecosystem, which organism would have the highest concentration in its system?

   A. grasshopper

   B. eagle

   C. frog

   D. crabgrass

116. Which trophic level has the highest ecological efficiency?

   A. decomposers

   B. producers

   C. tertiary consumers

   D. secondary consumers

117. A clownfish is protected by the sea anemone's tentacles. In turn, the anemone receives uneaten food from the clownfish. This is an example of:

   A. mutualism

   B. parasitism

   C. commensalisms

   D. competition

118. If the niches of two species overlap, what usually results?

   A. a symbiotic relationship

   B. cooperation

   C. competition

   D. a new species

119. Oxygen created in photosynthesis comes from the breakdown of:

   A. carbon dioxide

   B. water

   C. glucose

   D. carbon monoxide

120. Which photosystem makes ATP?

   A. photosystem I

   B. photosystem II

   C. photosystem III

   D. photosystem IV

121. All of the following gasses made up the primitive atmosphere except:

   A. ammonia

   B. methane

   C. oxygen

   D. hydrogen

122. The Endosymbiotic theory states that:

   A. eukaryotes arose from prokaryotes

   B. animals evolved in close relationships with one another

   C. the prokaryotes arose from eukaryotes

   D. life arose from inorganic compounds

123. Which aspect of science does not support evolution?

   A. comparative anatomy

   B. organic chemistry

   C. comparison of DNA among organisms

   D. analogous structures

124. Evolution occurs in:

   A. individuals

   B. populations

   C. organ systems

   D. cells

125. Which process contributes to the large variety of living things in the world today?

   A. meiosis

   B. asexual reproduction

   C. mitosis

   D. alternation of generations

126. The wing of bird, human arm and whale flipper have the same bone structure. These are called:

   A. polymorphic structures

   B. homologous structures

   C. vestigial structures

   D. analogous structures

127. Which biome is the most prevalent on Earth?

   A. marine

   B. desert

   C. savanna

   D. tundra

128. Which of the following is not an abiotic factor?

   A. temperature

   B. rainfall

   C. soil quality

   D. bacteria

129. DNA synthesis results in a strand that is synthesized continuously. This is the:

   A. lagging strand

   B. leading strand

   C. template strand

   D. complementary strand

130. Using a gram staining technique, it is observed that E. coli stains pink. It is therefore:

   A. gram positive

   B. dead

   C. gram negative

   D. gram neutral

131. A light microscope has an ocular of 10X and an objective of 40X. What is the total magnification?

   A. 400X

   B. 30X

   C. 50X

   D. 4000X

132. Three plants were grown. The following data was taken. Determine the mean growth.
   Plant 1: 10cm Plant 2: 20cm
   Plant 3: 15cm

   A. 5 cm

   B. 45 cm

   C. 12 cm

   D. 15 cm

133. Electrophoresis separates DNA on the basis of:

   A. amount of current

   B. molecular size

   C. positive charge of the molecule

   D. solubility of the gel

134. The reading of a meniscus in a graduated cylinder is done at the:

   A. top of the meniscus

   B. middle of the meniscus

   C. bottom of the meniscus

   D. closest whole number

135. Two hundred plants were grown. Fifty plants died. What percentage of the plants survived?

   A. 40%

   B. 25%

   C. 75%

   D. 50%

136. Which is not a correct statement regarding the use of a light microscope?

   A. carry the microscope with two hands

   B. store on the low power objective

   C. clean all lenses with lens paper

   D. Focus first on high power

137. Spectrophotometry utilizes the principle of:

   A. light transmission

   B. molecular weight

   C. solubility of the substance

   D. electrical charges

138. Chromotography is most often associated with the separation of:

   A. nutritional elements

   B. DNA

   C. proteins

   D. plant pigments

139. A genetic engineering advancement in the medical field is:

   A. gene therapy

   B. pesticides

   C. degradation of harmful chemicals

   D. antibiotics

140. Which scientists are credited with the discovery of the structure of DNA?

   A. Hershey & Chase

   B. Sutton & Morgan

   C. Watson & Crick

   D. Miller & Fox

141. Negatively charged particles that circle the nucleus of an atom are called:

   A. neutrons

   B. neutrinos

   C. electrons

   D. protons

142. The shape of a cell depends on its:

   A. function

   B. structure

   C. age

   D. size

143. The most ATP is generated through:

   A. fermentation

   B. glycolysis

   C. chemiosmosis

   D. Krebs cycle

144. In DNA, adenine bonds with _____, while cytosine bonds with _____.

   A. thymine/guanine

   B. adenine/cytosine

   C. cytosine/adenine

   D. guanine/thymine

145. The individual parts of cells are best studied using a (n):

   A. ultracentrifuge

   B. phase-contrast microscope

   C. CAT scan

   D. electron microscope

146. Thermoacidophiles are:

   A. prokaryotes

   B. eukaryotes

   C. bacteria

   D. archaea

147. Which of the following is not a type of fiber that makes up the cytoskeleton?

   A. vacuoles

   B. microfilaments

   C. microtubules

   D. intermediate filaments

148. Viruses are made of:

A. a protein coat surrounding a nucleic acid

B. DNA, RNA and a cell wall

C. a nucleic acid surrounding a protein coat

D. protein surrounded by DNA

149. Reproductive isolation results in:

A. extinction

B. migration

C. follilization

D. speciation

150. This protein structure consists of the coils and folds of polypeptide chains. Which is it?

A. secondary structure

B. quaternary structure

C. tertiary structure

D. primary structure

Answer Key

1. C	32. C	63. A	94. C	125. A
2. C	33. B	64. D	95. C	126. B
3. B	34. C	65. C	96. A	127. A
4. D	35. C	66. B	97. A	128. D
5. C	36. B	67. C	98. D	129. B
6. D	37. D	68. D	99. C	130. C
7. D	38. C	69. B	100. B	131. A
8. C	39. C	70. C	101. A	132. D
9. D	40. A	71. D	102. A	133. B
10. D	41. D	72. B	103. B	134. C
11. A	42. A	73. C	104. A	135. C
12. A	43. C	74. A	105. B	136. D
13. B	44. D	75. A	106. A	137. A
14. C	45. B	76. D	107. A	138. D
15. C	46. C	77. A	108. D	139. A
16. A	47. B	78. D	109. D	140. C
17. A	48. B	79. C	110. C	141. C
18. C	49. B	80. B	111. C	142. A
19. D	50. A	81. D	112. C	143. C
20. A	51. A	82. A	113. A	144. A
21. D	52. C	83. D	114. C	145. D
22. B	53. C	84. D	115. B	146. D
23. A	54. D	85. C	116. B	147. A
24. B	55. D	86. B	117. A	148. A
25. A	56. B	87. A	118. C	149. D
26. C	57. C	88. B	119. B	150. A
27. D	58. D	89. A	120. A	
28. C	59. B	90. A	121. C	
29. B	60. D	91. D	122. A	
30. D	61. B	92. C	123. B	
31. C	62. A	93. D	124. B	

Rationales with Sample Questions

1. A student designed a science project testing the effects of light and water on plant growth. You would recommend that she

   A. manipulate the temperature as well.
   B. also alter the pH of the water as another variable.
   C. omit either water or light as a variable.
   D. also alter the light concentration as another variable.

C. In science, experiments should be designed so that only one variable is manipulated at a time.

2. Identify the control in the following experiment. A student had four plants grown under the following conditions and was measuring photosynthetic rate by measuring mass. 2 plants in 50% light and 2 plants in 100% light.

   A. plants grown with no added nutrients
   B. plants grown in the dark
   C plants in 100% light
   D. plants in 50% light

C. The 100% light plants are those that the student will be comparing the 50% plants to. This will be the control.

3. In an experiment measuring the growth of bacteria at different temperatures, identify the independent variable.

   A. growth of number of colonies
   B. temperature
   C. type of bacteria used
   D. light intensity

B. The independent variable is controlled by the experimenter. Here, the temperature is controlled to determine its effect on the growth of bacteria (dependent variable).

TEACHER CERTIFICATION STUDY GUIDE

4. A scientific theory

   A. proves scientific accuracy.
   B. is never rejected.
   C. results in a medical breakthrough.
   D. may be altered at a later time.

D. Scientific theory is usually accepted and verified information but can always be changed at anytime.

5. Which is the correct order of methodology? 1) testing revised explanation, 2) setting up a controlled experiment to test explanation, 3) drawing a conclusion, 4) suggesting an explanation for observations, and 5) compare observed results to hypothesized results

   A. 4, 2, 3, 1, 5
   B. 3, 1, 4, 2, 5
   C. 4, 2, 5, 1, 3
   D. 2, 5, 4, 1, 3

C. The first step in scientific inquiry is posing a question to be answered. Next, a hypothesis is formed to provide a plausible explanation. An experiment is then proposed and performed to test this hypothesis. A comparison between the predicted and observed results is the next step. Conclusions are then formed and it is determined whether the hypothesis is correct or incorrect. If incorrect, the next step is to form a new hypothesis and the process is repeated.

6. Given a choice, which is the most desirable method of heating a substance in the lab?

   A. alcohol burner
   B. gas burner
   C. bunsen burner
   D. hot plate

D. A hotplate is the only heat source from the choices above that does not have an open flame. The use of a hot plate will reduce the risk of fire and injury to students.

SCIENCE: BIOLOGY

7. **Biological waste should be disposed of**

    A. in the trash can.
    B. under a fume hood.
    C. in the broken glass box.
    D. in an autoclavable biohazard bag.

D. Biological material should never be stored near food or water used for human consumption. All biological material should be appropriately labeled. All blood and body fluids should be put in a well-contained container with a secure lid to prevent leaking. All biological waste should be disposed of in biological hazardous waste bags.

8. **Chemicals should be stored**

    A. in a cool dark room.
    B. in a dark room.
    C. according to their reactivity with other substances.
    D. in a double locked room.

C. All chemicals should be stored with other chemicals of similar reactivity. Failure to do so could result in an undesirable chemical reaction.

9. **Given the choice of lab activities, which would you omit?**

    A. a genetics experiment tracking the fur color of mice
    B. dissecting a preserved fetal pig
    C. a lab relating temperature to respiration rate using live goldfish.
    D. pithing a frog to see the action of circulation

D. The use of live vertebrate organisms in a way that may harm the animal is prohibited. The observation of fur color in mice is not harmful to the animal and the use of live goldfish is acceptable because they are invertebrates. The dissection of a fetal pig is acceptable if it comes from a known origin.

TEACHER CERTIFICATION STUDY GUIDE

10. **Who should be notified in the case of a serious chemical spill?**

    I. the custodian
    II. The fire department
    III. the chemistry teacher
    IV. the administration

    A. I
    B. II
    C. II and III
    D. II and IV

D. For large spills, the school administration and the local fire department should be notified.

11. **The "Right to Know" law states**

    A. the inventory of toxic chemicals checked against the "Substance List" be available.
    B. that students are to be informed on alternatives to dissection.
    C. that science teachers are to be informed of student allergies.
    D. that students are to be informed of infectious microorganisms used in lab.

A. The right to know law pertains to chemical substances in the lab. Employees should check the material safety data sheets and the substance list for potential hazards in the lab.

12. **In which situation would a science teacher be liable?**

    A. a teacher leaves to receive an emergency phone call and a student slips and falls.
    B. a student removes their goggles and gets dissection fluid in their eye.
    C. a faulty gas line results in a fire.
    D. a students cuts themselves with a scalpel.

A. A teacher has an obligation to be present in the lab at all times. If the teacher needs to leave, an appropriate substitute is needed.

13. **Which statement best defines negligence?**

    A. failure to give oral instructions for those with reading disabilities
    B. failure to exercise ordinary care
    C. inability to supervise a large group of students.
    D. reasonable anticipation that an event may occur

B. Negligence is the failure to exercise ordinary or reasonable care.

14. **Which item should always be used when using chemicals with noxious vapors?**

    A. eye protection
    B. face shield
    C. fume hood
    D. lab apron

C. Fume hoods are designed to protect the experimenter from chemical fumes. The three other choices do not prevent chemical fumes from entering the respiratory system.

15. **Identify the correct sequence of organization of living things.**

    A. cell – organelle – organ system – tissue – organ – organism
    B. cell – tissue – organ – organ system – organelle – organism
    C. organelle – cell – tissue – organ – organ system – organism
    D. tissue – organelle – organ – cell – organism – organ system

C. An organism, such as a human, is comprised of several organ systems such as the circulatory and nervous systems. These organ systems consist of many organs including the heart and the brain. These organs are made of tissue such as cardiac muscle. Tissues are made up of cells, which contain organelles like the mitochondria and the Golgi apparatus.

16. **Which is not a characteristic of living things?**

    A. movement
    B. cellular structure
    C. metabolism
    D. reproduction

A. Movement is not a characteristic of life. Viruses are considered non-living organisms but have the ability to move from cell to cell in its host organism.

17. Which kingdom is comprised of organisms made of one cell with no nuclear membrane?

   A. Monera
   B. Protista
   C. Fungi
   D. Algae

A. Monera is the only kingdom that is made up of unicellular organisms with no nucleus. Algae is a protist because it is made up of one type of tissue and it has a nucleus.

18. Potassium chloride is an example of a(n)

   A. non polar covalent bond
   B. polar covalent bond
   C. ionic bond
   D. hydrogen bond

C. Ionic bonds are formed when one electron is stripped away from its atom to join another atom. Ionic compounds are called salts and potassium chloride is a salt; therefore, potassium chloride is an example of an ionic bond.

19. Which of the following is a monomer?

   A. RNA
   B. glycogen
   C. DNA
   D. amino acid

D. A monomer is the simplest unit of structure for a particular macromolecule. Amino acids are the basic unit that comprises a protein. RNA and DNA are polymers consisting of nucleotides and glycogen is a polymer consisting of many molecules of glucose.

20. Which of the following are properties of water?

    I. High specific heat
    II. Strong ionic bonds
    III. Good solvent
    IV. High freezing point

    A. I, III, IV
    B. II and III
    C. I and II
    D. II, III, IV

A. All are properties of water except strong ionic bonds. Water is held together by polar covalent bonds between hydrogen and oxygen.

21. Which does not affect enzyme rate?

    A. increase of temperature
    B. amount of substrate
    C. pH
    D. size of the cell

D. Temperature and pH can affect the rate of reaction of an enzyme. The amount of substrate affects the enzyme as well. The enzyme acts on the substrate. The more substrate, the slower the enzyme rate. Therefore, the only chance left is D, the size of the cell, which has no effect on enzyme rate.

22. Sulfur oxides and nitrogen oxides in the environment react with water to cause

    A. ammonia
    B. acidic precipitation
    C. sulfuric acid
    D. global warming

B. Acidic precipitation is rain, snow, or fog with a pH less than 5.6. It is caused by sulfur oxides and nitrogen oxides that react with water in the air to form acids that fall down to Earth as precipitation.

23. The loss of an electron is _____ and the gain of an electron is _____.

   A. oxidation, reduction
   B. reduction, oxidation
   C. glycolysis, photosynthesis
   D. photosynthesis, glycolysis

A. Oxidation-reduction reactions are also known as redox reactions. In respiration, energy is released by the transfer of electrons by this process. The oxidation phase of this reaction is the loss of an electron and the reduction phase is the gain of an electron.

24. **The product of anaerobic respiration in animals is**

   A. carbon dioxide
   B. lactic acid
   C. pyruvate
   D. ethyl alcohol

B. In anaerobic lactic acid fermentation, pyruvate is reduced by NADH to form lactic acid. This is the anaerobic process in animals. Alcoholic fermentation is the anaerobic process in yeast and some bacteria resulting in ethyl alcohol. Carbon dioxide and pyruvate are the products of aerobic respiration.

25. **In the comparison of respiration to photosynthesis, which statement is true?**

   A. oxygen is a waste product in photosynthesis but not in respiration
   B. glucose is produced in respiration but not in photosynthesis
   C. carbon dioxide is formed in photosynthesis but not in respiration
   D. water is formed in respiration but not in photosynthesis

A. In photosynthesis, water is split and the oxygen is given off as a waste product. In respiration, water and carbon dioxide are the waste products.

26. Carbon dioxide is fixed in the form of glucose in:

   A. Krebs cycle
   B. the light reactions
   C. the dark reactions (Calvin cycle)
   D. glycolysis

C. The ATP produced during the light reaction is needed to convert carbon dioxide to glucose in the Calvin cycle.

27. During the Kreb's cycle, 8 carrier molecules are formed. What are they?

   A. 3 NADH, 3 FADH, 2 ATP
   B. 6 NADH and 2 ATP
   C. 4 $FADH_2$ and 4 ATP
   D. 6 NADH and 2 $FADH_2$

D. For each molecule of CoA that enters the Kreb's cycle, you get 3 NADH and 1 $FADH_2$. There are 2 molecules of CoA so the total yield is 6 NADH and 2 $FADH_2$ during the Kreb's cycle.

28. Which of the following is not posttranscriptional processing?

   A. 5' capping
   B. intron splicing
   C. polypeptide splicing
   D. 3' polyadenylation

C. The removal of segments of polypeptides is a posttranslational process. The other three are methods of posttranscriptional processing.

29. Polymerase chain reaction

   A. is a group of polymerases
   B. technique for amplifying DNA
   C. primer for DNA synthesis
   D. synthesis of polymerase

B. PCR is a technique in which a piece of DNA can be amplified into billions of copies within a few hour.

30. Homozygous individuals

A. have two different alleles
B. are of the same species
C. have the same features
D. have a pair of identical alleles

D. Homozygous individuals have a pair of identical alleles and heterozygous individuals have two different alleles.

31. The two major ways to determine taxonomic classification are

A. evolution and phylogeny
B. reproductive success and evolution
C. phylogeny and morphology
D. size and color

C. Taxonomy is based on structure (morphology) and evolutionary relationships (phylogeny).

32. Man's scientific name is Homo sapiens. Choose the proper classification beginning with kingdom and ending with order.

A. Animalia, Vertebrata, Mammalia, Primate, Hominidae
B. Animalia, Vertebrata, Chordata, Mammalia, Primate
C. Animalia, Chordata, Vertebrata, Mammalia, Primate
D. Chordata, Vertebrata, Primate, Homo, sapiens

C. The order of classification for humans is as follows: Kingdom, Animalia; Phylum, Chordata; Subphylum, Vertebrata; Class, Mammalia; Order, Primate; Family, Hominadae; Genus, Homo; Species, sapiens.

33. The scientific name Canis familiaris refers to the animal's:

A. kingdom and phylum names
B. genus and species names
C. class and species names
D. order and family names

B. Each species is scientifically known by a two-part name, or binomial. The first word in the name is the genus and the second word is its specific epithet (species name).

34. Members of the same species:

A. look identical
B. never change
C. reproduce successfully among their group
D. live in the same geographic location

C. Species are defined by the ability to successfully reproduce with members of their own kind.

35. What is necessary for diffusion to occur?

A. carrier proteins
B. energy
C. a concentration gradient
D. a membrane

C. Diffusion is the ability of molecules to move from areas of high concentration to areas of low concentration (a concentration gradient).

36. Which is an example of the use of energy to move a substance through a membrane from areas of low concentration to areas of high concentration?

A. osmosis
B. active transport
C. exocytosis
D. phagocytosis

B. Active transport can move substances with or against the concentration gradient. This energy requiring process allows for molecules to move from areas of low concentration to high concentration areas.

37. A plant cell is placed in salt water. The resulting movement of water out of the cell is called:

A. facilitated diffusion
B. diffusion
C. transpiration
D. osmosis

D. Osmosis is simply the diffusion of water across a semi-permeable membrane. Water will diffuse out of the cell if there is less water on the outside of the cell.

38. As the amount of waste production increases in a cell, the rate of excretion

   A. slowly decreases
   B. remains the same
   C. increases
   D. stops due to cell death

C. Homeostasis is the control of the differences between internal and external environments. Excretion is the homeostatic system that regulates the amount of waste in a cell. As the amount of waste increases, the rate of excretion will increase to maintain homeostasis.

39. A type of molecule not found in the membrane of an animal cell is

   A. phospholipid
   B. protein
   C. cellulose
   D. cholesterol

C. Phospholipids, protein, and cholesterol are all found in animal cells. Cellulose, however, is only found in plant cells.

40. Which type of cell would contain the most mitochondria?

   A. muscle cell
   B. nerve cell
   C. epithelium
   D. blood cell

A. Mitochondria are the site of cellular respiration where ATP is made. Muscle cells have the most mitochondria because they use a great deal of energy.

41. The first cells that evolved on earth were probably of which type?

   A. autotrophs
   B. eukaryotes
   C. heterotrophs
   D. prokaryotes

D. Prokaryotes date back to 3.5 billion years ago in the first fossil record. Their ability to adapt to the environment allows them to thrive in a wide variety of habitats.

42. According to the fluid-mosaic model of the cell membrane, membranes are composed of

   A. phospholipid bilayers with proteins embedded in the layers
   B. one layer of phospholipids with cholesterol embedded in the layer
   C. two layers of protein with lipids embedded the layers
   D. DNA and fluid proteins

A. Cell membranes are composed of two phospholipids with their hydrophobic tails sandwiched between their hydrophilic heads, creating a lipid bilayer. The membrane contains proteins embedded in the layer (integral proteins) and proteins on the surface (peripheral proteins).

43. All the following statements regarding both a mitochondria and a chloroplast are correct except

   A. they both produce energy over a gradient
   B. they both have DNA and are capable of reproduction
   C. they both transfer light energy to chemical energy
   D. they both make ATP

C. Cellular respiration does not transfer light energy to chemical energy. Cellular respiration transfers electrons to release energy. Photosynthesis utilizes light energy to produce chemical energy.

44. This stage of mitosis includes cytokinesis or division of the cytoplasm and its organelles

   A. anaphase
   B. interphase
   C. prophase
   D. telophase

D. The last stage of the mitotic phase is telophase. Here, the two nuclei form with a full set of DNA each. The cell is pinched into two cells and cytokinesis, or division of the cytoplasm and organelles, occurs.

45. Replication of chromosomes occurs during which phase of the cell cycle?

   A. prophase
   B. interphase
   C. metaphase
   D. anaphase

B. Interphase is the stage where the cell grows and copies the chromosomes in preparation for the mitotic phase.

46. Which statement regarding mitosis is correct?

   A. diploid cells produce haploid cells for sexual reproduction
   B. sperm and egg cells are produced
   C. diploid cells produce diploid cells for growth and repair
   D. it allows for greater genetic diversity

C. The purpose of mitotic cell division is to provide growth and repair in body (somatic) cells. The cells begin as diploid and produce diploid cells.

47. In a plant cell, telophase is described as

   A. the time of chromosome doubling
   B. cell plate formation
   C. the time when crossing over occurs
   D. cleavage furrow formation

B. During plant cell telophase, a cell plate is observed whereas a cleavage furrow is formed in animal cells.

48. Identify this stage of mitosis

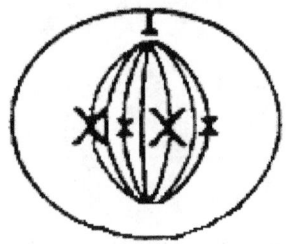

A. anaphase
B. metaphase
C. telophase
D. prophase

B. During metaphase, the centromeres are at opposite ends of the cell. Here the chromosomes are aligned with one another.

49. Identify this stage of mitosis

A. prophase
B. telophase
C. anaphase
D. metaphase

B. Telophase is the last stage of mitosis. Here, two nuclei become visible and the nuclear membrane resembles.

50. Identify this stage of mitosis

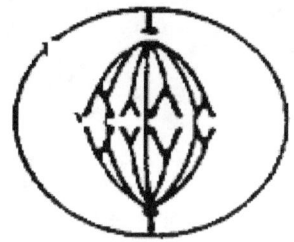

- A. anaphase
- B. metaphase
- C. prophase
- D. telophase

A. During anaphase, the centromeres split in half and homologous chromosomes separate.

51. Oxygen is given off in the

- A. light reactions of photosynthesis
- B. dark reactions of photosynthesis
- C. Krebs cycle
- D. reduction of NAD+ to NADH

A. The conversion of solar energy to chemical energy occurs in the light reactions. Electrons are transferred by the absorption of light by chlorophyll and causes water to split, releasing oxygen as a waste product.

52. In the electron transport chain, all the following are true except

- A. it occurs in the mitochondrion
- B. it does not make ATP directly
- C. the net gain of energy is 30 ATP
- D. most molecules in the electron transport chain are proteins.

C. The end result of the electron transport chain is 34 molecules of ATP.

TEACHER CERTIFICATION STUDY GUIDE

53. The area of a DNA nucleotide that varies is the

    A. deoxyribose
    B. phosphate group
    C. nitrogen base
    D. sugar

C. DNA is made of a 5 carbon sugar (deoxyribose), a phosphate group, and a nitrogenous base. There are four nitrogenous bases in DNA that allow for the four different nucleotides.

54. A DNA strand has the base sequence of TCAGTA. Its DNA complement would have the following sequence

    A. ATGACT
    B. TCAGTA
    C. AGUCAU
    D. AGTCAT

D. The complement strand to a single strand DNA molecule has a complementary sequence to the template strand. T pairs with A and C pairs with G. Therefore, the complement to TCAGTA is AGTCAT.

55. Genes function in specifying the structure of which molecule?

    A. carbohydrates
    B. lipids
    C. nucleic acids
    D. proteins

D. Genes contain the sequence of nucleotides that code for amino acids. Amino acids are the building blocks of protein.

56. What is the correct order of steps in protein synthesis?

    A. transcription, then replication
    B. transcription, then translation
    C. translation, then transcription
    D. replication, then translation

B. A DNA strand first undergoes transcription to get a complementary mRNA strand. Translation of the mRNA strand then occurs to result in the tRNA adding the appropriate amino acid for an ending product of a protein.

SCIENCE: BIOLOGY

TEACHER CERTIFICATION STUDY GUIDE

57. This carries amino acids to the ribosome in protein synthesis

    A. messenger RNA
    B. ribosomal RNA
    C. transfer RNA
    D. DNA

C. The tRNA molecule is specific for a particular amino acid. The tRNA has an anticodon sequence that is complementary to the codon. This specifies where the tRNA places the amino acid in protein synthesis.

58. A protein is sixty amino acids in length. This requires a coded DNA sequence of how many nucleotides?

    A. 20
    B. 30
    C. 120
    D. 180

D. Each amino acid codon consists of 3 nucleotides. If there are 60 amino acids in a protein, then 60 x 30 = 180 nucleotides.

59. A DNA molecule has the sequence of ACTATG. What is the anticodon of this molecule?

    A. UGAUAC
    B. ACUAUG
    C. TGATAC
    D. ACTATG

B. The DNA is first transcribed into mRNA. Here, the DNA has the sequence ACTATG; therefore the complementary mRNA sequence is UGAUAC (remember, in RNA, T are U). This mRNA sequence is the codon. The anticodon is the complement to the codon. The anticodon sequence will be ACUAUG (remember, the anticodon is tRNA, so U is present instead of T).

60. The term "phenotype" refers to which of the following?

   A. a condition which is heterozygous
   B. the genetic makeup of an individual
   C. a condition which is homozygous
   D. how the genotype is expressed

D. Phenotype is the physical appearance of an organism due to its genetic makeup (genotype).

61. The ratio of brown-eyed to blue-eyed children from the mating of a blue-eyed male to a heterozygous brown-eyed female would be expected to be which of the following?

   A. 2:1
   B. 1:1
   C. 1:0
   D. 1:2

B. Use a Punnet square to determine the ratio.

	b	b
B	Bb	Bb
b	bb	bb

B = brown eyes, b = blue eyes

Female genotype is on the side and the male genotype is across the top.

The female is heterozygous and her phenotype is brown eyes. This means the dominant allele is for brown eyes. The male expresses the homozygous recessive allele for blue eyes. Their children are expected to have a ratio of brown eyes to blue eyes of 2:2; or 1:1.

62. The Law of Segregation defined by Mendel states that

   A. when sex cells form, the two alleles that determine a trait will end up on different gametes
   B. only one of two alleles is expressed in a heterozygous organism
   C. the allele expressed is the dominant allele
   D. alleles of one trait do not affect the inheritance of alleles on another chromosome

A. The law of segregation states that the two alleles for each trait segregate into different gametes.

63. When a white flower is crossed with a red flower, incomplete dominance can be seen by the production of which of the following?

   A. pink flowers
   B. red flowers
   C. white flowers
   D. red and white flowers

A. Incomplete dominance is when the F_1 generation results in an appearance somewhere between the parents. Red flowers crossed with white flowers results in an F_1 generation with pink flowers.

64. Sutton observed that genes and chromosomes behaved the same. This led him to his theory which stated

   A. that meiosis causes chromosome separation
   B. that linked genes are able to separate
   C. that genes and chromosomes have the same function
   D. that genes are found on chromosomes

D. Sutton observed how mitosis and meiosis confirmed Mendel's theory on "factors." His Chromosome Theory states that genes are located on chromosomes.

65. Amniocentesis is

   A. a non-invasive technique for detecting genetic disorders
   B. a bacterial infection
   C. extraction of amniotic fluid
   D. removal of fetal tissue

C. Amniocentesis is a procedure in which a needle is inserted into the uterus to extract some of the amniotic fluid surrounding the fetus. Some genetic disorders can be detected by chemicals in the fluid.

66. A child with type O blood has a father with type A blood and a mother with type B blood. The genotypes of the parents respectively would be which of the following?

   A. AA and BO
   B. AO and BO
   C. AA and BB
   D. AO and OO

B. Type O blood has 2 recessive O genes. A child receives one allele from each parent; therefore each parent in this example must have an O allele. The father has type A blood with a genotype of AO and the mother has type B blood with a genotype of BO.

67. Any change that affects the sequence of bases in a gene is called a(n)

   A. deletion
   B. polyploid
   C. mutation
   D. duplication

C. A mutation is an inheritable change in DNA. They may be errors in replication or a spontaneous rearrangement of one ore more segments of DNA. Deletion and duplication are type of mutations. Polyploidy is when and organism has more than two complete chromosome sets.

68. The *lac* operon

   I. contains the *lac Z, lac Y, lac A* genes
   II. converts glucose to lactose
   III. contains a repressor
   IV. is on when the repressor is activated

   A. I
   B. II
   C. III and IV
   D. I and III

D. The *lac* operon contains the genes that encode for the enzymes used to convert lactose into fuel. It contains three genes: *lac A, lac Z,* and *lac Y*. It also contains a promoter and repressor. When the repressor is activated, the operon is off.

69. Which of the following factors will affect the Hardy-Weinberg law of equilibrium, leading to evolutionary change?

   A. no mutations
   B. non-random mating
   C. no immigration or emigration
   D. Large population

B. There are five requirements to keep the Hardy-Weinberg equilibrium stable: no mutation, no selection pressures, an isolated population, a large population, and random mating.

70. If a population is in Hardy-Weinberg equilibrium and the frequency of the recessive allele is 0.3, what percentage of the population would be expected to be heterozygous?

   A. 9%
   B. 49%
   C. 42%
   D. 21%

C. 0.3 is the value of q. Therefore, $q^2 = 0.09$. According to the Hardy-Weinberg equation, $1 = p + q$.

$1 = p + 0.3$.
$p = 0.7$
$p^2 = 0.49$

Next, plug q^2 and p^2 into the equation $1 = p^2 + 2pq + q^2$.

$1 = 0.49 + 2pq + 0.09$ (where 2pq is the number of heterozygotes).
$1 = 0.58 + 2pq$
$2pq = 0.42$

Multiply by 100 to get the percent of heterozygotes to get 42%.

71. **Crossing over, which increases genetic diversity occurs during which stage(s)?**

    A. telophase II in meiosis
    B. metaphase in mitosis
    C. interphase in both mitosis and meiosis
    D. prophase I in meiosis

D. During prophase I of meiosis, the replicated chromosomes condense and pair with homologues in a process called synapsis. Crossing over, the exchange of genetic material between homologues to further increase diversity, occurs during prophase I.

72. **Cancer cells divide extensively and invade other tissues. This continuous cell division is due to**

    A. density dependent inhibition
    B. density independent inhibition
    C. chromosome replication
    D. Growth factors

B. Density dependent inhibition is when the cells crowd one another and consume all the nutrients; therefore halting cell division. Cancer cells, however, are density independent; meaning they can divide continuously as long as nutrients are present.

73. **Which process(es) results in a haploid chromosome number?**

    A. both meiosis and mitosis
    B. mitosis
    C. meiosis
    D. replication and division

C. In meiosis, there are two consecutive cell divisions resulting in the reduction of the chromosome number by half (diploid to haploid).

74. **Segments of DNA can be transferred from the DNA of one organism to another through the use of which of the following?**

    A. bacterial plasmids
    B. viruses
    C. chromosomes from frogs
    D. plant DNA

A. Plasmids can transfer themselves (and therefore their genetic information) by a process called conjugation. This requires cell-cell contact.

TEACHER CERTIFICATION STUDY GUIDE

75. Which of the following is not true regarding restriction enzymes?

   A. they do not aid in recombination procedures
   B. they are used in genetic engineering
   C. they are named after the bacteria in which they naturally occur
   D. they identify and splice certain base sequences on DNA

A. A restriction enzyme is a bacterial enzyme that cuts foreign DNA at specific locations. The splicing of restriction fragments into a plasmid results in a recombinant plasmid.

76. A virus that can remain dormant until a certain environmental condition causes its rapid increase is said to be

   A. lytic
   B. benign
   C. saprophytic
   D. lysogenic

D. Lysogenic viruses remain dormant until something initiates it to break out of the host cell.

77. Which is not considered to be a morphological type of bacteria?

   A. obligate
   B. coccus
   C. spirillum
   D. bacillus

A. Morphology is the shape of an organism. Obligate is term used when describing dependence on something. Coccus is a round bacterium, spirillum is a spiral shaped bacterium, and bacillus is a rod shaped bacterium.

78. Antibiotics are effective in fighting bacterial infections due to their ability to

   A. interfere with DNA replication in the bacteria
   B. prevent the formation of new cell walls in the bacteria
   C. disrupt the ribosome of the bacteria
   D. All of the above.

D. Antibiotics can destroy the bacterial cell wall, interfere with bacterial DNA replication, and disrupt the bacterial ribosome without affecting the host cells.

SCIENCE: BIOLOGY

79. Bacteria commonly reproduce by a process called binary fission. Which of the following best defines this process?

   A. viral vectors carry DNA to new bacteria
   B. DNA from one bacterium enters another
   C. DNA doubles and the bacterial cell divides
   D. DNA from dead cells is absorbed into bacteria

C. Binary fission is the asexual process in which the bacteria divide in half after the DNA doubles. This results in an exact clone of the parent cell.

80. All of the following are examples of a member of Kingdom Fungi except

   A. mold
   B. algae
   C. mildew
   D. mushrooms

B. Mold, mildew, and mushrooms are all fungi. Brown algae and golden algae are members of the kingdom protista and green algae are members of the plant kingdom.

81. Protists are classified into major groups according to

   A. their method of obtaining nutrition
   B. reproduction
   C. metabolism
   D. their form and function

D. The chaotic status of names and concepts of the higher classification of the protists reflects their great diversity in form, function, and life styles. The protists are often grouped as algae (plant-like), protozoa (animal-like), or fungus-like based on the similarity of their lifestyle and characteristics to these more derived groups.

82. In comparison to protist cells, moneran cells

   I. are usually smaller
   II. evolved later
   III. are more complex
   IV. contain more organelles

   A. I
   B. I and II
   C. II and III
   D. I and IV

A. Moneran cells are almost always smaller than protists. Moneran cells are prokaryotic; therefore they are less complex and have no organelles. Prokaryotes were the first cells on Earth and therefore evolved before than the eukaryotic protists.

83. Spores characterize the reproduction mode for which of the following group of plants?

   A. algae
   B. flowering plants
   C. conifers
   D. ferns

D. Ferns are non-seeded vascular plants. All plants in this group have spores and require water for reproduction. Algae, flowering plants, and conifers are not in this group of plants.

84. Water movement to the top of a twenty foot tree is most likely due to which principle?

   A. osmostic pressure
   B. xylem pressure
   C. capillarity
   D. transpiration

D. Xylem is the tissue that transports water upward. Transpiration is the force that pulls the water upwards. Transpiration is the evaporation of water from leaves.

SCIENCE: BIOLOGY

85. What are the stages of development from the egg to the plant?

   A. morphogenesis, growth, and cellular differentiation
   B. cell differentiation, growth, and morphogenesis
   C. growth, morphogenesis, and cellular differentiation
   D. growth, cellular differentiation, and morphogensis

C. The development of the egg to form a plant occurs in three stages: growth; morphogenesis, the development of form; and cellular differentiation, the acquisition of a cell's specific structure and function.

86. In angiosperms, the food for the developing plant is found in which of the following structures?

   A. ovule
   B. endosperm
   C. male gametophyte
   D. cotyledon

B. The endosperm is a product of double fertilization. It is the food supply for the developing plant.

87. The process in which pollen grains are released from the anthers is called

   A. pollination
   B. fertilization
   C. blooming
   D. dispersal

A. Pollen grains are released from the anthers during pollination and carried by animals and the wind to land on the carpels.

TEACHER CERTIFICATION STUDY GUIDE

88. Which of the following is not a characteristic of a monocot?

   A. parallel veins in leaves
   B. petals of flowers occur in multiples of 4 or 5
   C. one seed leaf
   D. vascular tissue scattered throughout the stem

B. Monocots have one cotelydon, parallel veins in their leaves, and their flower petals are in multiples of threes. Dicots have flower petals in multiples of fours and fives.

89. What controls gas exchange on the bottom of a plant leaf?

   A. stomata
   B. epidermis
   C. collenchyma and schlerenchyma
   D. palisade mesophyll

A. Stomata provide openings on the underside of leaves for oxygen to move in or out of the plant and for carbon dioxide to move in.

90. How are angiosperms different from other groups of plants?

   A. presence of flowers and fruits
   B. production of spores for reproduction
   C. true roots and stems
   D. seed production

A. Angiosperms do not have spores for reproduction. They do have true roots and stems as do all vascular plants. They do have seed production as do the gymnosperms. The presence of flowers and fruits is the difference between angiosperms and other plants.

91. Generations of plants alternate between

   A. angiosperms and bryophytes
   B. flowering and nonflowering stages
   C. seed bearing and spore bearing plants
   D. haploid and diploid stages

D. Reproduction of plants is accomplished through alteration of generations. Simply stated, a haploid stage in the plant's life history alternates with a diploid stage.

SCIENCE: BIOLOGY

92. Double fertilization refers to which choice of the following?

A. two sperm fertilizing one egg
B. fertilization of a plant by gametes from two separate plants
C. two sperm enter the plant embryo sac; one sperm fertilizes the egg, the other forms the endosperm
D. the production of non-identical twins through fertilization of two separate eggs

C. In angiosperms, double fertilization is when an ovum is fertilized by two sperm. One sperm produces the new plant and the other forms the food supply for the developing plant (endosperm).

93. Characteristics of coelomates include:

I. no true digestive system
II. two germ layers
III. true fluid filled cavity
IV. three germ layers

A. I
B. II and IV
C. IV
D. III and IV

D. Coelomates are triplobastic animals (3 germ layers). They have a true fluid filled body cavity called a coelom.

94. Which phylum accounts for 85% of all animal species?

A. Nematoda
B. Chordata
C. Arthropoda
D. Cnidaria

C. The arthropoda phylum consists of insects, crustaceans, and spiders. They are the largest group in the animal kingdom.

95. Which is the correct statement regarding the human nervous system and the human endocrine system?

   A. the nervous system maintains homeostasis whereas the endocrine system does not
   B. endocrine glands produce neurotransmitters whereas nerves produce hormones
   C. nerve signals travel on neurons whereas hormones travel through the blood
   D. he nervous system involves chemical transmission whereas the endocrine system does not

C. In the human nervous system, neurons carry nerve signals to and from the cell body. Endocrine glands produce hormones that are carried through the body in the bloodstream.

96. A muscular adaptation to move food through the digestive system is called

   A. peristalsis
   B. passive transport
   C. voluntary action
   D. bulk transport

A. Peristalsis is a process of wave-like contractions. This process allows food to be carried down the pharynx and though the digestive tract.

97. The role of neurotransmitters in nerve action is

   A. turn off sodium pump
   B. turn off calcium pump
   C. send impulse to neuron
   D. send impulse to the body

A. The neurotransmitters turn off the sodium pump which results in depolarization of the membrane.

98. Fats are broken down by which substance?

A. bile produced in the gall bladder
B. lipase produced in the gall bladder
C. glucagons produced in the liver
D. bile produced in the liver

D. The liver produces bile which breaks down and emulsifies fatty acids.

99. Fertilization in humans usually occurs in the

A. uterus
B. ovary
C. fallopian tubes
D. vagina

C. Fertilization of the egg by the sperm normally occurs in the fallopian tube. The fertilized egg is then implanted on the uterine lining for development.

100. All of the following are found in the dermis layer of skin except

A. sweat glands
B. keratin
C. hair follicles
D. blood vessels

B. Keratin is a water proofing protein found in the epidermis.

101. Which is the correct sequence of embryonic development in a frog?

A. cleavage – blastula – gastrula
B. cleavage – gastrula – blastula
C. blastula – cleavage – gastrula
D. gastrula – blastula – cleavage

A. Animals go through several stages of development after fertilization of the egg cell. The first step is cleavage which continues until the egg becomes a blastula. The blastula is a hollow ball of undifferentiated cells. Gastrulation is the next step. This is the time of tissue differentiation into the separate germ layers: the endoderm, mesoderm, and ectoderm.

102. Food is carried through the digestive tract by a series of wave-like contractions. This process is called

   A. peristalsis
   B. chyme
   C. digestion
   D. absorption

A. Peristalsis is the process of wave-like contractions that moves food through the digestive tract.

103. Movement is possible by the action of muscles pulling on

   A. skin
   B. bones
   C. joints
   D. ligaments

B. The muscular system's function is for movement. Skeletal muscles are attached to bones and are responsible for their movement.

104. All of the following are functions of the skin except

   A. storage
   B. protection
   C. sensation
   D. regulation of temperature

A. Skin is a protective barrier against infection. It contains hair follicles that respond to sensation and it plays a role in thermoregulation.

105. Hormones are essential to the regulation of reproduction. What organ is responsible for the release of hormones for sexual maturity?

   A. pituitary gland
   B. hypothalamus
   C. pancreas
   D. thyroid gland

B. The hypothalamus begins secreting hormones that help mature the reproductive system and development of the secondary sex characteristics.

106. A bicyclist has a heart rate of 110 beats per minute and a stroke volume of 85 mL per beat. What is the cardiac output?

    A. 9.35 L/min
    B. 1.29 L/min
    C. 0.772 L/min
    D. 129 L/min

A. The cardiac output is the volume of blood per minute that is pumped into the systemic circuit. This is determined by the heart rate and the stroke volume. Multiply the heart rate by the stroke volume. 110 * 85 = 9350 mL/min. Divide by 1000 to get units of liters. 9350/1000 = 9.35 L/min.

107. After sea turtles are hatched on the beach, they start the journey to the ocean. This is due to

    A. innate behavior
    B. territoriality
    C. the tide
    D. learned behavior

A. Innate behavior are inborn or instinctual. The baby sea turtles did not learn from their mother. They immediately knew to head towards the ocean once they hatched.

108. A school age boy had the chicken pox as a baby. He will most likely not get this disease again because of

    A. passive immunity
    B. vaccination
    C. antibiotics
    D. active immunity

D. Active immunity develops after recovery from an infectious disease, such as the chicken pox, or after vaccination. Passive immunity may be passed from one individual to another (from mother to nursing child).

109. High humidity and temperature stability are present in which of the following biomes?

- A. taiga
- B. deciduous forest
- C. desert
- D. tropical rain forest

D. A tropical rain forest is located near the equator. Its temperature is at a constant 25 degrees C and the humidity is high due to the rainfall that exceeds 200 cm per year.

110. The biological species concept applies to

- A. asexual organisms
- B. extinct organisms
- C. sexual organisms
- D. fossil organisms

C. The biological species concept states that a species is a reproductive community of populations that occupy a specific niche in nature. It focuses on reproductive isolation of populations as the primary criterion for recognition of species status. The biological species concept does not apply to organisms that are completely asexual in their reproduction, fossil organisms, or distinctive populations that hybridize.

111. Which term is not associated with the water cycle?

- A. precipitation
- B. transpiration
- C. fixation
- D. evaporation

C. Water is recycled through the processes of evaporation and precipitation. Transpiration is the evaporation of water from leaves. Fixation is not associated with the water cycle.

112. All of the following are density independent factors that affect a population except

   A. temperature
   B. rainfall
   C. predation
   D. soil nutrients

C. As a population increases, the competition for resources is intense and the growth rate declines. This is a density-dependent factor. An example of this would be predation. Density-independent factors affect the population regardless of its size. Examples of density-independent factors are rainfall, temperature, and soil nutrients.

113. In the growth of a population, the increase is exponential until carrying capacity is reached. This is represented by a (n)

   A. S curve
   B. J curve
   C. M curve
   D. L curve

A. An exponentially growing population starts off with little change and then rapidly increases. The graphic representation of this growth curve has the appearance of a "J". However, as the carrying capacity of the exponentially growing population is reached, the growth rate begins to slow down and level off. The graphic representation of this growth curve has the appearance of an "S".

114. Primary succession occurs after

   A. nutrient enrichment
   B. a forest fire
   C. bare rock is exposed after a water table recedes
   D. a housing development is built

C. Primary succession occurs where life never existed before, such as flooded areas or a new volcanic island. It is only after the water recedes that the rock is able to support new life.

115. Crabgrass – grasshopper – frog – snake – eagle If DDT were present in an ecosystem, which organism would have the highest concentration in its system?

- A. grasshopper
- B. eagle
- C. frog
- D. crabgrass

B. Chemicals and pesticides accumulate along the food chain. Tertiary consumers have more accumulated toxins than animals at the bottom of the food chain.

116. Which trophic level has the highest ecological efficiency?

- A. decomposers
- B. producers
- C. tertiary consumers
- D. secondary consumers

B. The amount of energy that is transferred between trophic levels is called the ecological efficiency. The visual of this is represented in a pyramid of productivity. The producers have the greatest amount of energy and are at the bottom of this pyramid.

117. A clownfish is protected by the sea anemone's tentacles. In turn, the anemone receives uneaten food from the clownfish. This is an example of

- A. mutualism
- B. parasitism
- C. commensalisms
- D. competition

A. Neither the clownfish nor the anemone cause harmful effects towards one another and they both benefit from their relationship. Mutualism is when two species that occupy a similar space benefit from their relationship.

118. If the niches of two species overlap, what usually results?

   A. a symbiotic relationship
   B. cooperation
   C. competition
   D. a new species

C. Two species that occupy the same habitat or eat the same food are said to be in competition with each other.

119. Oxygen created in photosynthesis comes from the breakdown of

   A. carbon dioxide
   B. water
   C. glucose
   D. carbon monoxide

B. In photosynthesis, water is split; the hydrogen atoms are pulled to carbon dioxide which is taken in by the plant and ultimately reduced to make glucose. The oxygen from the water is given off as a waste product.

120. Which photosystem makes ATP?

   A. photosystem I
   B. photosystem II
   C. photosystem III
   D. photosystem IV

A. Photosystem I is composed of a pair of chlorophyll *a* molecules. It makes ATP whose energy is needed to build glucose.

121. All of the following gasses made up the primitive atmosphere except

   A. ammonia
   B. methane
   C. oxygen
   D. hydrogen

C. In the 1920s, Oparin and Haldane were to first to theorize that the primitive atmosphere was a reducing atmosphere with no oxygen. The gases were rich in hydrogen, methane, water, and ammonia.

122. The Endosymbiotic theory states that

   A. eukaryotes arose from prokaryotes
   B. animals evolved in close relationships with one another
   C. the prokaryotes arose from eukaryotes
   D. life arose from inorganic compounds

A. The Endosymbiotic theory of the origin of eukaryotes states that eukaryotes arose from symbiotic groups of prokaryotic cells. According to this theory, smaller prokaryotes lived within larger prokaryotic cells, eventually evolving into chloroplasts and mitochondria.

123. Which aspect of science does not support evolution?

   A. comparative anatomy
   B. organic chemistry
   C. comparison of DNA among organisms
   D. analogous structures

B. Comparative anatomy is the comparison of characteristics of the anatomies of different species. This includes homologous structures and analogous structures. The comparison of DNA between species is the best known way to place species on the evolution tree. Organic chemistry has nothing to do with evolution.

124. Evolution occurs in

   A. individuals
   B. populations
   C. organ systems
   D. cells

B. Evolution is a change in genotype over time. Gene frequencies shift and change from generation to generation. Populations evolve, not individuals.

125. Which process contributes to the large variety of living things in the world today?

   A. meiosis
   B. asexual reproduction
   C. mitosis
   D. alternation of generations

A. During meiosis prophase I crossing over occurs. This exchange of genetic material between homologues increases diversity.

126. The wing of bird, human arm and whale flipper have the same bone structure. These are called

   A. polymorphic structures
   B. homologous structures
   C. vestigial structures
   D. analogous structures

B. Homologous characteristics have the same genetic basis (leading to similar appearances) but are used for a different function.

127. Which biome is the most prevalent on Earth?

   A. marine
   B. desert
   C. savanna
   D. tundra

A. The marine biome covers 75% of the Earth. This biome is organized by the depth of water.

128. Which of the following is not an abiotic factor?

   A. temperature
   B. rainfall
   C. soil quality
   D. bacteria

D. Abiotic factors are non-living aspects of an ecosystem. Bacteria is an example of a biotic factor—a living thing in an ecosystem.

129. DNA synthesis results in a strand that is synthesized continuously. This is the

  A. lagging strand
  B. leading strand
  C. template strand
  D. complementary strand

B. As DNA synthesis proceeds along the replication fork, one strand is replicated continuously (the leading strand) and the other strand is replicated discontinuously (lagging strand).

130. Using a gram staining technique, it is observed that E. coli stains pink. It is therefore

  A. gram positive
  B. dead
  C. gram negative
  D. gram neutral

C. A Gram positive bacterium absorbs the stain and appears purple under a microscope because of its cell wall made of peptidoglycan. A Gram negative bacterium does not absorb the stain because of its more complex cell wall. These bacteria appear pink under a microscope.

131. A light microscope has an ocular of 10X and an objective of 40X. What is the total magnification?

  A. 400X
  B. 30X
  C. 50X
  D. 4000X

A. To determine the total magnification of a microscope, multiply the ocular lens by the objective lens. Here, the ocular lens is 10X and the objective lens is 40X.

  (10X) X (40X) = 400X total magnification

TEACHER CERTIFICATION STUDY GUIDE

132. Three plants were grown. The following data was taken. Determine the mean growth.
    Plant 1: 10cm Plant 2: 20cm Plant 3: 15cm

    A. 5 cm
    B. 45 cm
    C. 12 cm
    D. 15 cm

D. The mean growth is the average of the three growth heights.

$$\frac{10 + 20 + 15}{3} = 15\text{cm average height}$$

133. **Electrophoresis separates DNA on the basis of**

    A. amount of current
    B. molecular size
    C. positive charge of the molecule
    D. solubility of the gel

B. Electrophoresis uses electrical charges of molecules to separate them according to their size.

134. **The reading of a meniscus in a graduated cylinder is done at the**

    A. top of the meniscus
    B. middle of the meniscus
    C. bottom of the meniscus
    D. closest whole number

C. The graduated cylinder is the common instrument used for measuring volume. It is important for the accuracy of the measurement to read the volume level of the liquid at the bottom of the meniscus. The meniscus is the curved surface of the liquid.

SCIENCE: BIOLOGY

135. Two hundred plants were grown. Fifty plants died. What percentage of the plants survived?

   A. 40%
   B. 25%
   C. 75%
   D. 50%

C. This is a proportion. If 50 plants died, then 200 – 50 = 150 survived. The number of survivors is the numerator and the total number of plants grown is the denominator.

$$\frac{150}{200} = 0.75 \quad \text{Multiply by 100 to get percent} = 75\% \text{ survive}$$

136. Which is not a correct statement regarding the use of a light microscope?

   A. carry the microscope with two hands
   B. store on the low power objective
   C. clean all lenses with lens paper
   D. Focus first on high power

D. Always begin focusing on low power. This allows for the observation of microorganisms in a larger field of view. Switch to high power once you have a microorganism in view on low power.

137. Spectrophotometry utilizes the principle of

   A. light transmission
   B. molecular weight
   C. solubility of the substance
   D. electrical charges

A. Spectrophotometry uses percent of light at different wavelengths absorbed and transmitted by a pigment solution.

138. Chromotography is most often associated with the separation of

   A. nutritional elements
   B. DNA
   C. proteins
   D. plant pigments

D. Chromatography uses the principles of capillarity to separate substances such as plant pigments. Molecules of a larger size will move slower up the paper, whereas smaller molecules will move more quickly producing lines of pigment.

139. A genetic engineering advancement in the medical field is:

   A. gene therapy
   B. pesticides
   C. degradation of harmful chemicals
   D. antibiotics

A. Gene therapy is the introduction of a normal allele to the somatic cells to replace a defective allele. The medical field has had success in treating patients with a single enzyme deficiency disease. Gene therapy has allowed doctors and scientists to introduce a normal allele that would provide the missing enzyme.

140. Which scientists are credited with the discovery of the structure of DNA?

   A. Hershey & Chase
   B. Sutton & Morgan
   C. Watson & Crick
   D. Miller & Fox

C. In the 1950s, James Watson and Francis Crick discovered the structure of a DNA molecule as that of a double helix.

141. Negatively charged particles that circle the nucleus of an atom are called

- A. neutrons
- B. neutrinos
- C. electrons
- D. protons

C. Neutrons and protons make up the core of an atom. Neutrons have no charge and protons are positively charged. Electrons are the negatively charged particles around the nucleus.

142. The shape of a cell depends on its

- A. function
- B. structure
- C. age
- D. size

A. In most living organisms, its structure is based on its function.

143. The most ATP is generated through

- A. fermentation
- B. glycolysis
- C. chemiosmosis
- D. Krebs cycle

C. The electron transport chain uses electrons to pump hydrogen ions across the mitochondrial membrane. This ion gradient is used to form ATP in a process called chemiosmosis. ATP is generated by the movement of hydrogen ions off NADH and $FADH_2$. This yields 34 ATP molecules.

144. In DNA, adenine bonds with ____, while cytosine bonds with ____.

- A. thymine/guanine
- B. adenine/cytosine
- C. cytosine/adenine
- D. guanine/thymine

A. In DNA, adenine pairs with thymine and cytosine pairs with guanine because of their nitrogenous base structures.

145. The individual parts of cells are best studied using a (n)

    A. ultracentrifuge
    B. phase-contrast microscope
    C. CAT scan
    D. electron microscope

D. The scanning electron microscope uses a beam of electrons to pass through the specimen. The resolution is about 1000 times greater than that of a light microscope. This allows the scientist to view extremely small objects, such as the individual parts of a cell.

146. Thermoacidophiles are

    A. prokaryotes
    B. eukaryotes
    C. protists
    D. archaea

D. Thermoacidophiles, methanogens, and halobacteria are members of the archaea group. They are as diverse from prokaryotes as prokaryotes are to eukaryotes.

147. Which of the following is not a type of fiber that makes up the cytoskeleton?

    A. vacuoles
    B. microfilaments
    C. microtubules
    D. intermediate filaments

A. Vacuoles are mostly found in plants and hold stored food and pigments. The other three choices are fibers that make up the cytoskeleton found in both plant and animal cells.

148. Viruses are made of

    A. a protein coat surrounding a nucleic acid
    B. DNA, RNA and a cell wall
    C. a nucleic acid surrounding a protein coat
    D. protein surrounded by DNA

A. Viruses are composed of a protein coat and a nucleic acid; either RNA or DNA.

149. Reproductive isolation results in

A. extinction
B. migration
C. follilization
D. speciation

D. Reproductive isolation is caused by any factor that impedes two species from producing viable, fertile hybrids. Reproductive isolation of populations is the primary criterion for recognition of species status.

150. This protein structure consists of the coils and folds of polypeptide chains. Which is it?

A. secondary structure
B. quaternary structure
C. tertiary structure
D. primary structure

A. Primary structure is the protein's unique sequence of amino acids. Secondary structure is the coils and folds of polypeptide chains. The coils and folds are the result of hydrogen bonds along the polypeptide backbone. Tertiary structure is formed by bonding between the side chains of the amino acids. Quaternary structure is the overall structure of the protein from the aggregation of two or more polypeptide chains.

Go to xamonline.com for our latest product offerings including:

Extra Sample Tests
Flash Cards
Expanded Study Guides
Newsletter / Blogs
Digital Content